The Trouble with Unity

The Trouble with Unity

Latino Politics and the Creation of Identity

Cristina Beltrán

OXFORD

UNIVERSITY PRESS

2010

OXFORD
UNIVERSITY PRESS

Oxford University Press, Inc., publishes works that further
Oxford University's objective of excellence in research, scholarship,
and education.

Oxford   New York
Auckland   Cape Town   Dar es Salaam   Hong Kong   Karachi
Kuala Lumpur   Madrid   Melbourne   Mexico City   Nairobi
New Delhi   Shanghai   Taipei   Toronto

With offices in
Argentina   Austria   Brazil   Chile   Czech Republic   France   Greece
Guatemala   Hungary   Italy   Japan   Poland   Portugal   Singapore
South Korea   Switzerland   Thailand   Turkey   Ukraine   Vietnam

Copyright © 2010 by Oxford University Press, Inc.

"Poem in Lieu of a Preface," by Alurista from *Aztlan: Chicano Journal
of the Social Sciences and the Arts* 1, no. 1 (1970): ix. Copyright 1970 by
Alurista. Reprinted with permission of the author and the publisher, UCLA
Chicano Studies Research Center Press, Los Angeles.

Published by Oxford University Press, Inc.
198 Madison Avenue, New York, New York 10016

www.oup.com

Oxford is a registered trademark of Oxford University Press

Library of Congress Cataloging-in-Publication Data
Beltrán, Cristina.
The trouble with unity : Latino politics and the creation of identity / Cristina Beltrán.
p. cm.
Includes bibliographical references and index.
ISBN 978-0-19-537590-9 (hardcover); 978-0-19-537591-6 (pbk.)
1. Hispanic Americans—Ethnic identity. 2. Hispanic Americans—Civil rights.
3. Hispanic Americans—Politics and government. 4. Political participation—United
States. 5. Voting—United States. 6. Power (Social sciences) —United States. I. Title.

E184.S75B45   2010
973'.0468—dc22   2009047289

Printed in the United States of America
on acid-free paper

To my mother, Margie "Jona" Beltrán (1940–2001),
and my grandmother Isabelle Lopez (1911–2005).
For their spirit and their love.

Acknowledgments

To work at the intersection of political theory and Latino studies is to venture into unfamiliar terrain. As with any intellectual journey, such work can be a rather lonely business. In my case, the absence of any easy "home" has drawn me into a number of scholarly communities. Such crossings have given me a wealth of friends and colleagues whose varied intellectual projects continue to stimulate my own thinking, and I am grateful for their friendship, support, and critical engagement. Without them, this work would not be possible.

I am indebted to several colleagues who read draft chapters of the manuscript and whose feedback, criticism, encouragement, and guidance were of enormous value: Paul Apostolidis, Edwina Barvosa, Arlene Dávila, Louis DeSipio, Ange-Marie Hancock, Kirstie McClure,Gary Segura, George Shulman, Tracy Strong, and Elizabeth Wingrove. Special thanks to Mary Hawkesworth, whose intellectual discernment and generosity have been a gift to me and so many feminist scholars.

It is my good fortune to be part of a sizable cohort of political theorists whose introduction to the possibilities of our chosen vocation began at the University of California at Santa Cruz under the guidance of Peter Euben and Jack Schaar. Their creativity, rigor, and intellectual capaciousness continue to serve as models for my own teaching and research. Not until I took other political science courses did I discover that not everyone taught Plato alongside Thomas Pynchon, or Maria Lugones and Elizabeth Spelman with Alexis de Tocqueville. That my own work explores the nature of Latino political identity through the writings of (among others) Jean-Jacques Rousseau, Michael Warner, Hannah Arendt, and postmodern feminism speaks to my experience at UCSC. I am especially grateful to Peter Euben for encouraging me to pursue a doctorate in the field of political theory; his encouragement and keen interest were crucial to putting me on the path I'm on today.

I am thankful to have so many friends and colleagues whose conversations and intellectual camaraderie sustain me in the study of politics. I owe a special debt to the participants in the Feminist Theory and Latino Politics workshops at the Western Political Science Association, as well as the Latino Caucus and the Race, Ethnicity and Politics section of the American Political Science Association. My APSA, WPSA, and Association for Political Theory colleagues have provoked my thinking, and our conversations continue to be a source of pleasure and insight. At the risk of overlooking some of the many people to whom I am appreciative, I extend particular thanks to Martha Ackelsberg, Tony Affigne, Janni Aragon, Manuel Avalos, Lawrie Balfour, Christina Bejarano, John Bretting, Romand Coles, Jennifer Culbert, Heath Fogg Davis, Rodolfo de la Garza, Jodi Dean, Christine Di Stefano, Rudy Espino, Kathy Ferguson, Kennan Ferguson, Michaele Ferguson, Henry Flores, Joshua Foa Dienstag, Luis Fraga, Jason Frank, John A. Garcia, Lisa García Bedolla, Jen Gaboury, Kim Geron, Alfonso Gonzales, Michael Goodhart, Judith Grant, Vicky Hattam, Rodney Hero, Michael Jones-Correa, Jessica Lavariega Monforti, Robyn Marasco, Patchen Markell, Benjamin Marquez, Lori Marso, Valerie Martinez-Ebers, Dean Mathiowetz, Keally McBride, Susan McWilliams, Melissa Michelson, Josh Miller, Celeste Montoya-Kirk, Jeanne Morefield, Davide Panagia, Adrian Pantoja, Paul Passavant, Héctor Perla Jr., Ricardo Ramirez, Mark Reinhardt, Ray Rocco, Rodolfo Rosales, Anna Sampaio, Mark Sawyer, Ron Schmidt Sr., John Seery, Torrey Shanks, Christine M. Sierra, Anna Marie Smith, Verity Smith, Holloway Sparks, Joan Tronto, and Chip Turner.

This project was greatly improved by the opportunity to give talks at various colleges and universities and through presenting my research at a number of workshops and colloquia. I would like to thank participants in the Philadelphia Political Theory Workshop at the University of Pennsylvania; the Latino Cultural Center and the Yale Women's Center at Yale University; the Van Ek Speaker Series and Department of Political Science at the University of Colorado at Boulder; the Department of Women's and Gender Studies at Rutgers University; the Political Theory Workshop and the Center for the Study of Race, Ethnicity, and Politics at UCLA; the Department of Social and Cultural Analysis at New York University; and the political science departments of Siena, Union, and Swarthmore colleges.

During my years at Rutgers University, I was able to work with a truly outstanding group of scholars. Cyndi Daniels, Sue Carroll, and Linda Zerilli made the field of women and politics an incredibly exciting intellectual endeavor. I am especially grateful for the seminars I was able to take with Linda Zerilli, whose teaching and scholarship have had a more profound influence on my thinking than she might ever imagine. My deepest thanks go to Ben Barber, a democratic theorist of the first rank whose support and conscientiousness made him an exemplary teacher and adviser. Jane Junn has taught me much about the politics of pan-ethnicity, race, and American politics; I thank her for her encouragement and friendship. And I am exceedingly grateful to have had the opportunity to learn from and work with Carey McWilliams, a man whose brilliance was matched only by his enormous kindness and generosity. I wish he were here to see the completion of this project and to join me in a celebratory Manhattan.

Thanks also to my graduate cohort in political science, especially Isabelle Barker, Jeff Becker, Anand Commissiong, Rose Corrigan, David Gutterman, Christine Kelly, Jennet Kirkpatrick, Isis Leslie, Deb Liebowitz, Jill Locke, Anne Manuel, Laurie Naranch, Ron Schmidt Jr. (honorary), Claire Snyder-Hall, Matt Voorhees, Eric Williams, and Karen Zivi. I remain a proud member of the "Rutgers mafia" and am indebted to you all for your friendship and general awesomeness.

I thank Haverford College and the Department of Political Science for their continued support and assistance. Special thanks to Haverford's Hurford Humanities Center, Angela Hobart, and the Centro Incontri Umani in Ascona, Switzerland, for providing me with the opportunity to work without interruption in a beautiful and intellectually generative environment. My colleagues at Haverford and the Tri-College Consortium of Bryn Mawr and Swarthmore have sustained me with their friendship and commitment to intellectual community, particularly Craig Borowiak, Israel Burshatin, Roberto Castillo, Jeremy Elkins, Hank Glassman, Harvey Glickman, Lisa Jane Graham, Laurie Hart, Anita Isaacs, Steve Marr, Barak Mendelsohn, Jerry Miller, Bethel Saler, Steve Salkever, Bethany Schneider, David Sedley, Gus Stadler, Jill Stauffer, Catherine Stringer, Sid Waldman, Susanna Wing, and Tina Zwarg. I owe a particular debt of gratitude to my Latino studies colleagues in the Tri-Co, especially Miguel Díaz-Bárriga, Margaret Dorsey, and Lázaro Lima. Very special thanks to Laz for his generosity of spirit, insightful advice, and efforts to create a vibrant community of scholars in the area of U.S. Latino studies.

My Oxford editor, Angela Chnapko, has been a pleasure to work with, serving as a continual source of enthusiasm, insightful advice, and editorial acumen; thanks as well to Dave McBride for his vision and early interest in this project. I am also indebted to the three anonymous reviewers for Oxford whose exceptionally thoughtful feedback helped bring the book to fruition, and to the entire Oxford team, particularly Susan Ecklund for her meticulous editing. Portions of chapter 5 appeared previously as "Going Public: Hannah Arendt, Immigrant Action and the Space of Appearance," *Political Theory* 37, no. 5 (October 2009); I thank Mary Dietz and Sage Publications for granting permission to reprint the material. Abundant thanks to Alberto Urista (Alurista) for graciously allowing me to reprint his "Poem in Lieu of Preface" in chapter 3.

Throughout my various intellectual undertakings, I have been sustained by a very special group of dear friends: Darío Arena, Jen Arena, Becky Compton, Roxanne Euben, Susan Liebell, Jeremy Meyer, Bethel Saler, and Vic Tulli have all enriched my life in more ways than I can say. Particular thanks to a group of women who have been my close friends for a *shocking* number of years: Lisa Adler, whose amazing spirit and humor are a continual source of delight; Ronnee Schreiber, for her remarkable friendship, innumerable power walks and for always being forthright, funny, and spot-on; and Stephanie Volmer, for her extraordinary heart, cookies on demand, and willingness to join me for any number of work days and writing retreats.

Finally, I want to thank my family, whose support was crucial to this project's successful completion. First and foremost, I am grateful to my parents, two individuals of enormous intellect, charisma, ambition, and eloquence who have made the world better through their presence; I thank them for sharing their passion for politics and vigorous debate with me. I am grateful to my father, Pete Beltran, whose love and faith in my abilities have always been complete and unstinting. His years as an organizer and labor leader and his commitment to participatory democracy, workers' rights, and social justice remain a source of inspiration. I thank my in-laws, Ken and Sheila Budman, for the love they have shown me over the years and for being an ongoing source of stability and support in my life. My amazing brother, David Stanley, gives me hope for the future and for the true possibility of family; I remain forever grateful to have him as both a sibling and a friend. Thanks also to his mother, Elizabeth Stanley, for her friendship and strength, and to my entire extended family (Beltran, Budman, Carroll, Lopez, Montoya, Stanley, and beyond) for the devotion and encouragement they have shown me over the years.

My grandmother Isabelle Lopez was a wonderful storyteller, as well as an anchor of love and emotional sustenance throughout my life; her independence, resilience, and love of life are a continual source of inspiration to me. My mother, Margie Beltrán, was a born intellectual; a voracious and eclectic reader, she took enormous pleasure in conversation and believed passionately in the power of ideas. By instilling in me her love of books and words, she gave me the tools to craft my life. I find it beyond my ability to express how her love, intelligence, indefatigability, and capacity for self-invention made our lives possible. It is my deepest regret that she and my grandmother did not live to see this project to completion. I dedicate this book to them.

Finally, I want to thank my husband, Matthew Budman, editor extraordinaire, whose love and unstinting support have made this journey conceivable. The patience and good humor he has shown living with what has sometimes seemed an interminable project have been truly remarkable. I thank him for his many hours spent reading and editing the manuscript, as well as for the book's main title. My deepest thanks for his journalistic acuity and—more important—for bringing so much joy, love, and laughter into my life. All errors and omissions that remain in the following pages are, of course, my own.

Contents

The Trouble with Unity

Introduction: Sleeping Giants and Demographic Floods

Latinos and the Politics of Emergence

The Sleeping Giant has awakened and will not sleep again.

—Eugene Nelson, activist, September 1966[1]

The Hispanic giant in the United States is awakening and coming out of his labyrinth of solitude—to use the evocative phrase coined by Mexican poet Octavio Paz. As he stirs himself, this giant will continue to get bigger.

—Geoffrey Godsell, journalist, April 1980[2]

For many years, people were saying that Latinos were a sleeping giant. . . . . That giant is getting up now. Times are changing.

—Gaddi Vasquez, Orange County supervisor, 1991[3]

The United States is becoming a Latino nation. In the next century, every critical decision that this country makes will have to pass through the filter of the Latino vote. That's where the numbers, and this country, are headed.

—Jorge Ramos, journalist, 2004[4]

The sleeping Latino giant is finally awake.

—Jaime Contreras, activist, 2006[5]

Latinos in the United States have long been characterized as subjects on the cusp of political power and influence. Enmeshed in what feels like a recurring cycle of emergence, discussions of Latino political power elicit new allusions to old metaphors. Again and again, we are told that a sleeping giant is waking and that a demographic wave is about to crash upon American shores.

This metaphor of imminent mobilization, of a giant beginning to stir, is particularly prevalent in the realm of electoral politics, where Latinos find themselves discovered anew every two years.[6] More than 45 million strong and growing four times faster than the general population, Latinos recently surpassed African Americans as the country's largest minority group and are projected to increase to 102.6 million, or 24 percent of the nation's total population, by 2050.[7] Often characterized as a "swing vote" with the potential of providing the margin of victory in close races, Latinos represent the electorate's fastest-growing segment; both Republicans and Democrats depict them as a crucial component of state and national electoral strategies. The focus has been particularly intense in the realm of presidential politics, since Latinos are concentrated in electorally rich California, Florida, Illinois, New York, and Texas.

Yet this enduring depiction of Latinos as untapped potential is intrinsically linked to an impression of Latinos as politically passive and difficult to mobilize: the giant that seemingly *cannot* be roused from its slumber. So how should we understand this incoherent political characterization of Latinos as fundamentally passive, forever new, *and* perpetually emergent? What are we to make of this Latino Leviathan, this narcoleptic colossus that seems to periodically stir only to fall back into civic obscurity?

The widespread invocation of Latinos as a sleeping giant is more than an inaccurate political cliché or a simple metaphor for political agency. At a deeper level, the image presumes the existence of civic cohesion within these populations—particularly when invoked by advocates of Latino empowerment.[8] An implicit assumption of the metaphor is that Latinos will behave politically as an "ethnic bloc." The giant, then, signifies consciousness by materializing and expressing the collective will of the Latino community.[9] This performance of consensus is often defined in terms of a unified Latino vote or some other sort of embodied action (the immigrant marches of spring 2006 are a powerful example of this).[10] In this way, the very phrase "sleeping giant" implies a certain homogeneity—the belief that in some crucial way, Latinos perceive themselves as part of some larger whole, a political community with shared interests and a common policy agenda.

This development is partly the result of *Latinidad*—the sociohistorical process whereby various Latin American national-origin groups are understood as sharing a sense of collective identity and cultural consciousness.* Rather than speaking in

---

*According to Juana Rodriguez, the term *Latinidad* "serves to define a particular geopolitical experience" while also containing within it "complexities and contradictions of immigration, (post)(neo) colonialism, race, color, legal status, class, nation, language, and the politics of location." See Rodríguez, *Queer Latinidad*; Flores, *From Bomba to Hip-Hop*; Dávila, *Latinos, Inc*; and Aparicio and Chávez-Silverman, *Tropicalizations*.

terms of *specific and distinct* ethnic subgroups (Mexicans, Cubans, Puerto Ricans, Dominicans, etc.), "Latino" and "Hispanic" have become the shorthand designations of choice among journalists, politicians, advertising executives, academics, and other influential elites.[†] In this way, the terminology of *Latinidad* has entered America's mainstream; from Spanish-language television to presidential speeches, "Latino" and "Hispanic" are now the most commonly used terms to describe what is generally understood to be a culturally distinct and nationally visible minority group. This shift in terminology has become so entrenched over the past thirty years that few Americans have given it a moment's thought. Yet as scholars have noted, the process of *Latinidad* is both complex and contradictory, involving issues of immigration, colonialism, conquest, race, color, gender, sexuality, class, and languae.

Understood as a *political* category, *Latinidad* presumes that Latinos as a group share a common collective consciousness. Moreover, as the metaphoric embodiment of *Latinidad*, the sleeping giant reflects a series of widely held aspirations regarding how this pan-ethnic collective *ought* to behave politically. The giant reflects the belief that this large and growing population is most empowered when it functions as a united community, animated by a common agenda and striding across the national stage with direction and intent. Among Latinos themselves, the giant represents the long-standing desire to be seen as a vital and inescapable part of the national political landscape, a demographic powerhouse that has earned its right to both representation and recognition. In this way, the giant functions as a symbol of *presence*, a figure whose size makes it impossible to ignore and whose growing influence will surely impact every aspect of American cultural and political life.

[†]Throughout the book, I use the terms "Latino" and "Hispanic" interchangeably, since both are widely used to refer to individuals living in the United States who trace their ancestry to the Spanish-speaking regions of Latin America and the Caribbean. Of course, as Victoria Hattam writes, "the term Hispanic is by no means settled; it remains highly contested" (*In The Shadow of Race*, p. 121). Historically, it denotes ties to the Iberian Peninsula, and many, including U.S. government agencies, define "Hispanic" broadly, to include people of Spanish or Portuguese heritage as well as those of Latin American descent. The political implications of such nettlesome semantic issues arose recently with the U.S. Supreme Court nomination of Judge Sonia Sotomayor; some argued (unconvincingly) that Justice Benjamin Cardozo, of Portuguese ancestry, was the first Hispanic justice to sit on the Court.

When discussing particular ethnic groups, I will refer to them by national origin (Mexican American/Chicano, Cuban, Puerto Rican, etc.). Yet overall, I tend to favor the term "Latino." My approach echoes that of Arlene Dávila in her analysis and defense of the term "Latino" (rather than gender-neutral options such as "Latinos/as" or "Latinas"). For Dávila, the purposeful use of "Latino" signifies "the ubiquitous use of this term by the media and the mainstream press, which neither signals nor marks differences in gender, race, ethnicity, and other variables when making nationwide generalizations." For Dávila, the use of the term "Latino" signals "how this dominant generic designation also contributes to the whitewashing of this group" (*Latino Spin*, p. 7). I discuss the creation and political use of the terms "Latino" and "Hispanic" more fully in chapter 4.

Not surprisingly, then, Latino unity has emerged as *the* identifying characteristic necessary to produce the successful coalescing of this pan-ethnic Leviathan. And here my reference to Thomas Hobbes is quite intentional, for it is precisely the imagery in Abraham Bosse's famous frontispiece etching for Hobbes's *Leviathan*[11]—of a confederation of individuals personified as a single massive "artificial person"—that captures the political logic of *Latinidad* implicit in the metaphor of the sleeping giant. Only when its constituent parts come together is Latino political activity acknowledged and recognized; only then is the giant perceived as alive and "awake."

Yet it is precisely this confederation of disparate parts that makes the Latino Leviathan so susceptible to fragmentation and dissolution. For while the sleeping giant is composed of Latino subjects, it lacks the explicit presence of sovereign will as displayed in Bosse's etching. And while the mass media and other political elites often portray Latinos as a collective body with common interests, the actual existence of Latino unity—of a collective political consciousness and will distinct among Latinos—is far less certain. Much of this has to do with the all-encompassing quality of *Latinidad* itself, for as a category of identification, "Hispanic" and "Latino" are terms whose descriptive legitimacy is premised on a startling lack of specificity. The categories encompass any and all individuals living in the United States who trace their ancestry to the Spanish-speaking regions of Latin America and the Caribbean; Latinos hail from Colombia, Mexico, Paraguay, Puerto Rico, and beyond—more than twenty countries in all. Such inclusivity is part of the problem: "Hispanic" and "Latino" tell us nothing about country of origin, gender, citizenship status, economic class, or length of residence in the United States. An undocumented immigrant from Guatemala is Hispanic; so is a third-generation Mexican American lawyer. Moreover, both categories are racially indeterminate: Latinos can be white, black, indigenous, and every combination thereof. In other words, characterizing a subject as either "Hispanic" or "Latino" is an exercise in opacity—the terms are so comprehensive that their explanatory power is limited. When referring to "Latinos in the United States," it is far from immediately clear whether the subjects under discussion are farmworkers living below the poverty line or middle-class homeowners, urban hipsters or rural evangelicals, white or black, gay or straight, Catholic or Jewish, undocumented Spanish monolinguals or fourth-generation speakers of English-only.

While the homogenizing tendencies of *Latinidad* obscure the serious and significant differences within these populations, the tendency to conflate populations is neither accidental nor incomprehensible. Instead, as the following chapters show, the commitment to *Latinidad* reflects the diverse political impulses of numerous communities. When confronting an interest-group paradigm that rewards national over regional interests and sees strength in numbers, Latino political elites have found it beneficial to portray Latinos as a large and cohesive group capable of being mobilized around a recognizable set of issues. For these advocates, locating subjects under the "pan-ethnic" umbrella expands the population and geographic base for Latinos, projecting them into the national political arena.[12] In other words, by defining themselves in terms of *Latinidad*, Latino political elites and their advocates believe they are better able to both secure federal resources and gain national exposure.

The internal logic of *Latinidad* is not only strategic but also emotive and experiential. *Latinidad* is a historical practice constituted through the homogenizing effects of racism experienced by Latinos and other people of color. As with African Americans, a racialized "otherness" has been applied to the diverse communities of Latinos living in the United States. In other words, Latino pan-ethnicity has been fostered by a climate of xenophobia in which the regional and cultural history of all people of Latin American descent has been erased. As scholar Suzanne Oboler notes, despite internal and racial group differences, "people of Latin American descent in the United States have long been perceived homogeneously as 'foreign' to the image of 'being American' . . . regardless of the time and mode of their incorporation into the United States or their subsequent status as citizens of this nation."[13] Given this type of broad-based discrimination, it is unsurprising that *Latinidad* emerged as a productive response to prejudice and racial stereotyping.[14] In this sense, *Latinidad* represents an effort to expose group-based inequality, providing people with a shared history of racial struggle and a powerful sense of linked fate that has emerged as the basis for collective politics.

Yet despite such justified appropriation, disregard for specificity continues to cut both ways. Homogenizing depictions of Latinos continue to be invoked by those who fear the rapid growth of the United States' Latino population. For these Americans, Latinos are still monolithically "foreign," a racially and culturally distinct group who resist assimilation and whose high birth rates and regressive cultural practices threaten to undermine the country's unity and civic values. In *Who Are We? The Challenges to America's National Identity*, political scientist Samuel P. Huntington puts forward an especially dystopian vision of civic *Latinidad*:

> The cultural division between Hispanics and Anglos will replace the racial division between blacks and whites as the most serious cleavage in American society. A bifurcated America with two languages and two cultures will be fundamentally different from the America with one

language and one core Anglo-Protestant culture that has existed for over three centuries.[15]

For Huntington, Latinos are an indistinguishable yet racialized mass—an ever-spreading economic and cultural *threat* whose inability and/or unwillingness to integrate into American society threatens to wreak national havoc. Citing the growing number of Latinos in both the Southwest and Miami, Huntington erases the differences between the various Latino subgroups in order to fan the flames of xenophobia. In this way, he both accepts and then deploys the logic of *Latinidad*.[16] Such are the ironies of metaphor: the image of the sleeping giant is capable of moving effortlessly across America's racial divide. Put somewhat differently, both advocates *and* adversaries of Latino power make use of a homogenizing logic that portrays Latinos as culturally distinct and engaged in a transformative endeavor capable of reshaping America's political landscape. As Arlene Dávila notes, Americans seem unable to decide whether Latinos are "friends or foes." Nativists and anti-immigrant groups view Latinos as "America's most impending threat," while others view them as "the single most important up and coming ethnic group."[17] In both scenarios, Latino cohesion is naturalized as both liberals and conservatives presume the existence of a common consciousness among diverse Latino populations. For one constituency, this shared civic sensibility symbolizes hope; for the other, fear.

Latino politics has been caught in this discordant yet eerily familiar clash of characterizations for some time now: emergent and influential yet passive and powerless, a long-standing presence yet forever new, loyal patriots whose distinct culture threatens America's social cohesion. No wonder the sleeping giant is such a lumbering colossus! The civic face of *Latinidad* embodies impulses and aspirations that are constantly pulling in multiple directions and across different ideological divides. Among 45 million Latinos, one can *always* find simultaneous signs of assimilation and separatism, emergence and decline, civic gains and losses, participatory activism and political retreat. Given such deep diversity, should we be surprised that characterizations of this Leviathan appear so contradictory and incoherent? And no wonder the giant seems to emerge and then disappear with such rapidity: there is simply no clear way to pin down the presence and actions of a figure so murky and ambiguous. How does one "awaken" a political figure whose very political existence is so uncertain?

Let Sleeping Giants Lie

Amid these contradictory portrayals, this book does not seek to resolve the hetero-geneity implicit in *Latinidad*. I am uninterested in smoothing the terrain by ac-knowledging Latino multiplicity only to impose yet another meta-narrative, one based on the dubious presumption that Latinos are a political demographic with shared interests and a common policy agenda. I have no wish to create unity out of diversity; I offer no civic prescriptions to wake the sleeping giant.

Instead, a central contention of *The Trouble with Unity* is that there is no sleeping giant—only political subjects whose variegated actions and intentions are obscured by this limited vision of Latino empowerment. By embracing multi-plicity and letting sleeping giants lie, we will be better able to both observe and appreciate the political possibilities of these diverse subjects, communities, and populations. In other words, rather than attempting to uncover the unitary core that legitimates *Latinidad* (language, *mestizaje*, racism, etc.), this book takes a more poststructural approach, recognizing Latino identity as always historically and discursively constructed. In doing this, I draw on the insights of postmodern feminists and their insistence that "the category of women *produces* what it claims to *represent*."[18] Arguing that feminists could no longer seek recourse to an unprob-lematized women's "experience," Judith Butler has proposed reconceiving the category of women as "permanently open, permanently contested, permanently contingent, in order not to foreclose in advance future claims for inclusion."[19] In a similar vein, it is my contention that "Latino," like the category "women," should be reconceived as a site of permanent political contestation. In the following pages, *Latinidad* is approached as a site of ongoing resignifiability—as a *political* rather than merely *descriptive* category.

To engage the construction of Latino subjectivity as a political problematic in need of theoretical interrogation, *The Trouble with Unity* examines three critical moments in U.S. Latino political history: the Chicano and Puerto Rican civil rights movements of the late 1960s and early 1970s, the emergence of Latinos as a pan-ethnic voting bloc during the 1980s (the "decade of the Hispanic"), and the immigrant-rights protests throughout the United States in April and May 2006. In considering these moments when subjects were engaged in the effort to constitute themselves as a people (a Latino "we," as it were), I am not attempting to offer an exhaustive account of these events and their possible democratic implications. Instead, my readings draw on the work of social and political theorists as a way of evaluating the democratic and antidemocratic implications of several important phases of Latino politics.

In doing this, I am particularly interested in analyzing the underlying assumptions that shape how Latino activists in the United States construct themselves as political subjects. How do Latino civic elites[20] understand the nature of *power* (particularly political power), and how does this understanding impact how they approach their own ideological heterogeneity? What strategic and philosophical assumptions surround the concept of Latino unity, and has *Latinidad* emerged as a necessary precondition for visibility and political influence? Moreover, how do advocates of Latino empowerment perceive and negotiate the relationship between identity and political agreement? How is *disagreement* being theorized within contemporary Latino political thought and practice? Is there a tendency within Latino politics to conflate identity and political agreement? If so, what are the political and theoretical costs of such conflation?

Ranging over the past four decades and drawing on a diverse range of texts across multiple genres, the following chapters analyze the impulse toward group unity both in the pan-ethnic turn toward *Latinidad* and in the social justice movements of ethnic-specific subgroups (Mexican Americans and Puerto Ricans). By analyzing both electoral and protest politics—elite institutions as well as the grass roots—I seek to provide a critical and theoretically driven account of how political power, racial/ethnic identity, and ideological diversity have been theorized and debated within U.S. Latino politics.

Methodological Framework

As is probably already apparent, my approach to the field of Latino politics is less quantitative and more theoretically focused than most research on Latinos in the social sciences. Situated primarily within the tradition of political theory, *The Trouble with Unity* places canonical texts and authors in a sustained conversation with central readings in the field of Latino politics. As an argumentative reassessment of how Latino political identity is understood and talked about in contemporary life, the project also utilizes poetry, historical monographs, and recent poll data surveying Latino political behavior and opinion (including the recent Latino National Survey, the Latino National Political Survey, and the Pew Hispanic Center/Kaiser Family Foundation's National Survey of Latinos).

In situating this work, I should note that the goal of this project is *not* to provide an exhaustive account of the political and discursive practices of each Latino subgroup living in the United States. Instead, my analysis centers primarily on two groups, Chicanos/Mexican Americans and Puerto Ricans. Scholars have written comparatively little about the political behavior of Central and South Americans in the United States, and generating that sort of research is beyond this project's scope. By contrast, there is a significant body of research on Chicanos and Puerto Ricans that could benefit from a more theoretical analysis. Another, more significant reason is demographics: Chicanos and Puerto Ricans constitute the oldest and largest communities of U.S. Latinos (of the approximately 45 million Latinos in the United States, 64 percent are Mexican and 9 percent are Puerto Rican). In addition to accounting for some three-quarters of all U.S. Latinos, the two groups are also the most geographically dispersed throughout the nation.[21]

More important, the history and civic practices of Chicanos and Puerto Ricans established the assumptions and practices that have set the terms for Latinos as a political community, creating the discursive framework for all the groups that have followed. The Chicano and Puerto Rican movements of the late 1960s and early 1970s focused national attention on these communities; the movements were crucial to introducing Latinos into the American public sphere as political and historical subjects. These two movements also produced the largest group of Latino civic elites, a collection of activists, academics, and professionals who continue to influence Latino politics at the national level. Even at state and local levels, Chicano and Puerto Rican civic elites continue to head the vast majority of institutions serving the wider Latino community. Put somewhat differently, the political history, assumptions, and strategies of the two oldest and largest Latino subgroups created the discursive framework for all the groups that have followed.

As many scholars have noted, despite their potential as an intriguing site to examine issues of identity and democracy, Latinos as a political community have been underresearched in political science. As Rodney Hero observes, "Latinos in the United States have not received much attention in political science research, and there has been little effort to bring together or systematically discuss the implications of the analyses that do exist."[22] By drawing on the insights of political theory in order to analyze Latino political practices, my research seeks to respond to the analytical problematic that Hero and others have identified: developing a critical framework and vocabulary better able to analyze the central concepts undergirding the intellectual terrain of Latino political thought.

Much of the research in the subfield of Latino politics consists of either historical examinations of various organizations and social movements or empirical examinations of voting behavior and institutional participation. In the former category, research focuses on the movement politics of the late 1960s and early 1970s, particularly in the Puerto Rican and Chicano communities.[23] While such scholarship has been indispensable in shedding light on these political organizations' histories and internal workings, movement scholars too often take for granted the very categories and practices they ought to be analyzing and calling into question. For example, given that group unity is a defining preoccupation within movement thought, one would assume that scholars have sought to analyze and critique the concept—but, interestingly, this is rarely the case.[24] Instead, movement scholars consistently claim that lack of consensus seriously weakened the Chicano and Puerto Rican movements, and that future Latino empowerment will require "improvement" in this area.[25] By naturalizing racial unity and treating it as a political prerequisite, movement scholarship is often unable to fully theorize the costs and implications of these assumptions. Indeed, movement scholarship often participates in the very impulses it seeks to examine.

Probably the largest body of research that defines the study of Latino politics is that which focuses on Latinos' voting patterns and participation rates, alongside Latinos' efforts to win public office. Often based on state and national survey data, this research generally seeks to uncover and understand Latinos' political behavior and values and explain lower voting rates and the general underrepresentation of Latinos in political office. Such research often focuses on the obstacles to Latino political advancement (language barriers, citizenship requirements, racism, poverty) and offers possible solutions to the problem of institutional underrepresentation.[26] This research has provided the field of Latino politics with data essential to understanding the actual opinions and voting practices of Latinos in the United States. Prior to this research, both scholars and pundits were often guilty of characterizing these populations in ways that could be neither proved nor disproved. Today, notwithstanding pundits' lingering mischaracterizations of these communities, news outlets, elected officials, and policy advocates finally have access to a large and growing body of rigorous survey data and analysis.

Another significant body of research within Latino politics involves historical research and/or ethnographic studies in particular American cities (New York, Miami, Los Angeles, San Antonio, Chicago, etc.). Focusing on local movements, organizations, and practices, this type of qualitative research has been crucial to establishing a rich body of historically engaged and deeply contextualized knowledge exposing and analyzing the challenging conditions that Latinos in the public realm face, as well as the creativity and resourcefulness of Latino politics at the local level.[27] Interdisciplinary in nature, this research often looks beyond the electoral realm in considering questions of power and politics.

Yet despite the importance and value of both quantitative and qualitative research in the field of Latino politics, both bodies of scholarship tend to naturalize rather than theorize concepts central to their analysis—concepts such as community, unity, identity, and experience. Without a more theoretically engaged body of scholarship, scholars in the field of Latino politics will be unable to critically engage the very questions of democracy and power they seek to address.

While it is my contention that the near absence of political theory in the field of Latino politics reflects a gap in the literature that needs to be remedied, it is also true that for the most part, political theorists have ignored the field of Latino studies and Latino politics.[28] A number of scholars are doing important and theoretically engaged work in the field of Latino studies, but such work is mostly located in the fields of English, cultural and American studies, anthropology, comparative literature, media studies, and performance studies.[29] In these fields, Latino identity practices and the concept of pan-ethnicity (*Latinidad*) are often theorized, but rarely is there an explicit or sustained focus on political advocacy groups, mobilization, minority representation, or electoral politics. Instead, the works address literary genres, language, popular culture, marketing, and globalization.[30] This research is often extremely incisive and theoretically sophisticated but, unsurprisingly, generally inattentive to the intellectual concerns that animate political science and political theory—concerns related to representation, participation, rights, political institutions, and the relationship between conflict and community. My research draws on the rich theoretical insights of this scholarship, while seeking to apply these observations to Latino civic practices in the United States.

Performing Membership: Chapter Road Map

One of this book's central arguments is that while the pan-ethnic practice of *Latinidad* represents a relatively recent political phenomenon, the underlying logic driving contemporary assumptions of Latino unity has its roots in the Chicano and Puerto Rican social movements of the late 1960s and early 1970s. In many ways, these two movements continue to serve as emotional and strategic touchstones for many Latino elites regarding what Latino politics once was and what it could and should be. So while no longer characterized by radical nationalism or inflammatory rhetoric, contemporary Latino politics still echoes critical elements of movement thought, particularly the continuing conflation of unity with visibility and empowerment and the anxiety over internal dissent and disagreement. To consider these issues, chapters 1 and 3 provide analyses of various elements of movement thought, exploring how this early political privileging of racial unity continues to define the ideals and parameters of contemporary Latino politics.

I am mindful of the fact that different readers will approach this text—an interdisciplinary work of democratic theory with a focus on Latinos in the United States—with varying levels of familiarity with the Chicano and Puerto Rican movements. For those readers less conversant in this history, chapter 1 offers an overview of the two movements, with a particular focus on Latina feminism and the tensions created by efforts to reconcile racial unity with feminist action. Readers already familiar with the history of the Chicano and Puerto Rican movements should feel free to skim this chapter and move quickly to chapter 2, which begins the process of reading Latino politics through the lens of democratic theory. To gain a deeper insight into the unitary logic of *Latinidad*, this chapter turns to the work of social and political theorists who promote the value of social heterogeneity while criticizing disciplinary forms of community. Drawing on the work of Iris Marion Young, Gloria Anzaldúa, Cherríe Moraga, Chela Sandoval, Bernice Johnson Reagon, Susan Bickford, Michael Warner, Sheldon Wolin, and Alan Keenan, this chapter argues that the assumptions and practices of Latino politics can be best understood when located within the contradictions and chalenges of democracy. Drawing on the agonistic resources of feminist theory, this chapter approaches the concept of *Latinidad* through a consideration of Wolin's discussion of "fugitive democracy" alongside Keenan's recent discussion of democratic openness and the inevitably incomplete nature of democracy.

The following chapter explores the complicated relationship among identification, participation, deliberation, and the nondeliberative practices that sometimes characterize Latino politics. During the Chicano and Puerto Rican movements, for example, activists displayed a dual impulse toward ideological consensus and mass participation at the local level. But given that internal political cohesion is inevitably challenged by the deep diversity arising from enhanced and expanded participation, how were these contradictory and contending impulses to be reconciled? How could these movements be both inclusive *and* unified?

In chapter 3, I argue that movement activists bridged the gap between their contending desires for inclusive, participatory democracy and racial unity through the self-conscious staging of citizenship through public performance. Transposing Jean-Jacques Rousseau's concept of *identification* onto the field of movement politics, I suggest that Chicano and Puerto Rican activists approached citizenship in Rousseauian terms—as a set of practices that were participatory yet primarily nondeliberative. Anxious about the dissension that erupts when members of the civic body engage in agonistic debate and contestation, Rousseau turns to performative civic practices that transcend disagreement, uniting subjects understood as naturally separate and independent while avoiding the inequalities implicit in eloquent speech, as well as the pitfalls of sociability and dependency. Similarly, Chicano and Puerto Rican movement leaders sought to shape activists' political subjectivity through public gatherings that emphasized linked fate through expressive enactments of membership, particularly poetry events, fiestas, and conferences. I suggest that such embodied affiliations can be best understood as Rousseauian exercises in identification, giving Chicano and Puerto Rican activists a newfound sense of themselves as a people: unified and capable of political agency.

During the movement's heyday, activists displayed a belief that political life necessarily exceeded the realm of the legislative assembly: rallies, *teatros*, and poetry readings served to provide the Chicano and Puerto Rican body politic with a civic education that promoted identification through participatory action. Such performed affiliations provided participants with a heady sense of the community's power and potential, creating conditions of community while avoiding the political differences made present when subjects engaged in deliberative public speech. Moreover, the movement's performative practices sought to downplay and avoid agonistic deliberation and legitimate democratic debate. By theorizing how each movement distinguished between *participatory* and *deliberative* forms of democratic engagement, I address a central problematic in democratic theory: how movements founded on progressive visions of inclusion, empowerment, and enhanced presence can simultaneously limit opportunities for democratic discussion and debate. A particular instance of such limits appears in my analysis of movement-era feminists and the political challenge posed by their criticisms of gender bias and homophobia. The contentious speech of Latina feminists, accused of being disloyal and divisive, illustrates the difficulty in presuming that shared culture can transcend complex social and ideological divisions.

Moving from New Left radicalism to the realm of contemporary electoral politics, chapter 4 argues that contemporary Latino politics has seriously neglected the movement's legacy of participatory and expressive enactments of citizenship, while maintaining its unhealthy focus on group unity. Following the mass protests of the 1960s and 1970s, Latino politics became increasingly focused on *representation* via electoral politics and the increasing potential of the "Latino vote" in American political life. Yet despite this shift from performative identification to electoral representation, the contemporary discourse of civic *Latinidad* continues to share the movement's earlier aversion to contentious deliberation, equating group unity with civic health. In the pan-ethnic paradigm of civic *Latinidad*, the transformation from diversity to homogeneity is theorized as a necessary precondition for Latino empowerment—without it, Latino elites are unable to invoke the representative "we" that sustains discussion of the "Latino vote" and other markers of the pan-ethnic project.

In considering the political implications of civic *Latinidad*—as well as the related issues of embodiment, political visibility, participation, and deliberative public speech—chapter 5 focuses on the immigrant mobilizations of 2006 and the heightened presence of politically active immigrants (both documented and undocumented) in the United States. While other theorists have turned to Hannah Arendt's analysis of statelessness and superfluity to consider questions of immigration, "illegality," and the status of noncitizens, I argue that Arendt's account of labor and her nonconsequentialist account of action offer a richer optic for considering the undocumented in the United States. Rereading Arendt's notion of *animal laborans*, my analysis explores the limitations of noncitizens invoking labor as a way to gain civic standing. Rather than defining "success" in terms of replicability or immediate legislative results, this chapter offers an alternate account of the 2006 demonstrations. Considering recent discussions of subaltern counterpublics alongside Arendt's theory of action, I argue that the demonstrations can be best understood as a moment of *initiation* and an inaugural performance of the political.

Throughout this work, I draw attention to two impulses within Latino politics that I believe are of particular importance: first, a commitment to unity that is anxious about contentious speech and that naturalizes the existence of linked fate within these populations; second, an impressive tradition of mass participation and innovative performativity that has been underappreciated by both scholars and practitioners of contemporary Latino politics.[31] Advocates of Latino empowerment should draw on this legacy and build on the democratic and political possibilities expressed by participatory performance. Yet alongside this enhanced appreciation of Latino performativity, advocates must recognize the reality of ideological diversity among Latinos and accept the legitimacy and value of agonistic deliberation and debate. Such a task will not be easy, for we still inhabit a world in which the actions and intentions of Latino publics continue to be distorted and misunderstood.

The 2006 marches of immigrants and their allies offer a particularly good example of how Latino mass action reveals the existence of both too much and too little political imagination. The mass actions exposed some Americans' uninformed and often excessive hysteria concerning immigration; for them, the massive demonstrations implied *invasion* rather than *membership*—an irredentist effort by Mexican and Mexican American radicals and communists to "reconquer" the Southwest. Alongside this excess of apprehension, many Latino civic elites revealed an opposite tendency: the failure to appreciate the political possibilities of embodied action and public performance. Rather than considering the creative political potential of mass action to reshape the parameters of democratic belonging, Latino elites displayed an overwhelming tendency to view collective mass action instrumentally—as the performative precursor to "real participation," typically defined by electoral politics and the act of mobilizing the "Latino vote." Both the national punditry and Latino civic elites characterized the protests as yet another example of the sleeping giant waking, ready to emerge as and develop into a united Latino electorate.

While recognizing the enormous importance of voting and gaining legislative victories, *The Trouble with Unity* contends that too much is being lost in viewing Latino mass participation as a mere precursor to participation in the electoral process. Drawing on Michael Warner's notion of "counterpublics," I show how the embodied action of Latinos does not simply reflect but actively *constructs* communities and solidarities within the public realm. Performance and the physical claiming of public space is capable of producing a shared sense of membership, particularly for those who have historically found the public realm to be a site of silence, alienation, and invisibility. In other words, embodied performance is a particularly powerful practice when seeking to challenge prevailing discourses and/or engender new political possibilities.

Political Theory and Latino Politics: Border Crossings

In focusing on the relationships among democratic participation, visibility, embodiment, and public speech, *The Trouble with Unity* is one of the first books to put traditional works of political philosophy into a sustained conversation with contemporary scholarship on Latino politics in the United States. Yet in stressing this work's theoretical underpinnings, I am not attempting to shore up theory's constitutive borders. Rather, I seek to engage this philosophical tradition while expanding my gaze outside the discipline to include fields of thought and inquiry central to the study of Latinos in the United States. In doing this, my approach is indebted to what political theorist Wendy Brown describes as a "contrapuntal" approach to political theory. For Brown, the future vibrancy of the field of political theory depends on developing contrapuntal strategies whereby theorists "productively consort with those who are not our kind—those from other fields and other foci."[32] Considering Latino politics through the field of political theory is just such an effort to work and move in this larger and less clearly demarcated intellectual terrain.

Borrowing from the arts—music in particular—counterpoint articulates an idea by means of juxtaposition, reflecting an antihegemonic sensibility by complicating a single theme through the addition of contrasting themes. As Brown notes, such contrasting elements featured simultaneously do not simply harmonize, blend, or compete. Instead, counterpoint's multiplicity brings out complexities "that cannot emerge through a monolithic or single melody. This complexity does not add up to a whole but rather sets off a theme by providing it an elsewhere."[33] Counterpoint "sets off or articulates a thematic by means of contrast or juxtaposition; it highlights dominance through a kind of reverse othering."[34]

In making such crossings, I seek to do more than demonstrate parallels between the leading ideas and concepts of Latino politics and those within the field of political theory. This project looks to construct an encounter between democratic theory and Latino politics in order to comprehend the diverse and sometimes paradoxical ways in which Latinos lay claim to the public realm. Such a reading must resist glossing over important differences in historical context, as well as the attempt to reconcile the many disjunctions that exist between these bodies of thought. This effort requires a method of theorizing that involves "thinking with and against" the theorists and movements I seek to engage.[35] Such acts of appropriation and amendment can lead to forms of "reverse othering" that help defamiliarize the categories and practices of *Latinidad* that I seek to call into question. Moreover, instead of seeing identity politics as fundamentally *outside* the larger tradition of modern political thought, contrapuntal practices reveal the contradictions and challenges of democracy—decentering whiteness by engaging the assumptions and practices of Latinos living in the United States.

In taking this approach, I do not mean to imply that those who engaged in the political acts I examine consciously understood their actions in the terms I am describing. Nor am I suggesting that the theorists on whom I draw in each chapter fully encompass the dynamics at play. Rather than turning to Arendt to explore the immigrant-rights protests and to Rousseau to highlight the affective dimensions of the Chicano and Puerto Rican movements, I could have discussed the Nietzschean elements of the 2006 marches—or drawn on Arendt to analyze the Chicano and Puerto Rican movements. Clearly, one can establish productive juxtapositions and theoretical counterpoints in many different ways. My argument is simply that a reconsideration of these events through work of the theorists I have selected allows us to appreciate elements of Latino thought and practice we might otherwise not see.

In the concluding pages, I consider the implications of approaching *Latinidad* as a site of permanent political contest. Drawing on William Connolly's Deleuzean approach to pluralization, I propose a new, more explicitly political understanding of Latino identity, in which political subjectivity is recognized as inescapably fragmented and where agonistic identities are understood as foundational to its democratic project. Approaching *Latinidad* as action—as something we *do* rather than something we *are*—this definition sees Latino politics as inherently coalitional. Such an approach offers no guarantees regarding the ideological content of *Latinidad*. However, by approaching the category "Latino" as an assertion rather than an answer, the essentially contested quality of *Latinidad* avoids the trap of unitary inclusiveness that has often characterized Latino politics in the United States. By contrast, this reading of *Latinidad* acknowledges the presence of some and the absence of others. In this vision of politics, energy is directed at building majorities based on shared political visions of social justice rather than the solace (but ultimate frustration) of equating political agreement with identity. Such an approach emphasizes the importance of shared principles and shared beliefs while recognizing that exclusion and ideological competition are a legitimate and even necessary aspect of political community. In doing this, *The Trouble with Unity* concludes by sketching out some of the political possibilities that emerge when "Latino" is approached as a site of ongoing resignifiability—as protean yet not unrecognizable.

1 El Pueblo Unido

Visions of Unity in the Chicano and Puerto Rican Movements

During the late 1960s and 1970s, Mexican American and Puerto Rican activists put forward a politically charged critique of American politics. Bringing together a paradoxical mix of cultural nationalism, liberal reformism, radical critique, and romantic idealism, the Chicano and Puerto Rican movements created a new political vocabulary, one emphasizing resistance, recognition, cultural pride, authenticity, and fraternity (*hermanidad*). The movements—organizations, issues, and events—left a profound legacy.

Unlike the civil rights struggles of African Americans or the protest politics surrounding the Vietnam War, the Chicano and Puerto Rican movements represent a decidedly underexplored aspect of 1960s New Left radicalism. Outside of the communities themselves, the names, places, and events of these two movements are virtually unknown. Yet as many scholars of Chicano and Puerto Rican politics have noted, despite their short duration, both movements produced a disproportionate number of political leaders, academics, and artists whose influence persists to this day.[1] According to Rodolfo de la Garza, many of today's Chicano political elites were members of a "political generation" created by the Chicano movement.[2] Similarly, Andrés Torres and José Velázquez characterize Puerto Rican movement activists as continuing to shape contemporary Puerto Rican politics and culture. In the preface to *The Puerto Rican Movement: Voices from the Diaspora*, Torres and Velázquez describe the movement's legacy:

This is a generation that has produced leaders in civic, religious, and labor organizations and has even propelled a few elected officials into local and national government. And yes, some even have made their mark in the corporate world . . . they are a significant force in cultural, advocacy, electoral and community-building strategies wherever there are concentrations of Latinos. They direct social service agencies. . . . They teach in schools and colleges. . . . As musicians, artists, and writers, they are leading a renaissance in the arts. . . . They counsel youth and run health programs . . . operate cultural and educational programs . . . and help to strengthen labor unions and organize for workers' rights.[3]

Beyond the cultivation of a significant sociopolitical class, both movements produced institutions that continue to shape Latino political and cultural discourse. As New Left historian Van Gosse has noted, "The least-told story of U.S. history in the late twentieth century is how the social movements of the Sixties institutionalized themselves."[4] This is certainly true for Latino politics: national organizations such as the Mexican-American Legal Defense and Education Fund, National Council of La Raza, Institute for Puerto Rican Policy, and Congressional Hispanic Caucus all trace their political roots to these movements and continue to influence Latino politics at the national level, yet their roots are rarely discussed or acknowledged.[5] The movement's institutional legacy can also be seen in the realm of higher education: Chicano and Puerto Rican studies programs are the product of these movements and continue to play a key role in providing Latinos with a "civic education" that both politicizes and produces particular conceptions of Latino identity and subjectivity.

Interestingly, the recent rise of Latinos to high-profile political positions has led to increased (albeit distorted) attention to these organizations and their radical past. In 2003, during the California gubernatorial recall election, Lieutenant Governor Cruz Bustamante, the most prominent Democrat on the ballot, was questioned repeatedly about being a member of the Movimiento Estudiantil Chicano de Aztlán (MEChA) while attending California State University, Fresno, in the 1970s. Right-wing pundits demanded that Bustamante denounce an organization they characterized as "as racist as the Ku Klux Klan."[6] Similarly, in 2009, when Sonia Sotomayor was preparing for congressional hearings for her appointment to the Supreme Court, she was accused of being a racist for her involvement with "radical" organizations such as the Puerto Rican Legal Defense and Education Fund and the National Council of La Raza.[7] The fact that so many Latino elites were once members of these organizations speaks to the role these movements and organizations played in the creation of a significant sociopolitical class. Simultaneously, the fact that today these individuals and organizations are not radical but, rather, liberal to moderate speaks to both the movements' success and their limits—success at being catalysts for the creation and institutionalization of Latino advocacy organizations, failure for the inability to institutionalize a more radical critique of U.S. society. Sadly, right-wing politicians' and pundits' tarring prominent Latinos as "secret" radicals and racist nationalists speaks to widespread ignorance and the context of discrimination in which those views emerged. Yet despite such misinformation, as Laura Pulido writes in *Black, Brown, Yellow, and Left*, the radical activism of the 1960s and 1970s has left a lasting impression on contemporary progressive politics: "Even though the movement itself has collapsed, its legacy and impact can be seen in the greater empowerment of people of color, as well as in the coalitions and organizations forged out of the experiences and networks of that era."[8]

This chapter is divided into four sections: the first section provides a brief history of the Chicano and Puerto Rican movements; the second examines the principles and political impulses that both movements share; the third explores how the concept of unity was central to the overall ethos of both the Chicano and Puerto Rican movements; and the final section discusses the politics of Latina feminism and how women in both movements continued to deploy the concept of unity, even as its disciplinary ideal often served to silence feminist critique.

The Chicano and Puerto Rican Movements

Described as "the most traumatic and profound social movement to ever occur among Mexicans on the U.S. side of the Rio Grande," the Chicano movement led to a fundamental shift in the way Mexican Americans saw themselves, practiced politics, and related to American society.[9] Characterized by intense political activity and (at times) a militant cultural nationalism, the movement enjoyed a relatively brief heyday, from around 1965 to 1975. But during that tumultuous decade, it involved thousands of participants and encompassed a number of distinct (though related) issues. In George Mariscal's words, the movement was "a mass mobilization dedicated to a wide range of social projects, from ethnic separatism to socialist internationalism, from electoral politics to institutional reform and even armed insurrection."[10]

Prior to the movement, particularly in the years between 1920 and 1960, Mexican American politics was decidedly liberal in character. During this period, assimilation, integration, and participation in electoral politics were the norms governing Mexican American politics in the United States. The focus was on individual advancement and access to the political mainstream, what historian Mario Barrera calls the "egalitarian ideal" in Mexican American politics.[11] Organizations such as the American G.I. Forum, the Pan American Progressive Association, and the League of United Latin American Citizens (LULAC) fought discrimination by encouraging voter turnout and working through the courts. Internally, these organizations also placed a strong emphasis on loyalty, assimilation, leadership development, and youth programs. The LULAC program, for example, emphasized "our unquestionable loyalty to the ideals, principles and citizenship of the United States of America."[12] These themes were often echoed in the *LULAC News*, the group's official newspaper. In his 1939 article "Our Americanism," LULAC member Ezequiel Salinas wrote that the organization's members would "accept no theory . . . adhere to no doctrine . . . follow no ideology which does not carry the star spangled symbol as its standard."[13]

Mexican American civic elites sought political and socioeconomic advancement not by building mass movements or promoting community cohesion but through strengthening their ties to the Democratic Party and other traditional bastions of political power.[14] Mexican American politics during this era was dominated by businessmen and other members of the Mexican American middle class.[15] LULAC sought explicitly to distinguish its middle-class membership from the influx of recent Mexican newcomers.[16] A liberal organization that fought on behalf of the poorer segments of the population (including braceros and other migrant workers), LULAC nevertheless restricted its membership to American citizens. This emphasis on citizenship was also central to the American G.I. Forum, an organization dedicated to assisting Mexican American war veterans.[17] Emphasizing the relationship between service and membership, the G.I. Forum invoked patriotic symbols and rhetoric to secure benefits and defend Mexican American civil rights.

Despite the efforts of middle-class leaders and activists, by the late 1960s, ongoing discrimination and widespread inequality left Mexican Americans disillusioned with the "egalitarian ideal" and its emphasis on Americanism, assimilation, and individualism. For example, while LULAC won significant victories in the courts in the late 1940s over de jure school segregation, during the 1960s de facto segregation continued to be the reality for the majority of Mexican American youth.[18] At this time, the high school dropout rate was still over 50 percent for Mexican Americans, with a majority of students attending overcrowded, underfunded schools. Mexican American history and literature were virtually absent from school curricula, and most schools had few, if any, Mexican American teachers or administrators.[19]

By the late 1960s, Mexican Americans continued to face serious barriers to socioeconomic advancement despite efforts to prove themselves loyal and legitimate members of the American polity. The rise of the Chicano movement, then, was a reaction to ongoing inequality as well as the earlier strategies of Mexican American civic elites. Dissatisfied with their elders' assimilationist politics and inspired by the black civil rights movement, antiwar protests, and national liberation struggles in Europe and the Third World, Chicano students emerged as some of the community's most politicized and active members. Unlike the earlier generation of middle-class leaders, movement activists emphasized mass protest and grassroots participation. For Chicano students, fighting for citizenship rights meant organizing rallies, sit-ins, marches, "blow-outs," and demonstrations, both on campuses and in the streets.[20] Chicano activists protested the Vietnam War by organizing the Chicano Moratorium, one of the largest antiwar demonstrations ever by a community of color.[21] Across the United States, students fought for Chicano studies programs and demanded "better educational and social opportunities for their communities and for their generation."[22]

More than a brief burst of youthful radicalism, the Chicano movement represented a radical shift in group consciousness that was shaped by labor activism, property rights, electoral activism, and cultural production through the arts. In California, César Chavez, along with Dolores Huerta, founded the National Farm Workers Association, later to become the United Farm Workers of America. Throughout the Southwest, Chavez and the UFW organized the largely (though not exclusively) Mexican farmworkers through strikes, nationally publicized pilgrimages, hunger strikes, and consumer boycotts in an effort to win labor contracts from growers, improve labor conditions, and better the lives of migrant farmworkers. In Los Angeles, a paramilitary group calling itself the Brown Berets "captured the imagination of young people and the media" by encouraging student protest, creating a free clinic, and "calling for an end to the Vietnam War before that demand became widespread."[23] In New Mexico, Reies López Tijerina founded the Alianza Federal de Mercedes (Federated Alliance of Land Grants), an organization dedicated to restoring ownership of common-use land (*ejidos*) taken from Mexican individuals and small farming communities left landless as a result of the 1846–48 Mexican-American War.[24] In Colorado, Rodolfo "Corky" Gonzáles organized barrio youth through his Chicano civil rights organization, Crusade for Justice. In Texas, Jose Angel Gutiérrez founded La Raza Unida, an independent political party that won control of the Crystal City city council.[25] The 1970 electoral victory of La Raza Unida marked the first time since the Mexican-American War that the Chicanos of Crystal City had political control of their community's schools.[26] Culturally, the movement was also crucial to bringing about an artistic renaissance: Chicano cultural production in art, music, and literature exploded during the late 1960s and early 1970s, with many prominent muralists, musicians, poets, playwrights, and writers emerging during this period.[27]

One of the Chicano movement's most striking elements was its heterogeneity. Rural farmworkers, urban youth, disenfranchised land-grant owners, university students, labor organizers, artists, community activists—at times, the movement seemed to embody the historical, regional, and social diversity of the Chicano body politic. Yet within this broad spectrum of issues and actions, the movement was characterized by tremendous overlap and interconnected involvement. Nowhere was this overlap more apparent than within the student movement, where issues of self-identity, personal experience, and historical memory were understood as crucial components of a progressive politics.[28]

In contrast to the earlier focus on assimilation and integration, Chicano politics of the late 1960s and early 1970s can be best understood through the emerging ideology of cultural nationalism, dubbed *Chicanismo*. According to Ignacio García, *Chicanismo* can be understood as a "militant version of self-help and racial solidarity."[29] Focusing on racial pride and the celebration of cultural difference, Chicano cultural nationalists sought to transcend social and class divisions by emphasizing a shared history of racial discrimination and extolling the virtues of a shared indigenous past.[30] One of the most potent and successful symbols of reimagining Chicano identity through the use of history and myth was the concept of Aztlán, a term that entered the movement's cultural discourse in 1969 at the Chicano Youth Liberation Conference. Organized by "Corky" Gonzáles and sponsored by his Crusade for Justice, the conference's goal was to unite the student movement and connect college students to barrio youth.[31] It was here that *El Plan Espiritual de Aztlán* was first introduced and read aloud to the 1,500 attendees.[32] Initially a pre-Cortesian myth of origin, Aztlán came to represent the geographic region known as the southwestern part of the United States.[33] Written and conceived by Chicano poet Alurista, *El Plan Espiritual de Aztlán* calls on its readers to recognize their Aztec origins and historical connection to the Mexican territories lost to the United States. As J. Jorge Klor de Alva notes, in a movement hungry for symbols, Aztlán is "still the single most distinguishing metaphor for Chicano activism. . . . [T]he term adorns countless poems, novels, painting, and organizations which display it as both a sign of their content and a mark of their political ideology."[34]

The appropriation of Aztlán has been described as "the most brilliant political maneuver of the Chicano cultural nationalists." Under no other sign or symbol from the left, right, or center "were as many Chicanos mobilized and as much enthusiasm galvanized into political action—except for the concept of *Chicanismo* itself."[35]

Following the 1969 conference, Chicano activists published and widely disseminated *El Plan Espiritual de Aztlán*. As a political manifesto, *El Plan* extols the ideals of Chicano unity and cultural nationalism. Rather than promoting pluralism and the politics of liberal individualism, the new ethos of *Chicanismo* stressed self-determination and communal empowerment. Defiant and combative, movement leaders disparaged the emphasis on loyalty and patriotism put forward by an earlier generation of Mexican American activists. Social inequality, community empowerment, pride, and fear of cultural disintegration were the major concerns of this new generation of activists.

While Chicano activists were mobilizing in California and throughout the Southwest, 3,000 miles away, Puerto Rican radicals were building a social movement that emphasized cultural pride, community control, direct action, and decolonization. As with the Chicano movement, the revolutionary nationalism of activists in the 1960s and 1970s transformed Puerto Rican politics.

Like those of their Chicano counterparts in the Southwest, Puerto Rican politics in the 1950s was dominated by the community's more moderate and middle-class members. According to scholar Roberto Rodríguez-Morazzani, assimilation was the dominant strategy of politically active Puerto Ricans during the 1950s and early 1960s.[36] That accommodationist strategy was something of an aberration: prior to World War II, Puerto Ricans had a long and rich history of political radicalism. Based primarily in New York City, Puerto Rican politics was dominated by leftist nationalists organizing for independence and against Spanish colonialism.[37] Following the Spanish-American War (when the island of Puerto Rico was ceded to the United States) and the passage of the Jones Act in 1917 (which imposed U.S. citizenship on the people of Puerto Rico), Puerto Ricans began to migrate to the United States in ever-greater numbers.

This earlier generation of Puerto Ricans was powerfully influenced by the growing presence of cigar makers (*tabaqueros*) and their participation in socialist and labor politics.[38] Cigar makers not only were skilled craftsmen—they also participated in the tradition of factory readings, in which a person was hired to read to the employees while they did their work.[39] The tradition of the *lectors* and their involvement in the labor movement made the *tabaqueros* "the most educated and politically advanced sector of the Puerto Rican working class."[40] Cigar workers were active in various independence, socialist, and labor organizations, including the American Federation of Labor and the Socialist Labor Party.[41]

Following World War II, working-class radicalism among Puerto Ricans began to decline.[42] Mechanization of the cigar industry and the movement of cigar factories away from New York to New Jersey, Pennsylvania, and other locations led to the deskilling and dispersal of cigar workers. Massive immigration to the mainland also changed the Puerto Rican political climate in the United States. The enormous influx of postwar immigration displaced the earlier community of leftists, transforming this former majority into a minority of the Puerto Rican community in New York. With the dissolution of this earlier political culture and community, Puerto Rican politics became more moderate, less tied to labor unions, and less focused on the grass roots. By the early 1960s, the majority of Puerto Ricans were unfamiliar with this radical past. Not until the movement's emergence would this early history be recuperated, as activists sought to link their struggle with the oppositional politics of an earlier era.

The Puerto Rican movement of the 1960s and 1970s can be defined by its consistent calls for a radical transformation of U.S. society while simultaneously promoting the independence of Puerto Rico.[43] Known as El Nuevo Despertar, this "New Awakening" of Puerto Rican radicalism was inspired and shaped by the growing militancy abroad and at home. Black Power, youth unrest (particularly against the Vietnam War), the War on Poverty, national liberation struggles in the Third World, Chicano and Native American militancy, gay and lesbian rights, and second-wave feminism are all part of the context that shaped the movement.

A number of significant organizations emerged during this period: the Young Lords Party, the Puerto Rican Socialist Party, El Comité-MINP (Puerto Rican National Left Movement), the Puerto Rican Student Union, the Movement for National Liberation, the Armed Forces for National Liberation, the Nationalist Party, and the Puerto Rican Independence Party.[44] Of the various organizations that constituted the Puerto Rican movement, the Young Lords left the most lasting legacy. In *Boricua Power: A Political History of Puerto Ricans in the United States*, José Ramón Sánchez describes the Young Lords as "more successful than most in getting the larger society to pay attention to Puerto Rican community needs and demands."[45] Beyond their influence on later Puerto Rican political and civic institutions, the Young Lords also distinguished themselves in their capacity "to capture the public's attention and imagination to a degree that no Puerto Rican politician or leader has been able to do since then."[46] For example, during the early months of 1970, fully 40 percent of all *New York Times* news reports on Puerto Ricans focused on the Young Lords.[47] Moreover, between 1969 and 1971, the Young

Lords "made it to the national media stage" almost as often as leading Puerto Rican politician Herman Badillo and actually had more featured stories on national television than Badillo.[48] Given the group's significance, my discussion of the Puerto Rican movement will focus on the practices and writings of the Young Lords Party and its leaders.[49]

Like its Chicano counterpart, the Puerto Rican left was a small but heterogeneous portion of the community. Characterizing the membership of the Young Lords, for example, former activist Iris Morales describes the organization as being composed of "former prison inmates, recovering heroin addicts and alcoholics, college students and high school drop-outs, young factory and hospital workers, parents and Vietnam veterans."[50] Compared with Chicanos, who had large and concentrated population centers (both urban and rural) throughout the southwestern United States, the Puerto Rican community was smaller in number, primarily urban, and concentrated in the Northeast and Midwest, particularly New York City and Chicago.

Ideologically, the Young Lords presented themselves as a socialist organization. In his book *We Took the Streets: Fighting for Latino Rights with the Young Lords*, Miguel "Mickey" Melendez described the organization as having a "philosophical likeness" with groups such as the Youth Against War and Fascism, the Communist Party USA, the Youth International Party (Yippies), La Casa de Las Americas, and the Movimiento Pro-Independencia.[51] As a "revolutionary nationalist party," their main goal was the "self-determination" and "liberation" of Puerto Ricans "on the island and inside the United States."[52] In practice, the Young Lords based much of their organizing on "serve the people programs," including free breakfast and clothing programs, door-to-door testing for lead poisoning and tuberculosis, a detox and drug rehabilitation program, and "liberation" schools that taught Spanish and Puerto Rican history to barrio children. The Young Lords organized conferences and marches, lobbied city officials to improve garbage pickup, and occupied city hospitals and churches to expose substandard conditions experienced by many mainland Puerto Ricans.[53] In doing this, the Young Lords built a significant mass base of support in the Puerto Rican community.

During their heyday, the Young Lords had a large and active base in New York, with branches in New Jersey, Pennsylvania, and Connecticut and on the island of Puerto Rico,[54] as well as ties to Puerto Rican groups in Massachusetts, Ohio, and Michigan. In New York City, the organization published a bilingual newspaper (*Pa'lante*) and produced its own radio show on WBAI.[55] Its effectiveness in using the mass media helped the Young Lords to organize some of the largest and most successful demonstrations of the Puerto Rican left (including a 1970 march of 10,000 from El Barrio (East Harlem) to the United Nations to protest police brutality and the colonial status of Puerto Rico).[56] The UN march is, to date, "the largest anti-colonial street demonstration set up by mainland Puerto Ricans."[57]

While Chicanos in the Southwest sought to emulate the paramilitary style of the Black Panthers by forming groups such as the Brown Berets, it was Puerto Rican organizations like the Young Lords that most self-consciously modeled themselves on the Black Power movement.

This cultural and political solidarity between African Americans and Puerto Ricans is not surprising; indeed, a number of scholars have noted the "long and profound" relationship the two groups have shared. According to Juan Flores, "New York Puerto Ricans have been at close living and working quarters with Blacks, perhaps closer than any other national group in the history of this country."[58] Moreover, the Afro-Caribbean origins of Puerto Ricans make them a people who have had to continually negotiate the black-white racial divide, both in the United States and in Puerto Rico. In the organization's analysis of race, the Young Lords explored the differences between *Afro-Boricuas* (Puerto Rican blacks) and *Jíbaros* (light-skinned Creoles). Capturing this distinction between light- and dark-skinned Puerto Ricans, Pablo Guzmán claimed, "before they called me a spic, they called me a nigger."[59] The resignation of Young Lords leader Denise Oliver and her subsequent membership in the Black Panther Party is further testimony to the close and interconnected political and racial relationship between Puerto Rican and African American leftists during this period.[60]

Chicanismo y el Nuevo Despertar: The Shared Vision of the Chicano and Puerto Rican Movements

While both movements placed a strong emphasis on nationalism, Chicano and Puerto Rican activists simultaneously displayed enormous ideological diversity, with liberals, socialists, feminists, and communists making a home for themselves in both movements. According to Ignacio García, this tendency to draw freely from an array of theories and ideologies was a consistent feature of movement politics. For García, *Chicanismo* was the culmination and coalescing of various philosophical and historical currents that existed in the Mexican American political community. The ethos of *Chicanismo* involved a radical shift in group consciousness, but as a political philosophy, it was far from coherent, developing through an uneven and evolutionary process.[61] The same can be said for the Puerto

Rican movement, in which the ideology of its participants evolved over time, and many resisted identifying with any particular political philosophy.

But despite the ideological heterogeneity that characterized both movements, Puerto Rican and Chicano politics shared a number of political impulses. The following section puts forward an analysis of key principles that I see as defining both movements: a critique of racism and inequality and an emphasis on community control—that is, communal advancement and the critique of individualism.

Racism, Social Inequality, and Cultural Pride

During this period, Latino artists did not shy away from taking on issues of racial and economic inequality; many artists displayed a newly politicized style of expression. The music, murals, literature, and theater of the movement period most often explored racial identity, cultural pride, and social inequality. Pedro Pietri's oft-cited poem "Puerto Rican Obituary" is representative of this developing aesthetic. It states:

> Here lies Juan
> Here lies Miguel
> Here lies Milagros
> Here lies Olga
> Here lies Manuel
> who died yesterday today
> and will die again tomorrow
> Always broke
> Always owing
> Never knowing
> that they are beautiful people
> Never knowing
> The geography of their complexion
>
> PUERTO RICO IS A BEAUTIFUL PLACE
> PUERTORRIQUEÑOS ARE A BEAUTIFUL RACE[62]

Poetry such as "Puerto Rican Obituary" highlights another significant aspect of movement thought: the shift from cultural shame to ethnic pride. Unlike earlier critiques of prejudice and discrimination, movement rhetoric and writings often focused on the emotional and psychic damage of racism, exploring the need to overcome internalized shame and self-hate.

Throughout this period, Latino activists articulated increasingly pointed critiques of assimilation, simultaneously developing forms of pride and racial consciousness that were not so much preexistent as they were produced and con-stituted by the movement's emerging ethos. Mickey Melendez describes this process when discussing a fellow member of the Young Lords during the organi-zation's inception:

> Paul had gone to Mexico for a Spanish-culture immersion and to learn the language of our people. . . . Upon his return, Paul was no longer Paul. Now he was Pablo. Not only did he become Pablo, he became Pablo "Yoruba" Guzmán—a complete transformation. That time had the power of altering hundreds of thousands of us in search of our identity, our true history and pride within ourselves.[63]

By depicting the shift whereby "Paul was no longer Paul," Melendez character-izes Guzmán's identity as both return and transformation. Melendez describes Guzmán as no longer the assimilated college student unable to speak Spanish but, rather, a man who had gained pride through the discovery of his "true" language, history, and identity. Yet this naturalized depiction of return fails to capture the complexities of *Latinidad* that define Guzmán's emerging sense of self. He is, after all, a young man who goes to Mexico to gain a deeper sense of his identity as a Puerto Rican.

While the complexities of identity were often essentialized during this era, the movement's analysis of racism and inequality offered Chicanos and Puerto Ricans a valuable framework for critiquing forms of defensive assimilation that involved proving their worth to the dominant culture. Instead, Anglo society had to prove itself to Chicanos and Puerto Ricans. This new perspective is clearly apparent in *El Plan de Santa Barbara*:

> For decades Mexican people in the United States struggled to realize the "American Dream." And some—a few—have. But the cost, the ultimate cost of assimilation, required turning away from *el barrio* and *la colonia*. In the meantime, due to the racist structure of this society, to our essentially different life style, and to the socio-economic functions assigned to our community by Anglo-American society—as suppliers of cheap labor and a dumping ground for the small-time capitalist entrepreneur—the *barrio* and *colonia* remained exploited, impoverished, and marginal.[64]

According to Berkeley professor Carlos Muñoz, the Chicano movement was a quest for identity, and both this search and the dilemmas it posed are key to understanding the Chicano and Puerto Rican student movement.[65] As Mario Barrera argues, the movement represented a distinct new ideological phase in which community, identity, and ethnic equality "were not only raised simultaneously, but were intimately linked."[66]

Activists' critique of racism and political and economic inequality represents one of the most important and successful aspects of the movement's legacy. The movement's approach to identity convinced a generation of Chicanos and Puerto Ricans that they did not have to choose between racial pride and social equality. More significantly, the collective act of exposing conditions, speaking out against economic exploitation, and drawing attention to issues of social injustice resonated powerfully with large segments of the Chicano and Puerto Rican communities. As Iris Morales notes, "Even those who disagreed with our tactics had to agree the injustices we pointed to were clear. . . . The organization touched people of conscience in our community."[67]

But while both movements put forward a powerful critique of the problems facing Chicanos and Puerto Ricans, they proved less effective when trying to transform their critique into an effective political strategy. In other words, movement activists were more successful as voices of opposition than as creators of substantive political and economic alternatives.

Community Control, Group Advancement, Cross-Class Solidarity, and the Critique of Individualism

El Plan de Santa Barbara also demonstrates a second principle of the movement: the celebration of community and the critique of American individualism. Both Chicano and Puerto Rican activists continually stressed the importance of community control of local institutions, arguing that oppression and inequality would never end until Chicanos and Puerto Ricans controlled the institutions that directly affected community life.[68] This analysis of community control is key in *El Plan Espiritual de Aztlán*, one of the earliest political manifestos to emerge from the Chicano movement. *El Plan* states:

> 2. ECONOMY: economic control of our lives and our communities can only come about by driving the exploiter out of our communities, our pueblos, and our lands and by controlling and developing our own talents, sweat, and resources. . . . Institutions in our community which do not serve the people have no place in the community. The institutions belong to the people.[69]

The Young Lords' thirteen-point platform makes almost identical demands:

6. WE WANT COMMUNITY CONTROL OF OUR INSTITUTIONS AND LAND.

> We want control of our communities by our people and programs to guarantee that all institutions serve the needs of our people. People's control of police, health services, churches, schools, housing, transportation, and welfare are needed. We want an end to attacks on our land by urban renewal, highway destruction, and university corporations. LAND BELONGS TO ALL THE PEOPLE!

For Chicano and Puerto Ricans, substandard housing, inferior health care, failing schools, dangerous and exploitive working conditions, and inadequate civil rights protection all helped encourage a nationalist critique among activists that institutions controlled by non-Latinos could not be trusted. In other words, material encounters with social inequality and racism led these movements to their critique of community control.

The demand for community control also highlights a related shift in perspective—the vision of Chicanos and Puerto Ricans as a distinct, separate, and cohesive community. In contrast to earlier narratives of advancement that presumed leaving the barrio in order to assimilate into the broader community, movement rhetoric stressed internal transformation and *group* advancement. In the Young Lords Party, even those who were *not* from the barrio were encouraged to take their place alongside the Latino working class. No longer a place to escape, the barrio became a place to sustain.

Moreover, the rhetoric of group advancement and community maintenance was at its most forceful in the writings of those segments of the community most likely to leave. University students were portrayed as having particularly deep and powerful obligations to the community. *El Plan de Santa Barbara*, for example, was written by Chicano graduate students and professors with regard to the relationship between the movement and higher education. Discussing the responsibilities that college students have to the broader community, it states:

> MEChA [a Chicano student organization] must bring to the mind of every young Chicano that the liberation of his people from prejudice and oppression is in his hands and this responsibility is greater than personal achievement and more meaningful than degrees, especially if they are earned at the expense of his identity and cultural integrity.[70]

In *El Plan de Santa Barbara*, a university education is refigured as an opportunity to better serve one's community. One leaves in order to return.

In examining the political philosophies of these two movements, what becomes clear is that both viewed American society and culture as defined by its overemphasis on the individual at the expense of the community. Describing the Young Lords' vision of the Puerto Rican community, Pablo Guzmán offers this critique of American individualism:

> We're brought up to be individuals who look out solely for themselves. In school we're taught that the first law of nature is self-preservation. We say that's bullshit—the first law of nature is preservation of the group, because as long as your nation exists, then you exist. See, people often run the line down to me, "Well, you know, you've got some brains—you could make it." Yeah, I could make it, I could—me, myself, Pablo "Yoruba" Guzmán. I could be into law, I could be into public relations, a number of fields I could have gone into, right. But that same thing does not hold true for my people. I become the exception rather than the rule, and we're trying to make a society where opportunity is the rule for everybody.[71]

As stated earlier, the Young Lords' emphasis on group advancement provides a compelling counternarrative to the politics of liberal individualism. Guzmán's critique also leads to the final point about the movement's approach to community: the need to identify and live in solidarity with those at the bottom of the socioeconomic ladder. The Young Lords, for example, originated as a Puerto Rican street gang.[72] In their ability to trace their roots from the Chicago streets to political organization, the Young Lords reflected the organization's identity as an organization that sought to create a "unity of the street people with students of working class background."[73] Similarly, Chicanos in the Southwest were aware of the class implications of their own naming practices. Discussing the newfound choice to self-identify as "Chicano," the writers of *El Plan de Santa Barbara* state:

> Culturally, the word *Chicano*, in the past a pejorative and class-bound adjective, has now become the root idea of a new cultural identity for our people. It also reveals a growing solidarity and the development of a common social praxis. The widespread use of the term *Chicano* today signals a rebirth of pride and confidence.[74]

In addition to their support for César Chavez and the farmworkers' struggle, Chicano activists consistently displayed solidarity with and compassion for "the poor, the imprisoned, the abused, and even the misguided criminal element."[75]

The creation of El Partido de la Raza Unida (La Raza Unida Party) in 1970 is a prime example of the drive for community control and the importance of cross-class solidarity. In addition to mobilizing Chicanos to vote, La Raza Unida also sought to run candidates who were themselves members of the community's working class. The 1970 election in Crystal City exemplifies this approach: the four candidates recruited by José Angel Gutiérrez were all working-class. Running for the school board were Mike Pérez, a dance-hall operator, and Arturo Gonzales, a twenty-one-year-old gas station attendant. The candidates for city council were Pablo Puente, a manager of a local auto-parts store, and Ventura Gonzales, a worker at the Del Monte packing and cannery plant just outside Crystal City.[76] According to García, the party worked explicitly to promote members of the Chicano community "who did not fit the Anglos' model of a candidate."[77] Not surprisingly, the opposition argued that Crystal City needed "responsible men for responsible jobs," arguing that "poor migrant farm workers, dance hall operators, gas-station attendants, and young radicals were not the right people to govern the city."[78]

The desire among movement activists to identify with their communities' most oppressed and despised segments implies a shared destiny with working-class members. It is a democratic ethos, reflecting a concern with conditions faced by the *majority* of Latinos in the United States. Moreover, this shift was a self-conscious inversion of the approach taken by the previous generation of Latino civic elites, who sought to avoid the stigma of poverty by emphasizing their constituents' middle-class status and/or aspirations.

But this "bottom-up" strategy also led movement activists to romanticize disadvantaged and disempowered Latinos, portraying them as the community's most "authentic" members. Depending on how this tendency was invoked and deployed, it was capable of producing both radical political solidarity and a fetishizing of the disadvantaged. Personal experience with poverty became a precondition for political credibility for movement activists, with some members becoming increasingly defensive about having assimilated and/or middle-class backgrounds and aspirations.

The movement's emphasis on community control had a similar double-edged function. On one level, community control represented the democratic desire for autonomy and self-sufficiency. For movement activists, community control was a much-needed response to institutions that had historically neglected Latinos, treating them as dependent, unimportant, and/or civically incompetent. In this context, community control was more than a claim for local power. Instead, as Agustín Laó notes in "Resources of Hope: Imagining the Young Lords and the Politics of Memory," it was "a radical democratic demand for self-management on behalf of those who work and those who are serviced."[79] However, community control *also* presumed that Chicano and Puerto Rican communities were always coherent and concentrated—monolithic communities with few "outsiders." In fact, many communities were more racially diverse and less spatially concentrated than movement rhetoric implied. During the 1960s and 1970s, Andrés Torres notes, Puerto Ricans as a group were clearly politically disempowered and experiencing racism and poverty, but they were also simultaneously experiencing increasing signs of assimilation, including greater English-language usage, the gradual adoption of U.S. customs and traditions, and an increase in marriages to non–Puerto Ricans.[80] The ideology of community control and self-help failed to take into consideration this reality of racially mixed communities and internal cultural diversity. Instead, movement activists often chose to rhetorically produce a more homogeneous vision of the community rather than grapple with this more complex reality.

Discernible within each of the principles discussed here is the belief that group *unity* was necessary for Chicano and Puerto Rican advancement. Racism and social inequality, for example, were collective experiences presumed to unite Latinos, thereby promoting a shared political perspective. In their critique of individualism and group advancement, movement activists asserted their belief that ethnicity (as opposed to shared class interests) was the essential component of political community.

This unitary impulse was shaped in large part by the nationalist ethos that defined Chicano and Puerto Rican politics during this period. But while nationalism powerfully informed activism in both groups, the movements differed in how they interpreted and enacted nationalist principles. The vast majority of Chicano activists, for example, were not ideologically committed to nation-building or separatism. The emphasis on Aztlán as the Chicano homeland was a rhetorical gesture that sought to connect Chicanos to their indigenous past while simultaneously reminding them of the colonial implications of the Mexican-American War. Aztlán, then, represented a mythic narrative suffused with nationalist sentiment that informed the Chicano movement rather than a serious call for the creation of a separate and sovereign state.[81]

In contrast to the Chicano experience, the Puerto Rican movement *did* call for the political independence of Puerto Rico and an end to the island's colonial status. But support for independence did not mean that Puerto Ricans in the United States would have to return to the island. Instead, like Chicanos, Puerto Ricans understood themselves to be a national minority in need of self-determination and community control *within* the United States as well.

In the following section, I explore the relationship between nationalism and unity in the Chicano and Puerto Rican movements. My contention is that the unitary impulse apparent in the Chicano movement is different from the unitary politics of the Puerto Rican movement, in part because they differ in their respective nationalist philosophies. In the Chicano movement, shared culture was seen as the primary precondition for a shared political perspective, whereas for Puerto Rican activists, movement politics was more explicitly Marxist and anticapitalist in perspective. These two forms can be characterized as *cultural* versus *revolutionary* nationalism. But despite their different perspectives, in both movements, group unity ultimately emerges as a dominant ethos shaping both movements.

Nationalism and the Politics of Unity

Puerto Rican Revolutionary Nationalism: Unity through Ideology

The Young Lords understood themselves to be a revolutionary nationalist party with an internationalist vision. According to Melendez, three texts formed the core of the Young Lords' political education program: Franz Fanon's *The Wretched of the Earth*, Mao Tse-tung's *Little Red Book*, and Che Guevara's *Man and Socialism: Transformation of the Individual*.[82] Grounded in Mao's critique of nationalism and Fanon's analysis of colonialism, as well as Vladimir Lenin's writings on imperialism and the national question, the nationalism of the Young Lords was much more ideologically explicit than that of most Chicano leaders. According to Agustín Laó, in the various writings of the Young Lords, members make a distinction between *cultural* nationalism and *revolutionary* nationalism. Pablo Guzmán writes:

> Now, there are some people who would say that there's a contradiction in being a revolutionary nationalist—in fact, they say you can't be a Nationalist and a Socialist at the same time. Well, that's wrong. See, for these people I would quote Mao, where he says that loving your people and your country and fighting to liberate your people is the best way to aid the struggle of all peoples around the world. It's ridiculous to say you're an internationalist and you're going to struggle for all oppressed people, without picking a particular segment of people you're gonna work in . . . revolutionary nationalism— that is the kind of nationalism that says, "Yes, we are proud to be Puerto Rican, we are proud to be number one—but we want everybody else to be number one too, and we're gonna help everyone else be number one." See, 'cause the other kind of nationalism is reactionary nationalism—where you say, "Well, I'm number one. Fuck everybody else."[83]

Despite the differences in ideological clarity, a unitary impulse is present in both Chicano and Puerto nationalism. For the Young Lords, revolutionary nationalism was linked to a "personal and collective decolonization that tran-scends mere cultural self-affirmation."[84] For the Lords, cultural liberation requires a process of decolonization that transforms one's "colonized mentality" of inter-nalized racism, sexism, and self-hate. Inspired by Che Guevara, the Young Lords sought to engage the internal struggle of the individual "to manifest change within himself in order to create a revolution in society."[85] Describing this process, Melendez writes:

> We were transformed from a dependent colonial people to a people capable of charting a path to social justice and independence. We publicly rejected the established norms and American values for the integration of our own cultural value system. We began to reject ideas that perpetuated the supremacy of the male, the dehumanization of homosexuals, and the inequality of our diverse racial origins.[86]

As Melendez's account makes clear, the Young Lords' self-conscious radicalism and their commitment to revolutionary change provided them with a political language capable of challenging the cultural status quo of both the dominant society *and* the Puerto Rican community. By contrast, the Chicano movement's emphasis on culture and tradition produced a more conservative nationalism that left less room for radical transformation. As I discuss later in this chapter, the differences between revolutionary nationalism and cultural nationalism become particularly stark when issues of gender and sexuality come to the fore. The Young Lords' anticolonial discourse was based on a notion of "false consciousness" that functioned to "justify the role of the party in enlightening (raising the conscious-ness) of the masses and giving them a track and a horizon."[87] Combined with their belief in themselves as a vanguard party, this discourse produced an ideological combination that led the Young Lords to view political disagreement as some-thing *external* to the Puerto Rican community—internalized racism, police agents, colonial brainwashing, and so forth. The Young Lords saw a lack of unity as rep-resenting an inability to follow "the correct line" rather than an array of legitimate viewpoints.

Early on, the Young Lords subscribed to the "divided nation" thesis, a theory that linked the liberation of Puerto Ricans in the United States with the island's struggle for independence as a sovereign nation-state. According to the thesis, Puerto Rico is a divided nation, with one-third of Puerto Ricans living in the United States and two-thirds living in Puerto Rico.[88] This vision of Puerto Rican unity is apparent in the Young Lords' description of the opening of the organiza-tion's first branch in Puerto Rico. The Central Committee writes:

In January 1971, we announced that we were going to open a branch in Puerto Rico. This came after fighting for a year and a half in the united states of amerikkka, in the belly of the monster.

You see, one-third of the Puerto Rican Nation is in the united states, and two-thirds of our people are in Puerto Rico. We always knew in our minds and our hearts that the Party would be expanding to Puerto Rico. . . . We saw right from the beginning that one of the first steps in our struggle for National Liberation would be the uniting of our nation.

And now it's done. The one-third and the two-thirds are together. We've opened two branches in Puerto Rico—one in Aquadilla, the home of Julio Roldan, and the other in El Caño. . . .

[W]e will win. Because our compañeras and compañeros everywhere are together. They are strong, dedicated, and filled with love.[89]

According to the "divided nation" thesis, the political interests of Puerto Ricans are the same both on and off the island; Puerto Ricans on the island and in the United States are understood as an organic whole divided by the external and unnatural divide of colonialism.[90] The Young Lords understood Puerto Ricans both as a national minority within the North American "multinational working class" and as a colonized people on the island. In this way, Puerto Rican identity can be seen as oscillating in ambiguity "between the national subject and the colonized subaltern."[91] But even as Puerto Rican subjectivity straddled the national and the subaltern, the Young Lords consistently envisioned the community as "compañeras and compañeros everywhere together . . . strong, dedicated, and filled with love." This romantic imagery is best summed up in the organization's slogan of U.S.-island unity: "*Tengo a Puerto Rico en mi corazón*" (Puerto Rico is in my heart). Not merely a political question, the status of the island is an issue as much about the head as about the heart.

Ultimately, the organization's outreach to Puerto Rico proved politically unsuccessful. As Mickey Melendez observed, "The plan was as ambitious as it was foolish. First-generation Puerto Ricans, born, raised and educated in the U.S., mainly from Northeastern urban cities, were going to export revolution to Puerto Rico. . . . We should have asked ourselves why they would need our brand of nationalism in light of their already established, and strong, nationalist tradition."[92] According to Central Committee member Pablo Guzmán, it made more sense to understand Puerto Ricans as an "oppressed national minority" in the United States.[93] Instead, the move to the island led to fewer resources in the States and to party offices closing throughout New York City.[94]

In contrast to the Chicano movement's ideologically diffuse ethnic populism, the Puerto Rican movement's main organizations were self-consciously socialist. Moreover, the Young Lords practiced a form of "democratic centralism," whereby the Central Committee made all the major decisions and set the organization's direction. According to Iris Morales, this emphasis on strict adherence to Central Committee directives "frequently stifled member creativity and initiative."[95] This increasing concern with ideological clarity—with having the "correct line"—reached a peak in 1973 when the Young Lords Party transformed itself into the Puerto Rican Revolutionary Workers Organization, a Maoist Third World party.[96] In their belief that ideological unity was the key to achieving revolutionary change, the Young Lords' leadership sought a strict definition of what constituted legitimate political interests. Such a unitary narrative meant that there was little room for competing political claims.[97] As Morales notes:

> When members raised differences of opinion with ideology or tactics or leaders, they were often subjected to name-calling and labeled "opportunists." The Central Committee even falsely accused some members of being police agents. During the Puerto Rican Revolutionary Workers' phase, the ruling group maintained control by accusing everyone who disagreed with them of being agents and collaborators. The accusations lost credibility and allowed real agents to continue to operate in the movement unexposed.[98]

According to Melendez, "ideological struggles . . . replaced garbage offensives and breakfast programs. . . . Deviation from the party line was not tolerated, and those who did not speak up were subject to psychological torture, kidnappings, and beatings."[99] Not surprisingly, public support diminished as the former Young Lords Party ceased its grassroots activism and degenerated into yet another segment of the far left consumed by sectarian infighting.

Cultural Nationalism in the Chicano Movement: Unity as Ideology

According to Carlos Munõz, the Chicano movement's most common ideological orientation was nationalism with "a heavy emphasis on cultural identification and cultural issues."[100] Under the heading "Nationalism," *El Plan Espiritual de Aztlàn* states: "Nationalism as the key to organization transcends all religious, political, class and economic factors or boundaries. Nationalism is the common denominator that all members of La Raza can agree on."[101]

In the nationalist philosophy of *El Plan Espiritual de Aztlàn*, ethnicity is what defines one's identity and loyalty. In a speech, movement leader Rodolfo "Corky" Gonzáles explains how a nationalist philosophy is capable of uniting the Chicano community:

> What are the common denominators that unite the people? The key common denominator is nationalism. . . . If Tony is a socialist, if my brother here is an independent, if my sister is a Republican—she might hit me later— if one of the others is a Democrat and one is a communist, and one from the Socialist Labor Party, what do we have in common? Nothing. We've been fighting over parties across the kitchen table, wives are Republicans and husbands are Democrats, sometimes, and we argue over a bunch of garbage. And the same Republicans and Democrats are having cocktails together at the same bar and playing golf together and kissing each other behind the scenes.
>
> So you tell me, what is the common denominator that will touch the barrio, the campo and the ranchitos? Are we going to go down there with some tremendous words of intellectualism which they cannot relate to . . . the revolution of 15 or 20 years from now is not going to feed a hungry child today.
>
> So what is the common denominator we use? It is nationalism.[102]

What is significant about the nationalist ethos of Gonzáles and *El Plan Espiritual Aztlán* is their belief that culture and shared historical experience are sufficient to produce political agreement. Unity would emerge through culture and national origin rather than shared class interests. In Gonzáles's vision of nationalism, there is a preexisting "core" set of cultural and philosophical values that can be "discovered" and that will serve all Chicanos equally well. Specific political beliefs are characterized as insignificant abstractions—"tremendous words of intellectualism . . . a bunch of garbage"—that fade in the face of shared identity and experience. Partisanship is meaningless: Republicans and Democrats are figured as "the same animal with two-heads that feeds from the same trough."[103] By contrast, Gonzáles characterizes his organization, the Crusade for Justice, as a space of participation, unity, and immediacy: "[I]n our group, we have dropped all the parliamentary procedure bull, we dropped all the *gringo* type of government, and we have a *concilio de la familia*."[104]

According to sociologist Maxine Baca Zinn, the Crusade for Justice operated on "a family principle: a system of family ties extending beyond the immediate family to a family of all Chicanos."[105] The movement's depiction of Chicanos as "La familia de la Raza" sought to unite Chicanos to struggle as a family tied together by a spirit of *carnalismo* (brotherhood). Baca Zinn has termed this fusing of cultural and political resistance "political familism."[106] This linkage between political pragmatism and romantic familism permeates both *El Plan Espiritual de Aztlán* and La Raza Unida Party.

As a mythic narrative, poet Alurista's reconceptualization of Aztlán in *El Plan Espiritual de Aztlán* functioned as an imaginative and powerful metaphor for Chicano unity. *El Plan*'s opening statement represents the text at its most ideological, as well as its most mythopoetic:

> In the spirit of a new people that is conscious not only of its proud historical heritage but also of the brutal "gringo" invasion of our territories, we, the Chicano inhabitants and civilizers of the northern land of Aztlán from whence came our forefathers, reclaiming the land of their birth and consecrating the determination of our people of the sun, declare that the call of our blood is our power, our responsibility, and our inevitable destiny. We are free and sovereign to determine those tasks which are justly called for by our house, our land, the sweat of our brows, and by our hearts. Aztlán belongs to those who plant the seeds, water the fields, and gather the crops and not foreign Europeans. We do not recognize capricious frontiers on the bronze continents.
>
> Brotherhood unites us, and love for our brothers makes us a people whose time has come and who struggles against the foreigner "gabacho" who exploits our riches and destroys our culture. With our hearts in our hands and our hands in the soil, we declare the independence of our mestizo nation. We are a bronze people with a bronze culture. Before the world, before all of North America, before all our brothers in the bronze continent, we are a nation, we are a union of free pueblos, we are Aztlán.[107]

In *El Plan*, Aztlán is portrayed as a space of blood and belonging ("Brotherhood unites us, and love for our brothers makes us a people"). Moreover, as a narrative of home and identity, Aztlán mirrors the contradictions of Chicano subjectivity. Like Chicanos themselves, Aztlán is *from* but not *in* Mexico, *in* but not *of* the United States. Aztlán is portrayed not as a return to Mexico but as the spiritual and territorial embodiment of Chicano aspirations. Most important, Aztlán came to symbolize "the spiritual union of the Chicanos, something that is carried within the heart, no matter where they may live or where they may find themselves."[108]

In the nationalist politics of the movement, Chicano unity is intimately linked to political agency. The politics of unity demand that differences be set aside to achieve common goals. Describing the unity produced by nationalism, *El Plan* states:

> *El Plan Espiritual de Aztlán* sets the theme that the Chicanos (La Raza de
> Bronze) must use their nationalism as the key or common denominator for
> mass mobilization and organization. Once we are committed to the idea
> and philosophy of *El Plan de Aztlán*, we can only conclude that social, eco-
> nomic, cultural and political independence is the only road to total libera-
> tion from oppression, exploitation, and racism. Our struggle then must
> be for the control of our barrios, campos, pueblos, lands, our economy,
> our cultural, and our political life. *El Plan* commits all levels of Chicano
> society—the barrio, the campo, the ranchero, the writer, the teacher, the
> worker, the professional—to la Causa.[109]

In *El Plan*, the group unity produced by nationalism represents the "common
denominator" that will lead to "mass mobilization and organization." Nationalism (rather than any particular ideology) is what mobilizes Chicano society
("the writer, the teacher, the worker, the professional"). Unity is what mobilizes to
move Chicanos forward; unity is what will make the group effective and successful.

During the movement, Chicano activists consistently called for "the political
unity of the Chicano people."[110] In fact, unity was the first organizational goal
listed in *El Plan Espiritual de Aztlán*, which states: "UNITY in the thinking of our
people concerning the barrios, the pueblo, the campo, the land, the poor, the
middle class, the professional—all committed to the liberation of La Raza."[111]

El Plan presents a vision of political community characterized by total agreement
("Unity in the thinking of our people"). For the authors of *El Plan*, the Chicano
community is envisioned as a site in which certain core values are beyond the
realm of diversity and disagreement. In the rhetorical realm of the *Plan*, the multiplicity of Chicano social locations inevitably gives way to a united Chicano perspective. The economic and social diversity of Chicanos is named ("the barrios,
the pueblo, the campo, . . . the poor, the middle class, the professional"), but in the
end, a deeper unity of identity prevails ("all committed to the liberation of
La Raza").

Because the idea for a Chicano political party came out of *El Plan Espiritual de
Aztlán*, it is unsurprising that the organization struggled with questions of ideology.
According to Ignacio García, party leaders "wanted a new system based on a
cultural nationalism that was not as yet defined in terms of political processes and
economic institutions."[112]

The creation of La Raza Unida Party in 1970 is a prime example of the belief that
shared cultural identity is a sufficient basis for political action and mobilization.

As the name itself makes clear, La Raza Unida was founded on the principle that Chicanos share a set of interests that transcend ideology and partisanship. Excerpts from a position paper by Armando Navarro, a graduate student and chief organizer of the Riverside–San Bernardino–Upland chapter, are notable because of the paper's many stated and unstated ideological and political claims. Navarro writes:

> La Raza Unida must become more than a political organization. It must symbolize the creation of a nation within a nation, a spiritual unification for effective action of all persons of Mexican descent in the United States. One principle dominates La Raza Unida thought—that the destiny of each Chicano is linked immutably to the destinies of every other Chicano. . . .
>
> Unity will only be achieved by the formation of an evolutionary doctrine which is compatible with the philosophy, culture, and life style of La Raza. This doctrine will seek to synthesize the diverse perspectives of La Raza so that ultimately one dominant perspective will prevail.[113]

As Carlos Muñoz notes, "very little was done to develop [La Raza Unida's] theory or ideology."[114] This lack of ideological development is clearly apparent in Navarro's position paper. It is never made clear or explicit just what type of "evolutionary doctrine" would be "compatible with the philosophy, culture, and life style of La Raza." Instead, Navarro's understanding of cultural identity veers into essentialism. Chicano identity is posited as sufficient foundation for creating the "one dominant perspective" that will eventually prevail. Here again, unity is equated with cultural identity rather than ideology.

Because unity was understood as a familial impulse crucial to the creation of a political agenda, little space existed for legitimate disagreement. Instead, disagreement is understood as the denial of self-determination. This approach to politics leads to a seemingly contradictory practice: the claim that Chicanos are an organic and united political community, combined with a vicious internal politics that demonizes those with whom it disagrees. This comment by Corky Gonzáles is typical in this regard:

> [W]e have to understand principle. And the man who says we can do it within the system—who says, "Honest, you can, look at me, I have a $20,000-a-year job"—he's the man who was last year's militant and this year's OEO [Office of Economic Opportunity] employee. And now he's keeping his mouth shut and he ain't marching anymore. We have to understand that he's not a revolutionary, that he's a counter-revolutionary. He's

not an ally, he becomes an enemy because he's contaminated. You can't walk into a house full of disease with a bottle full of mercurochrome and cure the disease without getting sick yourself.[115]

Here, disagreement is treated as pathology. Because group unity is organic, division is external and, hence, unnatural. In the politics of unity, someone or something must be found and blamed for divisions and disagreements. Hence José Angel Gutiérrez's claim that ideological diversity represents an excess of "prostituted thought" while Gonzáles sees Chicanos who work within the system as being "contaminated"—co-opted and made "sick" by the external disease of Anglo culture.

As I noted earlier, movement scholars often blame a lack of unity for weakness in the Chicano and Puerto Rican movements.[116] Scholars of La Raza Unida all acknowledge that the party lacked ideological coherence. According to Carlos Muñoz, "the most difficult problem in trying to establish the party as a permanent institution . . . was its inability to achieve ideological unity."[117] For Muñoz, the vagueness of the party's long-term goals and its inability to establish ideological consensus ultimately produced a liberal, reformist agenda couched in radical presentation.[118] In *United We Win*, Ignacio García agrees with Muñoz that "[i]deologically, the chapters never found common ground, and thus, there was no encompassing platform or political document acceptable to the majority."[119] Yet while García faults the party for lacking a clear philosophy and direction, he also argues that Muñoz's theoretical framework is too conceptually stringent and that the life span of the organization was too brief (less than eight years) to judge its ideological orientation. "[T]he life span of most of the party chapters," writes García, "is simply not enough time by which to judge whether La Raza Unida Party had, or better put, *would have had* an ideology."[120] Both authors, however, see ideological confusion as a major obstacle to the party's development. As Ernesto Chávez notes, the collapse of the movement organizations such as La Raza Unida Party resulted from "the failure of its constituent parts to recognize the dynamic and heterogeneous nature of the ethnic Mexican community in Los Angeles and, indeed, the nation."[121]

Unlike Muñoz and García, Chávez recognizes that the party's lack of ideological clarity was not simply an organizational weakness—it was fundamental to the organization's understanding of itself. The party's nationalist ethos was predicated on the belief that culture and racial identification would transcend ideology. Constructing a political strategy that no longer equated political agreement with identity would be to call the organization's very existence into question. To acknowledge that Chicanos were divided by contending economic interests and philosophical beliefs involved accepting the idea that the Chicano community was inescapably fragmented politically—an untenable realization.

The experience of Latina feminists represents a particularly telling example of the power of unity as the defining ethos of both the Chicano and Puerto Rican movements. Women active in the movement were often attacked for raising gender issues and accused of being divisive and undermining the movement's unity. Yet even as Latinas were viciously attacked under the guise of political familism and group unity, movement feminists did not challenge the legitimacy of these concepts. Thus, even while feminists experienced firsthand how the demand for unity silenced debate and rendered disagreement illegitimate, so strong was this ethos in movement politics that even feminists were unable and/or unwilling to resist the concept. Instead, Latinas argued that feminism would *increase* group unity rather than undermine it. Put somewhat differently, Latina feminists operated from the belief that group unity was still the discourse with the most political legitimacy.

Unity and the Challenge of Latina Feminism

> I remember when I first joined the party, the Central Committee and the officers would give a lot of speeches, and whenever they would be talking to people in the community, they would say, "And you *brothers* must be warriors! And we *men* must struggle together in the revolution!" You know, sisters were never mentioned. When any of us would point that out, we would get, like, jumped on. They would say, "Oh, that's that Women's Lib stuff."
>
> —Denise Oliver, Young Lords Party[122]

As Mary Hawkesworth notes, accounts of U.S. politics often "fail to mention the critical contributions of women to the development of inclusive and participatory practices."[123] This is certainly true of Latina feminists, whose demands for power and recognition led to new forms of democratic accountability and the establishment of gender-based issues and priorities. As for other women of the New Left, it was the experience of encountering sexism in the context of social justice movements that fueled the feminist critique. In the context of the Chicano and Puerto Rican movements, Latina feminism emerged as a challenge to traditional gender dynamics understood as oppressive and disempowering to Latinas. The presence of a feminist perspective within these movements exposed deep disagreements regarding women's liberation. Feminists were consistently accused of dividing the movement. Angela Jorge, for example, notes that raising the concerns of black Puerto Rican women is often viewed as an unacceptable act, "since it will be perceived as divisive precisely at a time when the Puerto Rican people need to be united."[124]

Chicana Feminists: Vendidas versus Loyalists

As scholars studying women's activism in the Chicano movement have noted, the movement involved new challenges related to gender and sexual equality.[125] "Never before," wrote Maxine Baca Zinn in 1975, "have Chicanos, both men and women, discussed so open and intensely questions relating to sex roles in the Chicano community."[126] Throughout the movement, Chicanas were writing, meeting, and organizing to discuss the changing role of women. At times, these questions led to mass action, as when the women of the East Los Angeles chapter of the Brown Berets resigned en masse to form a new organization, dubbed Las Adelitas de Aztlán. Criticizing the male leadership for treating them as "nothings, not as Revolutionary sisters," the women of the Brown Berets called on their fellow Chicanas to "join Las Adelitas de Aztlán . . . *porque somos una familia de hermanas*" (because we are a family of sisters).[127]

In challenging traditional gender relations, many Chicana activists were accused of being lesbians, "white identified," narcissistic, and antifamily. An example of this dynamic can be seen in Corky Gonzáles's speech "Chicano Nationalism: The Key to Unity for La Raza," in which Gonzáles expresses concerns regarding the growing feminist presence in the movement:

> [O]ne of the problems that I see, as one of the grass roots people that came out of the *barrios*, as someone who worked in the fields, is that I recognize too much of an influence of white European thinking in the discussion. I hope that our Chicana sisters can understand that they can be front runners in the revolution, they can be in the leadership of any social movement, but I pray to God that they do not lose their *Chicanisma* or their womanhood and become a frigid *gringa*. So I'm for equality, but still want to see some sex in our women.[128]

In his characterization of Chicana feminists, Gonzáles invokes his own cultural authenticity within the community ("one of the grass roots people," "someone who worked in the fields") in order to contrast this to the "European thinking" of *femenistas*. For Gonzáles, feminism is understood as a destructive force coming from *outside* the Chicano community.

Interestingly, men such as Gonzáles were not the only ones speaking out against feminism. While women were a large and active presence from the movement's inception, a number of Chicana activists were inarguably *not* feminists. An example of this diversity of opinion occurred in 1969, at the first Chicano Youth Liberation Conference. Participants in a workshop on the status of Chicanas emerged with a resolution stating that "it was the consensus of the group that the Chicana woman does not want to be liberated." This infamous resolution appalled feminists and led to increased debate regarding the status of women in the movement.[129] During this period, Chicanas in the movement were split between feminists and "loyalists"—antifeminists who argued that Chicanas should not organize around gender-specific issues. For loyalists, the subjugation of Chicanas was part of the larger problem of Chicano oppression: when inequality between men and women *did* occur, it was the fault of a racist society that oppressed men economically and socially. Loyalists consistently portrayed feminism as a divisive ideology, alien to Chicano culture and distracting the movement from the "real issues." As one loyalist wrote:

> I am concerned with the direction that the Chicanas are taking in the move-ment. Words such as liberation, sexism, male chauvinism . . . plus the theme of individualism is a concept of the Anglo society; terms prevalent in the Anglo Woman's movement. The *familia* has always been the strength in our culture. But it seems evident . . . that [you] are not concerned with the *familia* but are influenced by the Anglo Woman's movement.[130]

A related accusation leveled by loyalists was that feminists' individualistic ten-dencies would divide the community as feminists put their own personal develop-ment before the advancement of the community. According to movement feminist Anna NietoGomez, Chicanas in search of a new identity or new role in society were accused of being engaged in an "Anglo bourgeois trip" and not to be trusted.[131] As one loyalist put it:

> And since when does a Chicana need identity? If you are a real Chicana then no one regardless of their degrees needs to tell you about it. The only ones who need identity are the *vendidas* [sellouts], the *falsas* [false ones], and the opportunists. The time has come for the Chicanas to examine the direction they wish to take. Yes, we need recognition. Our men must give this to us. But there is danger in the manner we are seeking it. . . . We are going to have to decide what we value more, the culture or the individual (as Anglos do)? I hope it's not too late.[132]

In the Chicano movement, feminists were consistently accused of representing a destructive force coming from *outside* the community. In other words, Chicana feminists were not simply wrong about gender relations—they were *falsas* (false ones), no longer legitimate members of the community.

Accused of being cultural traitors creating conflict and fragmentation, Chicana feminists were often on the defensive. In part to prove that they were not "white identified," *femenistas* devoted a great deal of energy to criticizing the mainstream feminist movement (dismissed as the "Anglo women's movement"). For example, NietoGomez insists that "[t]he conflict between the feminists and the loyalists is the result of not clearly defining the differences and the similarities between the Anglo and Chicana feminist movement."[133] She writes:

> Historical differences determine the relationship between the Anglo woman and the Chicana woman. The Anglo woman is a product of Protestant and imperialistic Anglo-European capitalism. . . . The middle-class Anglo woman only shares with the Chicana the fact that they are both women. But they are women of different ethnic, cultural, and class status. All these factors determine the different political positions of these women.[134]

In her effort to convince critics of the differences between Chicana and white feminists, NietoGomez produces a monolithic vision of Anglo women. Ironically, the loyalist struggle complicates her claim that differences in "ethnic, cultural, and class status" are crucial to determining "the different political positions of these women." The *femenistas*, after all, share "ethnic, cultural and class status" with the loyalists. But despite common culture and experience, NietoGomez admits that "The loyalists do not recognize sexism as a legitimate issue in the Chicano movement," while "*femenistas* see sexism as an integrated part of the Chicana's struggle in conjunction with her fight against racism."[135] Yet despite such deep-seated conflict, she continues to presume that members of the movement are ultimately united in their vision of Chicano liberation.

Despite the tendency to essentialize white women, Chicana feminists' critique of the mainstream women's movement was often thoughtful and penetrating. Criticizing the movement's tendency to emphasize gender at the expense of race and class, NietoGomez notes that

> the Anglo-headed popular movement has only viewed Chicanas as potential members of the ranks of women because all women are oppressed by the sexist attitudes against them. It has then ignored the issues the Chicana must contend with as a member of a minority, culturally different lower

income group. In so doing, it has ignored how the Chicana's social and economic status as a woman is severely determined by her race as well as her sex.[136]

Chicana feminists criticized the women's movement for both its conservative and its radical tendencies. For example, while many Chicanas supported abortion rights, they were also attentive to the long history of sterilization abuse that haunted Latino communities.[137] Chicana activists formed organizations such as Comisión Femenil, which raised funds enabling a group of Chicanas to file a class-action civil rights lawsuit on behalf of women who had been coercively sterilized.[138] For these women, the right to choose involved not only the right to terminate a pregnancy but also the right to decide for themselves how many children they should have. In the context of the movement, the feminist language of *choice* demanded a new attentiveness to issues of class, race, language, and citizenship status.

Femenistas found the demand for female equality insufficient, since female inclusion did nothing to challenge the socioeconomic status quo. Moreover, Chicana feminists also opposed the separatist tendencies of some radical feminists, arguing that Chicano men were not the enemy but, rather, were part of a shared community that needed to be educated and struggled with. In an analysis of mainstream feminism, Adaljiza Sosa-Riddell captures the multiplicity of the Chicana feminist critique:

> Many Chicanas find the Women's Liberation movement largely irrelevant because more often than not is a move for strictly women's rights. While women's rights advocates are asking for a share of the "American" pie, Chicanas (and Chicanos) are asking for something other than parity. The end which is desired by Chicanas in the restoration of control over a way of life, a culture, an existence. For a Chicana to break with this goal is to break with her past, her present, and her people. For this reason, the concerns expressed by Chicanas for their own needs within the *Movimiento* cannot be considered a threat to the unity of the *Movimiento* itself.[139]

Sosa-Riddell's critique also reveals the effort by Chicana feminists to lay claim to a feminist tradition *within* Chicano culture. By emphasizing Chicana leadership and involvement in Chicano political history, *femenistas* sought to portray feminism as an indigenous—as opposed to an alien and divisive—feature of the community. In the essay "Our Feminist Heritage," Martha Cotera gives an overview of Mexicana/Chicana political history, arguing that "Chicana feminist activities have

been intricately interwoven into the entire fabric of the Chicano civil rights movement from 1848 to the present."[140]

By insisting that feminism had its roots in Chicano culture, Chicana feminists
sought to counter claims that they were being influenced by the "Anglo Woman's
Movement." Moreover, by laying claim to their own cultural authenticity, *femenistas* argued that the social and political empowerment of women would make the
community *more* united, not less.

Despite the fact that the call to group unity was one of the most effective ways
of isolating feminists and delegitimating the feminist critique, Chicana feminists
never sought to undermine the idea of unity as an ideal. For example, in founding
Las Adelitas de Aztlán, the women of the Brown Berets characterized themselves
as *"una familia de hermanas."* As Dionne Espinoza notes, this language of sisterhood "implicitly translated *carnalismo*, or 'brotherhood' . . . into a kinship of
women—that is, sisterhood."[141] Rather than challenging the political familism of
the movement, Chicana activists claimed it as their own. *Femenistas* certainly had
good reason to abandon this principle—they could have cited their experience to
show how nationalist narratives of unity treat agreement and community as
organic and disagreement as alien and destructive. Instead, Chicanas constructed
their own narrative of feminism as the basis for community cohesion, arguing that
the movement would become *more* unified once feminist demands were met. Like
their antifeminist counterparts, Chicana feminists continued to believe in the fundamental unity of the Chicano community. For feminists, once women's oppression was overcome, men and women would be a healthy, unified whole seeking
the liberation of their people. For loyalists, once the community expelled European norms and Anglo cultural practices and returned to their cultural roots, the
animating concept of *familia* would produce the unified whole. In both narratives,
division is unnatural and external to the community.

Puerto Rican Feminists: Uncertain Alliances

Like their feminist counterparts in the Chicano movement, Puerto Rican women
were initially criticized for demanding that the movement address issues of sexism
and women's oppression. And like Chicanos who celebrated the traditional patriarchal family, Puerto Rican activists also sought to appropriate cultural practices
for radical purposes. In the Young Lords, for example, machismo was initially
portrayed as a progressive force in Latino culture.[142] Feminists, however, argued
that machismo would never be a progressive or revolutionary tendency in Puerto
Rican politics. According to Young Lord Denise Oliver, "[s]aying 'revolutionary

machismo' is like saying 'revolutionary fascism' or 'revolutionary racism'—it's a contradiction."[143]

The critique of the mainstream women's movement put forward by Puerto Rican feminists was more nuanced and ideologically grounded than in the Chicano movement.[144] Describing the possibility of solidarity with members of the women's movement, Oliver writes:

> Now in the Women's Liberation Movement, you have different women from different classes (although primarily from the middle class) some of whom are very reformist, some of whom just want to turn the tables and just be the capitalist oppressors of everybody else, and a large number really, who are revolutionaries.
>
> We say right on to any women who are revolutionaries. . . . We support them, and they should support us in our struggle.[145]

Rather than essentializing white women as NietoGomez does, Oliver explores the ideological diversity that characterized the women's movement. Yet despite their willingness to make common cause, Puerto Rican feminists also expressed concerns regarding the women's liberation movement. Like Chicana feminists, women in the Young Lords were opposed to gender separatism in the women's movement. Oliver writes:

> The basic criticism that we have of our sisters in Women's Liberation is that they shouldn't isolate themselves, because in isolating yourselves from your brothers, you're making the struggle separate. . . . I don't believe that a group of women should get together just to educate themselves and not go out and educate the brothers.[146]

With this goal of community education in mind, the Young Lords formed caucuses for both women and men to discuss women's oppression, sexism, and the role of women in the revolution. Even more significantly, men in the Young Lords could be disciplined for male chauvinist behavior. In 1970, for example, Felipe Luciano was demoted from his position as Central Committee chairman and organization spokesperson for being unfaithful to his wife (who was also a member of the central staff). Many of the men viewed Luciano's infidelity as a private issue, but the women of the Young Lords argued that it was an organizational and political concern. Emphasizing the issue of "change from within" in order to create "outward revolution," the organization charged the former chairman with male chauvinist behavior, demoted him to a nonranking cadre, and sent him back for reeducation.[147]

Beyond challenging sex roles in the organization, the Young Lords' support for feminism and women's rights eventually led the leadership to speak out in favor of gay and lesbian liberation. Young Lords minister of information Pablo Guzmán describes the move from women's rights to gay liberation:

> [T]he second thing that made perhaps a greater impact on us was when we first heard about Gay Liberation. That's a whole other trip because we found out it's a lot quicker for people to accept the fact that sisters should be in front of the struggle, than saying that we're gonna have gay people in the Party. . . . Now I'm not gay, but maybe I should be. It would probably give me a better outlook on a whole lot of things. . . . Being gay is not the problem; the problem is that people do not understand what gay means. . . . The Gay struggle really rounds out the individual. . . . See, there is a biological division in sex right—however, this society has created a false division based on this thing called gender. Gender is a false idea, because gender is merely traits that have been attributed through the years to a man or a woman. . . . Because certain traits have been assigned to people historically by society, we've actually developed as half-people, as half-real. We're saying that to be totally real, it would be healthy for a man, if he wanted to cry, to go ahead and cry. It would also be healthy for a woman to pick up the gun, to use the gun.[148]

As Laura Pulido notes, while patriarchy "created tensions, reduced organizational efficacy, and warped individuals, such organizations also offered women of color an unprecedented opportunity to fight for their communities and develop themselves, and they offered men, at least those so inclined, an alternative way of claiming their masculinity."[149] Guzmán's effort to question normative sexuality and challenge the sex/gender divisions speaks to the radical and transformative possibilities that feminism brought to both the men and women of these movements. Furthermore, Guzmán's statement shows that, unlike Chicana feminists, the Young Lords did not have to contend with a large and organized antifeminist element among the female rank and file or within its leadership. Instead, as self-described revolutionaries, the Young Lords were willing to challenge traditional cultural norms, while groups such as the Crusade for Justice, MEChA, and the Brown Berets sought to unite themselves politically around a shared cultural identity that too often conflated culture with patriarchal norms. The logic of such gendered orthodoxies led Chicano antifeminists to accuse *femenistas* of cultural and political betrayal.

But despite their differences, it is important to note that neither movement challenged the legitimacy of unity as a guiding political principle. Like their male counterparts, Latina activists in both the Chicano and Puerto Rican movements believed in the fundamental unity of the Chicano and Puerto Rican people and that ethnicity was the site of their primary allegiance. Both feminists and antifeminists saw political disagreement within their respective communities as external and unnatural—the result of "false consciousness," "police agents," or inauthentic, culturally suspect sellouts. In other words, rather than viewing *both* white women and Latino men as potential (though not guaranteed) allies, Puerto Rican and Chicana feminists were ideologically compelled to privilege race over gender. For feminists in these movements, disagreement with Latino men was something to be *overcome*, since a natural unity lay beneath the disagreements. Conflict with white feminists was often viewed as *confirming* the fact that these women were not part of a shared community. This was particularly true for Chicana feminists: for Chicanas to embrace the idea of a transracial solidarity that cut across class lines would have exposed them to charges that they were "white identified"—an accusation about which many Chicanas were defensive. For *femenistas*, suspicion and hostility to white feminism were signs of cultural authenticity, crucial to the belief in the inherent unity of the Chicano people. In this way, the politics of group unity *narrowed*—rather than enlarged—the political alternatives available to Latina feminists.

2 The Incomplete and Agonistic "We"
Reading Latinidad into Democratic Theory

As the previous chapter suggests, when looking at the Chicano and Puerto Rican movements, we encounter political practices and assumptions both attractive and disturbing. The mass gatherings and protests that took place during the movements highlight citizens' desire to experience democracy as a form of political participation in which they feel a part of something larger than themselves. Beyond participation, the movements' passionate opposition to social inequality, vivid critique of liberal individualism, and unwillingness to leave anyone behind all reflect an ethos that America's democracy has failed to serve all its people equally well.

Yet even as the movements appeal to our democratic sensibilities, their desire to suppress difference should give us pause. Their undeniably powerful vision of community contained a disturbing unwillingness to accept the legitimacy of internal dissent so essential to democratic politics. The belief that shared culture could produce a unified political perspective was compellingly inclusive, but it turned disagreement into betrayal. The movements' perception of conflict as something external and unnatural to the community meant that those who challenged norms and traditions became culturally and politically suspect. The attack on Chicana feminists is a prime example of this phenomenon: feminists were vilified and lesbians silenced—in the name of community, unity, and *familia*.

And so we find ourselves at an impasse. We know that the ethos and practices of these two movements inspired and influenced the very project of contemporary Latino politics. But given our ambivalence, how are we to interpret this legacy? What should we celebrate? What should we resist?

In this chapter, I argue for drawing on the resources of democratic theory to consider the complexities of Latino political thought and practice. In doing this, my work is inspired by the work of other social and political theorists who emphasize the value of social heterogeneity while warning of the disciplinary exclusions that often inform such encounters. This strand of democratic theory calls for resisting disciplinary and homogenizing forms of community, empowering marginalized voices, and cultivating a critical responsiveness to difference. Yet in much of this work, theorists almost always characterize homogenizing and unitary depictions of community in terms of dominant populations (white, male, heterosexual, middle-class, etc.) while attaching issues of difference and exclusion to gender, racial, and sexual minorities.

While acknowledging the socioeconomic violence and political exclusions that occur when dominant subjectivities seek sameness and community, I urge democratic theorists to resist the tendency to read Latinos as carriers of difference who challenge settled notions of community. Rather than approaching excluded populations as "voices of difference," democratic theorists must more fully and critically engage the paradoxical impulses that exist *within* the marginalized communities they seek to include.

I propose considering Latino agency in terms of its emancipatory potential, as well as through the disciplinary tendencies that undermine its own democratic aspirations. Such an approach seeks to decenter whiteness by focusing on how the democratic actions of marginalized groups can also veer between democratic renewal and the suppression of the political. More specifically, my reading offers a vocabulary and ethos better equipped to accept the permanent instability of "Latino" as a political category. Inspired by insights of postmodern feminist and radical democratic theorists, I contend that the assumptions and practices of Latino politics reveal more than the potential of direct action, the limits of nationalism, the value of multicultural politics, or the problems of racism, sexism, and homophobia—they reflect the contradictions and challenges of democracy itself.

This chapter is divided into three sections. In the first section, I discuss some of the criticisms of community, unity, and homogeneity put forward by democratic theorists, with a particular focus on the work of Iris Marion Young. In the second section, I explore the democratic resources of Third World feminism, particularly its complex and agonistic account of membership and political community. Finally,

I discuss the idea of democratic openness and the politics of closure. My analysis here is particularly indebted to Sheldon Wolin's work on "fugitive democracy" and Alan Keenan's discussion of democratic openness and the contingent and unavoidably incomplete nature of democracy. Such incompleteness, I argue, is critical to any democratic definition of *Latinidad*.

The Ideal of Community and the Politics of Difference

In her seminal work *Justice and the Politics of Difference*, Iris Marion Young puts forward a critique of unity and community that, in many ways, inspires this very project. According to Young, the "ideal of community" fails as an appropriate alternative vision of a democratic polity: "The ideal of community denies and represses social differences. . . . This ideal expresses a desire for the fusion of subjects with one another which in practice operates to exclude those with whom the group does not identify."[1] According to Young, critical theory and advocates of participatory democracy share a tendency to suppress difference by conceiving the polity in terms of a unitary ideal that presumes an oppositional relationship between the universal and the particular. The binary logic of the universalist ideal has often operated to exclude from citizenship persons identified with the wrong side of these oppositions: with subjects identified with the private, the particular, emotion, and the body—including women, Jews, people of color, and gays and lesbians.[2] For Young, the communitarian impulse represents this urge to unity—the desire for security, symmetry, and social wholeness. Such an ideal reflects "a longing for harmony among persons, for consensus and mutual understanding."[3] By positing identification and agreement as its civic ideals, Young suggests that the communitarian ethos denies difference by valuing and enforcing homogeneity through practices that often exclude or oppress those experienced as different. Such exclusions have serious political consequences:

> [T]he myth of community operates strongly to produce defensive, exclusionary behavior: pressuring the Black family that buys a house on the block to leave, beating up the Black youths who come into "our" neighborhood, zoning against the construction of multiunit dwellings.
>
> The exclusionary consequences of valuing community, moreover, are not restricted to bigots and conservatives. Many radical political organizations founder on the desire for community. . . . Mutual identification as an implicit group ideal can reproduce a homogeneity that usually conflicts with the organization's stated commitment to diversity.[4]

Proposing alternatives to the exclusionary consequences of community, Young argues for forms of democratic participation that do not require "the submerging of social differences" whereby subjects are asked to set aside their particular identities and affiliations in order to perceive and produce a common good.[5] In her desire to affirm democratic diversity, Young also asks participatory democrats to be more attentive to the importance of nondeliberative and/or less deliberative practices. Rather than depoliticizing democratic actions by excluding practices deemed uncivil, irrational, and/or inappropriate, she argues for including forms of political communication that go beyond rational-critical arguments. Such practices include greetings, stories, rhetoric, political art, and protest. For Young, adopting this more expansive account of political discourse will foster more citizen participation in deliberative decision making, even under imperfectly democratic conditions.[6]

In considering the problems of exclusion and domination, Young criticizes deliberative democrats for privileging local, face-to-face relations. Citing instances of local participation in which people of color and members of the working class were less able to promote and protect their interests, she demonstrates how face-to-face participatory practices can actually disempower particular segments of a given political community.[7] For Young, participatory dreams of immediacy fail to appreciate the basic asymmetry of subjects, presuming instead what Jacques Derrida calls a metaphysics of presence—an ideal of transparency whereby "persons cease to be other, opaque, not understood, and instead become mutually sympathetic, understanding one another as they understand themselves, fused."[8] Such "metaphysical delusions" fail to acknowledge that mediation through the speech and actions of others is the fundamental condition of sociality.[9] Even under conditions of local participation, communication between subjects is always subject to misunderstanding and characterized by disparities of power, privilege, and ability. Moreover, because human beings often possess competing and opposing desires, subjects are never fully knowable, even to themselves:

> Because the subject is not a unity, it cannot be present to itself, know itself. I do not always know what I mean, need, want, desire, because meanings, needs, and desires do not arise from an origin in some transparent ego. . . . Subjects all have multiple desires that do not cohere; they attach layers of meanings to objects without being aware of each layer or the connections between them.[10]

As an alternative to a politics of distributive justice, Young seeks to characterize justice in terms of the elimination of domination and oppression.[11] In this effort to "foster justice and minimize domination and oppression," she proposes a "politics of difference" that argues for "specific representation of oppressed or disadvantaged groups."[12] Because the perspectives of oppressed groups might be silenced without explicit representation, her vision seeks to "give voice" to various disadvantaged groups. According to Young, "only if oppressed groups are able to express their interests and experience in the public on an equal basis with other groups can group domination through formally equal processes of participation be avoided."[13] The representation of social groups within various decision-making bodies would allow "each constituency to analyze economic and social issues from the perspective of its experience."[14] In calling for the specific representation of social groups, Young notes that she is not referring to "interest groups or ideological groups."[15] In contrast to groups who share a common policy desire or shared political beliefs, Young defines a social group as:

> a collective of persons differentiated from at least one other group by cultural forms, practices, or way of life. Members of a group have a specific affinity with one another because of their similar experience or way of life, which prompts them to associate with one another more than with those not identified with the group, or in a different way.[16]

For Young, social groups share common interests based on their "similar experience or way of life." Importantly for her, such affinities emerge from a common perspective based on their shared disadvantage and/or marginalization. In this way, Young characterizes a social group as a type of "constituency" that transcends ideology yet requires formal representation.

In *Justice and the Politics of Difference*, Young states that her concern with questions of justice and difference was ignited by discussions in the women's movement of the importance of acknowledging differences among women and, more generally, the social position of oppressed groups.[17] In her effort to create a workable ideal of justice, Young clearly committed to the laudable effort of displacing an exclusionary meaning of difference with an emancipatory one. In a further effort to resist idealizing conditions of immediacy and transparency, she proposes envisioning politics as "a relationship of strangers who do not understand one another in a subjective and immediate sense, relating across time and distance."[18] For Young, "city life" offers a normative ideal of such a relationship of strangers, celebrating the public encounter with difference, the pleasure of the unfamiliar, and the value of anonymity. In the capaciousness of cities, she finds the promise of "social differentiation without exclusion"—a normative ideal of city life that allows for belonging without dissolving into commonness.[19]

I find Young's analysis resonant, though perhaps in unexpected ways. For her, the "turn to difference" exists in opposition to the unitary ideal she criticizes. Yet as theorist Jodi Dean rightly notes, the effort to "suppress debate and claim unity in the face of plurality has been a major problem for a variety of groups and movements."[20] This unitary ideal is powerfully present within the social groups Young seeks to represent. For instance, when considering her analysis of transparency and identification, I recall the Young Lords' characterization of the Puerto Rican community as "compañeras and compañeros everywhere together . . . strong, dedicated, and filled with love."[21] In her critique of community and the tendency to idealize harmony and consensus, I hear echoes of the Chicano movement and its emphasis on *carnalismo* (brotherhood). In both movements, we witnessed a compelling critique of liberal individualism alongside presumptions of shared subjectivity that led to equating internal disagreement with civic decline and failure. Yet Young seems reluctant to grapple with these subjects' more ambiguous agency and capacity for disciplinary exclusions.

Homogenizing Multiplicity: Social Groups, Intersectionality, and the Limits of Difference

I turn now to conceptions of democratic politics put forward by feminist theorists focused at the intersections of race, class, and sexuality. Like Young's, my approach is indebted to the work of feminists of color and postmodern feminist theorists who have showed how claims in the name of "women" inevitably produce refusals by those who fail to recognize themselves in such demands. Such an approach seeks to acknowledge how both history and embodiment are constitutive of subjectivity yet never fully determinant.[22] Where I diverge from Young is at her effort to displace an exclusionary meaning of difference with an emancipatory one. Her call for the specific representation of marginalized social groups presumes the existence of a politics of difference whose internal logic is both inherently empowering and internally coherent. Despite the laudatory effort to critique mainstream feminism for its own exclusions and assumptions, Young's critique of social groups leads her to depict marginalized social groups as inherently transgressive. By contrast, I draw on the democratic tradition of Third World feminists and their willingness to criticize even those marginalized communities with whom they claim political affinity.[23] As Susan Bickford notes, these feminists offer a compelling conception of "democratic citizenship for our inegalitarian times . . . active, agonistic, and communicative."[24]

As many scholars have noted, the work of feminists of color is distinct for being self-consciously intersectional: building bridges while simultaneously challenging the exclusions and silences that exist within all forms of community.[25] According to Jodi Dean, unlike some white feminists who assumed a shared experience of oppression, "feminists of color used language and communication to construct a new experience of belonging."[26] Such an approach is visible in Norma Alarcón's critique of a "politics of unity" based solely on gender. For Alarcón, the "multiple-voiced" subjectivity of women of color reflects a "lived in resistance to competing notions for one's allegiance or self-identification."[27] Such "multiple-voiced" resistance constitutes what Kathy Ferguson sometimes refers to as "mobile subjectivities." According to Ferguson, women who are conscious of the fact that their race, class, gender, and erotic identities might be held against them "are less likely to invest themselves completely in any single dimension and more likely to realize that their likeness to others" is never complete.[28] This "pull of competing fragments and partial affiliations can be uncomfortable," for both those inhabiting such subjectivities and those confronting such subjects.[29] In the oft-cited essay "The Master's Tools," Audre Lorde discomfits her fellow feminists by claiming just such a form of feminist allegiance alongside a confrontational query, asking:

> If white American feminist theory need not deal with the differences between us, and the resulting difference in aspects of our oppression, then what do you do with the fact that the women who clean your houses and tend your children while you attend conferences on feminist theory are, for the most part, poor and third world women? What is the theory behind racist feminism?[30]

Similarly, in her poem "Between Ourselves," Lorde poses equally unsettling questions regarding the nature of community as a lesbian feminist engaging with black nationalism:

> Once when I walked into a room
> my eyes would seek out the one or two black faces
> for contact or reassurance or a sign
> I was not alone
> now walking into rooms full of black faces
> that would destroy me for any difference
> where shall my eyes look?
> Once it was easy to know
> who were my people.[31]

In her refusal to privilege harmony, Lorde challenges the myth of community in ways that both affirm and exceed Young's analysis. Writing in a similar vein, Gloria Anzaldúa declares: "I will not glorify those aspects of my culture which have injured me and which have injured me in the name of protecting me. So don't give me your tenets and your laws. Don't give me your lukewarm gods. What I want is an accounting with all three cultures—white, Mexican, Indian."[32] In her demand for "an accounting" with the many cultures and communities that define her identity, Anzaldúa articulates *una cultura mestiza*, an agonistic and innovative feminism whose democratic receptivity is characterized by its emphasis on contentious encounters that cut across multiple axes of difference.

Yet even here, Young's critique of transparency remains unexpectedly relevant—particularly when the democratic potential of feminist intersectionality finds itself haunted by its own ideal of community. For example, in "U.S. Third World Feminism: The Theory and Method of Oppositional Consciousness in the Post-modern World," Chela Sandoval argues that U.S. feminists of color have come together, made coalitions, and share a unified stance. Sandoval characterizes Third World feminists as having developed a particular theoretical and methodological standpoint she names "oppositional consciousness." Listing a wide array of Third World feminist texts and authors as examples of this common theoretical approach, she writes:

> *All the Blacks Are Men, All the Women Are White, But Some of Us Are Brave* or *This Bridge Called My Back*, titles which imply that women of color somehow exist in the interstices between the legitimated categories of the social order. . . . This in-between space, this third gender category, is also explored in the writings of such well-known authors as Maxine Hong Kingston, Gloria Anzaldúa, Audre Lorde, Alice Walker, and Cherríe Moraga, all of whom argue that U.S. third world feminists represent a different kind of human—new "mestizas," "Woman Warriors" who live and are gendered "between and among" the lines, "Sister Outsiders" who inhabit a new psychic terrain which Anzaldúa calls "the Borderlands," "la nueva Frontera."[33]

In this passage, Sandoval rhetorically removes the differences among this diverse set of Third World women writers, creating a sense of commonality and shared epistemology through the naming, listing, and interweaving of multiple titles. Such rhetorical practices have their place (my own discussion here of Third World feminism may well be guilty of similar erasures). Yet what makes this move prob-lematic is not the attempt to find common practices and perspectives—it is the presumption that a deeper, more organic form of consensus and identification exists at this site of community. In other words, while focusing on the tense and turbulent debates between white feminists and U.S. Third World feminists and across gender, Sandoval's analysis seems to do away with differences *between* Third World feminists. Not surprisingly, the inability to achieve this ideal of community becomes the site of democratic despair. In the foreword to the second edition of *This Bridge Called My Back*, Cherríe Moraga articulates this disappointment regarding the lack of unity she sees among feminists of color:

> At the time of this writing, however, I am feeling more discouraged than optimistic. The dream of a unified Third World feminist movement in this country as we conceived of it when we first embarked on the project of this book, seemed more possible somehow, because as of yet, less tried. It was waiting in the ranks begging to take form and hold. In the last three years I have learned that Third World feminism does not provide the kind of easy political framework that women of color are running to in droves. We are not so much a "natural" affinity group, as women who have come together out of political necessity. . . . There *are* many issues that divide us; and, recognizing that fact can make that dream at times seem quite remote. Still, the need for a broad-based U.S. women of color movement capable of spanning borders of nation and ethnicity has never been so strong.[34]

Like other Third World feminists, Moraga had come to terms with the alienation and agonism that characterized her relationships to men of color and white feminists. As discussed, such displacement was often painful, but it also functioned as a generative site of democratic renewal. Yet when envisioning the political relationships between women of color, new presumptions of homogeneity and transparency sometimes emerged. Intriguingly, this intersectional site of disenchantment has parallels to Young's description of the communitarian impulse toward "security, symmetry, and social wholeness." In the case of Moraga, her dream of a "unified Third World feminist movement" reflects a similar longing for immediacy and "harmony . . . consensus and mutual understanding."[35] Here, Moraga would do well to take up Young's call to envision the political as "a relationship of strangers who do not understand one another in a subjective and immediate sense, relating across time and distance."[36] In taking pleasure in the unfamiliar, feminists of color and other advocates of intersectionality would do well to extend the space of "strangeness" not only to the relationships between gays and straights or between white women and/or men of color but also among Third World feminists and other communities characterized as "home."

The concept of "home" has a complex and sometimes convoluted history within Third World feminism. In an oft-cited essay on coalition politics, for example, feminist activist and artist Bernice Johnson Reagon argues for the importance of not confusing home and coalition. According to Reagon, coalitions need to be understood as unsafe spaces, defined by the presence of strangers and character- ized by the dictates of survival: "The only reason you would consider trying to team up with somebody who could possibly kill you, is because that's the only way you can figure you can stay alive."[37] In the space of coalition, subjects feel "threatened to the core," as though they might "keel over and die." It is for these reasons that "you can't stay there all the time."[38] In contrast to coalition, Reagon characterizes home as refuge—the space of sameness, a potentially nurturing place where you "act out community" and "decide who you really are." Yet even here, she acknowl- edges that such spaces of enforced homogeneity (what she characterizes as "the barred room") can become destructive.[39] Read in light of Reagon, Moraga's "dream of a unified Third World feminist movement" reflects Moraga's misreading of feminists of color as signifying "home" rather than a coalition. Echoing Reagon's depiction of coalition as a form of survival, Moraga argues that this diverse group of women "are not so much a 'natural' affinity group as women who have come together out of necessity."

Yet despite offering a more contentious definition of community, Reagon's essay underproblematizes the concept of "home" itself. Written for a workshop at the West Coast Women's Music Festival, her remarks were given in the context of a black feminist speaking about coalition to a group of mostly white women; given the circumstances, it is hardly surprising that Reagon characterizes coalition as the "monster" that "never gets enough" and "always wants more."[40] This depiction highlights the burden of representation that feminists of color often feel doing coalition work in predominantly white environments. Yet Reagon's language of coalition sustains a dichotomy of community that leaves little room for the plea- sures of difference. Instead, the encounter with the unfamiliar is something with which to make peace rather than from which to take satisfaction. In contrast to home—where there exists at least the *possibility* of nurturance—Reagon depicts coalition in strictly instrumentalist terms, as a burdensome and disagreeable necessity. While understandable, such a reading of home works to sustain myths of community that equate sameness with sustenance and solace.

The strength of Reagon's analysis lies in her capacity to celebrate the necessity of an agonistic feminism that challenges the idea that women share a common experience simply by dint of being women. As she notes, "wherever women gather together it is not necessarily nurturing. It is coalition building."[41] Here, Reagon highlights a difficult reality: the work of democratic politics can be demanding and unpleasant. Encounters with heterogeneous others are often frustrating, exhausting, and fraught with misunderstanding. In its call to welcome such challenges, Reagon's analysis enriches contemporary democratic theory.

But what would it mean to refuse Reagon's demand that we "not confuse" home and coalition? What if we complicate the very idea of "home"? What if we argue that not only is coalition "not home"—*home itself* is "not home"? Gloria Anzaldúa evokes this possibility in a speech given at the National Women's Studies Association. She writes:

> Moving at the blink of an eye, from one space, one world to another, each world with its own peculiar and distinct inhabitants, not comfortable in anyone of them, none of them "home," yet none of them "not home" either. I'm flying home to South Texas after this conference, and while I'm there, I'm going to be feeling a lot of the same things that I'm feeling here—a warm sense of being loved and of being at home, accompanied by a simultaneous and uncomfortable feeling of no longer fitting, of having lost my home, of being an outsider. My mother, and my sister and my brothers, are going to continue to challenge me and to argue against the part of me that has community with white lesbians, that has community with feminism, that has community with other *mujeres-de-color,* that has a political community. Because I no longer share their world view, I have become a stranger and an exile in my own home. "When are you coming home again, Prieta," my mother asks at the end of my visit, of every visit. "Never, Momma."[42]

In blurring the lines between biological family and political community, Anzaldúa explores the ambivalent pleasure that comes from acknowledging the simultaneity of identification and estrangement. Here, Anzaldúa makes flesh what Bonnie Honig describes in her analysis of the saying "There's no place like home." Discussing the magical phrase spoken by Judy Garland as Dorothy in *The Wizard of Oz*, Honig calls upon us to consider the deep ambivalence and yearning these words contain:

> On its face, the phrase expresses a heartfelt home-yearning, as in "There's *no* place like home, [sigh]." Here the phrase suggests that home is so unique, wonderful, and irreplaceable a place (a "place where people know me, where I can just be," in Minnie Bruce Pratt's phrasing), that no other place ever lives up to it. However, the selfsame phrase unmasks this yearning for

home as a fantasy. Switch the emphasis to "There's no place *like* home," and the phrase now seems to suggest that there is no place as wonderful as home is mythologized to be, and that includes home itself.[43]

For Honig, the "uncanny, punlike character" of "There's no place like home" combines the yearning for home with the awareness that "the home so yearned for is a fantasy."[44]

As I hope the previous two sections make clear, democratic theory's critique of the unitary ideal of community speaks to the limits of liberal individualism and reflects a profound desire to promote agency among subjects experiencing real inequalities of power. Yet many of democratic theory's most penetrating insights are not applied to the communities identified as "oppressed." In the case of Young, her desire to confront oppressive and exclusive practices leads her to envision the communitarian impulse in unidirectional terms—dominant groups excluding marginalized ones. Rather than interrogating the internal dynamics of marginalized populations, Young equates justice with the procedural dream of attending to group-specific needs by affirming the positive identities of oppressed groups and "guaranteeing" group representation in decision making. Such an approach is comfortable considering such subjects in terms of the wrongs done to them and to their efforts to resist those wrongs. By contrast, my approach is indebted to the more agonistic elements of Latina feminism (and feminists of color more generally). At its best, the work of Third World feminists and other feminist theorists of intersectionality offers variations of agonistic allegiance from which democratic theorists would do well to learn.

Yet despite the fact that terms such as "experience" and "ways of life" appear increasingly unintelligible politically, the injustices and democratic deficits that concern Young persist. Even as the concept of "social groups" becomes increasingly opaque as populations and communities grow in both size and diversity, global capitalism and modern forms of state power continue to be implicated in increasing levels of socioeconomic inequality and democratic diminishment. Moreover, differences in race, gender, sexuality, and class often intensify and/or define such conditions of inequality. In other words, democratic theorists face the daunting task of envisioning a democratic politics capable of collective action in the face of increasingly inegalitarian conditions and deep, crosscutting forms of difference.

In facing these challenges, Latinos in the United States are a population who exemplify this democratic dilemma: increasingly internally diverse by subgroup and region, yet with majorities who continue to bear the brunt of global capital and state power.

Simultaneously, growing numbers of Latinos are experiencing upward mobility, educational advancement, and socioeconomic inclusion. What sort of democratic theory speaks to the complexities and paradoxes of this condition? While I offer no prescription for "solving" the democratic dilemmas inherent in *Latinidad*, it is clear that democratic theory needs to reconsider its tendency to see "difference" as adhering to raced bodies. Such an approach tends to make whiteness its referent, while locating Latino "difference" on the margins. This type of analysis is less able to explore the internal dynamics of the political communities under discussion.

In her passionate concern with social justice, Iris Marion Young identifies herself as a pragmatist, "theorizing with . . . practical intent" and concerned with "the elimination of institutionalized domination."[45] As a democratic theorist of identity who values the importance of problem solving and applied theory, I nevertheless want to push back against this prescriptive logic and impulse toward closure. Instead, while sustaining the agonism of Third World feminism alongside Young's critique of unity, I seek a shift in footing that is more attentive to the ambiguity and ongoing contingency that characterize democratic action. To make this move, I turn now to Sheldon Wolin's analysis of "fugitive democracy" and Alan Keenan's recent discussion of democratic openness and the inevitably incomplete nature of democracy. Incorporating these insights provides us with a vocabulary and ethos better equipped to accept the permanent instability and openness of "Latino" as a political category.

The Impulse to Closure: Democratic Uncertainties and Fugitive Moments

In his essay "Fugitive Democracy," Sheldon Wolin defines democracy as "a project concerned with the political potentialities of ordinary citizens . . . with their possibilities for becoming political beings through the self-discovery of common concerns and of modes of action for realizing them."[46] Related to his notion of the political, democracy involves the idea that "a free society composed of diversities can nonetheless enjoy moments of commonality, when, through public deliberations, collective power is used to promote or protect the wellbeing of the collectivity."[47] In a similar vein, Wolin argues for an understanding of democracy as "fugitive"—"a moment" rather than a form of government:

> The so-called "problem of contemporary democracy" is not, as is often alleged, that the ancient conception of democracy is incompatible with the size and scale of modern political societies. Rather it is that any conception

of democracy grounded in the citizen-as-actor and politics-as-episodic is incompatible with the modern choice of the State as the fixed center of political life and the corollary conception of politics as continuous activity organized around a single dominating objective, control of or influence over the State apparatus. . . .

Democracy needs to be reconceived as something other than a form of government: as a mode of being which is conditioned by bitter experience, doomed to succeed only temporarily, but is a recurrent possibility as long as the memory of the political survives.[48]

Unsettling and boundary denying, Wolin conceives of democracy as "born in transgressive acts"—those rare and rebellious moments when the political is "remembered and recreated."[49] Yet, as Wolin notes, this definition of democracy as "protean and amorphous" rejects the classical and modern conception "that ascribes to democracy 'a' proper or settled form."[50] Wrongly conflated with the institutionalization of authority and the competition and contestation over resources, democracy in the modern regime is understood not as a politics but as a *process*: "promotion of the economy, law enforcement, military preparedness, revenue collection," and so forth.[51] By contrast, Wolin argues that "democracy should be about forms rather than *a* form or constitution."[52] In other words, rather than conceiving of democracy as the effort to gain dominance over the state apparatus, democracy represents the fact that "at any moment," everyday people can show themselves capable of contesting forms of unequal power and creating "new cultural patterns of commonality."[53]

In *Democracy in Question: Democratic Openness in a Time of Political Closure*, Alan Keenan also highlights the link between democracy and the citizen-as-actor, offering what he describes as a "deconstructive reading of democracy" and collective self-rule. Arguing that today's citizens "largely find themselves reduced to spectator-voters, unable to influence the political agenda except in sporadic and marginal ways," Keenan echoes Wolin in his desire to more fully realize democracy's "radical promise."[54] Drawing on an array of prominent theorists, Keenan offers what he describes as a "deconstructive reading of democracy" and collective self-rule. Seeking to expose the fundamental uncertainty of all self-constituting practices, he traces this dilemma to Rousseau's discussion of foundings in *The Social Contract*. According to Keenan, Rousseau's paradox exposes the democratic problematic that "political community is never fully achieved *as* 'a people.'" Absent any authoritative grounds other than those claimed and affirmed by the people themselves, "the people must call itself into being before it exists."[55]

Keenan's depiction of the self-constituting character of "the people" helps explicate Wolin's claim that democracy is born in "transgressive acts," unsettling old boundaries and drawing new ones. Both recognize that such moments of revolutionary action contain the capacity for both violent closure and democratic renewal. Yet in its ongoing and fundamental incompleteness, democracy remains a recurrent possibility "as long as the memory of the political survives."[56] This characterization acknowledges a fundamental uncertainty that haunts every democratic society: that "the people form not so much a clear ground as the open site and object of permanent debate and contestation."[57] As Keenan notes, the effort to call a people into being involves speaking and acting prior to the consent of those for whom they claim to speak. Moreover, because such efforts to name a people inevitably occur from a not-yet-fully-democratic position, the legitimacy of such actions can be determined only retroactively.[58]

I want to suggest that reading Latino politics through this deconstructive lens sharpens our appreciation of *Latinidad* as the effort to inaugurate a new political "imaginary." This iteration of *Latinidad* involves a discourse of sociopolitical empowerment linked to a rethinking of subjectivity. Both the Chicano and Puerto Rican movements, for example, involved ordinary people creating new forms of commonality, discovering their political potentialities through contesting forms of unequal power. The self-constituting character of democratic belonging can be seen in both movements: when participants of the First National Chicano Liberation Youth Conference adopted the manifesto *El Plan de Aztlan* and declared themselves "a new people . . . a union of free pueblos . . . Aztlán," they were articulating a new theory of the subject whereby Mexican Americans became "Chicanos." In doing this, activists were speaking and acting prior to the consent of those they claimed to speak for. When the Young Lords called for the liberation of Puerto Ricans "on the Island and inside the United States," they were producing new cultural patterns of collectivity—an alternate imaginary—that nevertheless rested on sites of debate and contestation. Chicano and Puerto Rican activists were enacting what Keenan identifies as a central democratic problematic: the fact that "the people must call itself into being before it exists."[59]

Accepting the inherently incomplete nature of the democratic "we" reminds us that the significance of the movements' claim-making was itself subject to political and democratic contestation. Moreover, in trying to make sense of their diverse and unexpected sites of democratic belonging, both movements reflect Wolin's insight that democracy is "not about where the political is located but how it is experienced."[60] In each case, Puerto Rican and Chicano activists renewed the political by creating new paradigms of affinity—often with the poorest and most denigrated segments of their populations. During such democratic transgression, movement activists spoke from a not-yet-fully-democratic position, their speech not yet sanctioned by the larger, dominant (white) society or even the majority of their own communities. Yet in retrospect, both movements are recognized as moments of democratic expansion as Latinos across the United States engaged in new forms of resistance, participation, and subject formation. At the same time, both movements remain sites of contestation: debates continue to rage regarding the legitimacy (or illegitimacy) of the exclusions and limits that defined this particular political moment.[61]

While both Wolin and Keenan recognize the profoundly contingent nature of democracy, Keenan rejects the idea that democracy can emerge only sporadically, in "fugitive" appearances. Instead, he argues for a sustainable notion of democratic politics capable of continually negotiating its paradoxes and tensions. For Keenan, democracy's promise of radical openness (and its commensurate qualities of inclusion and revisability) inevitably involves exclusions and setting limits in order to defend or institutionalize a particular vision of the people. This demand for closure often risks taking on "dangerous, even violent, dimensions."[62] Such practices are an inescapable aspect of democratic politics. Yet democracy's paradox (as well as its promise) lies in its resistance to all forms of completion or achievement. Keenan describes this effort in terms of cultivating an ethic of democratic openness characterized as "nonclosure"—the recognition that the process by which a people calls itself into being can never be fully accomplished.[63] Rather than offering answers, democracy presents citizens and theorists alike with a set of queries regarding the nature of the people, what we hold in common, and how we should engage in self-rule. In this way, democracy must always remain a *question*, since democratic theory can never fully capture the lived experience of democratic politics.[64] In recognizing the impossibility of ever completing the democratic community once and for all, democracy is best understood as a project of eternally striving to produce (though never fully achieving) the communities we seek to name.

While I agree with this effort to consider democracy's dilemmas in a more continual way, Keenan's emphasis on democracy's ongoingness misses a crucial element of what is so powerful in Wolin's characterization of democracy as "fugitive." Wolin's depiction of democracy as rare, ephemeral, and sporadic captures a temporal aspect of political action that Keenan overlooks in his discussion of the "forever open, always incomplete" quality of democratic openness. In Wolin, we find an understanding of citizen-as-actor that recognizes the power of the democratic *moment*. Describing the elusive character of Wolin's approach to democracy, Nicholas Xenos writes:

> Democracy eludes definition because it has a protean nature, but it is not unrecognizable. It is transformative, but it leaves no institutional product. It exists in the moments when we open ourselves and our communities to the unfamiliar and the unsettling, then dissolves when a new familiarity and a new settlement take place.[65]

Wolin's approach to democracy recognizes the evanescent moments of democratic belonging *whose criteria cannot be sustainability*. These transgressive episodes—where boundaries are breached rather than renewed—have a special standing in our consciousness. At these moments, democracy becomes a mode of being. It becomes an experience.

Recognizing the ongoingness of democratic politics does not require a rejection of its fugitive appearances: indeed, the memory of such fugitive moments can be a critical element of how subjects come to cultivate a more enduring ethos of democratic openness. Such an approach recognizes the persistent tension between democracy's constitutive incompleteness and its simultaneous desire to secure its accomplishments. Yet in highlighting the ephemeral aspects of democracy, such postmodern initiatives neither seek a retreat from politics nor deny the possibility of agency. Instead, as Fred Dallmayr notes, approaching democracy as more than a form of government encourages new perspectives for political action, including the realization that "popular self-rule is fragile, but no mere illusion."[66]

Conclusion: Fugitive *Latinidad*

In discussing the always-existent possibility of democratic renewal, Wolin approvingly cites Polish Solidarity, as well as a variety of social movements throughout U.S. history ("the movement to abolish slavery and the abortive effort at reconstructing American life on the basis of racial equality; the Populist and agrarian revolts of the 19th century; the struggle for autonomous trade unions and for women's rights; the civil rights movement of the '60s and the anti-war, anti-nuclear, and ecological movements of recent decades").[67] Yet in celebrating such movements' ability to renew the political, Wolin is less attentive to how fugitive moments are often animated by their own dreams of democratic closure. Yet as Keenan reminds us, democracy is a concept inevitably pulled between politics and the political, between the deliberative and the nondeliberative, between openness and closure. As a case in point, the Chicano and Puerto Rican movements are an extraordinary example of how closure exceeds the constitutionalizing moment. Even in the context of fugitive action and democratic renewal, we can see moments of democratic attenuation as emancipatory movements display their own unwillingness to accept dissonant voices and alternate political visions.

As we saw in the previous chapter, the demand for closure was powerfully present in the movements' dreams of racial unity. In their efforts to constitute themselves as a people, movement activists were confronting the inevitable democratic dilemma that no political community is *ever* fully achieved. Nevertheless, both movements understood Chicano and Puerto Rican unity as not only politically necessary but in some sense achievable.

At their least successful, the movements' radical democratic imagination faltered as displays of internal diversity came to be seen as threats to the movements' past political accomplishments. In this way, both movements harbored visions of community whose parameters and legitimacy could be secured once and for all. Not surprisingly, the command logic of unity both produced and sought to conceal the ongoingness of political conflict, as new transgressions and subject formations were increasingly rendered suspect. In other words, the movements' fundamental flaw was not their specific instances of sectarianism and exclusion— *it was the assumption that closure was itself a goal to be achieved.* Rather than taking pleasure in the production of diverse new political formations, activists saw the movements as achievements to be preserved. Reading the challenges of democratic theory into Latino politics helps us understand the critical importance of that which is "fugitive" alongside the ongoing challenge of sustaining an ethos of nonclosure.

As I show in the following chapters, Latino politics over the past forty-plus years can be read as a history of democratic moments and their aftermath, between the desire for representation and the memory of participation. Reading democratic theory into Latino politics turns these qualities of contestation, incompletion, and provisionality into the radical potential of *Latinidad*. Forever torn between the ongoing demand of democratic openness and the demands of politics, an ethos of nonclosure represents the capacity to find value in the interruptions and disruptions that inevitably accompany efforts to speak for and on behalf of subjects marked "Latino."

Throughout this book, I approach the concept of *Latinidad* as itself fugitive, with roots in the transgressive histories of excluded subjects who come to understand themselves as political actors. In this way, we can understand *Latinidad* as a form of what Wolin describes as "evanescent homogeneity"—an experience of commonality whose existence is forever possible yet never guaranteed. Drawing on the resources of democratic theory helps us see "Latino politics" not as an object or practice to be identified and permanently defined but, rather, as an ongoing argument whose effectiveness and legitimacy can be understood only over time. Approached as a site of permanent political contestation, *Latinidad*'s indeterminacy is not its failure but its promise. Such internal diversity should be creatively confronted rather than merely endured.

3 "The Bacchanalia of the Political"

Jean-Jacques Rousseau and the Dream of Latino Identification

Is the concept of *Latinidad* haunted by its movement past? Does the movement's legacy of democratic encounter help us envision the future anew? Or is Latino politics a project defined by loss?

In this chapter, I analyze various practices of *identification* central to movement politics—in particular, rallies, conferences, and poetry events. In focusing on events that emphasize identification through expressive enactments of membership, I ask: How were such moments produced, and what political lessons were drawn from such encounters? How was conflict perceived, and what was the relationship between conflict and questions of identification, deliberation, and public speech? Does the memory of such passionate and participatory politics inspire future political action—or does it render all that follows a disappointment?

To consider these questions, I turn to the political thought of Jean-Jacques Rousseau. More than most, Rousseau is a theorist attentive to the emotive power of democratic encounter. In his conception of democracy as grounded in the citizen-as-actor, Rousseau speaks to the importance of both passionate and participatory encounters in the public sphere. Yet his theory of identification, transparency, and nondeliberative public speech also reveals practices and assumptions that hinder democratic politics. I want to suggest that this combination of the radically democratic alongside the antidemocratic helps us understand how practices of passionate identification operated within the Chicano and Puerto Rican movements. In other words, the impulses and assumptions of movement politics can be better understood if we conceive Chicano and Puerto Rican activists as practicing a *Rousseauian* form of politics, emphasizing civic practices understood as passionate, performative, and familial.*

The relationship among identification, deliberation, and public speech is another significant element of the Rousseauian impulse in movement politics. A deep and abiding anxiety regarding political speech infuses both traditions: deliberative practices that uncover difference and conflict are characterized as damaging and dangerous, confirmation of political decline and decay. Yet while Rousseau's depiction of public speech is always characterized by risk, the practice itself is not always corrosive. Public speech among members of the political body *can* succeed, so long as deliberation and identification coexist. Rousseau articulates precisely this type of deliberative public speech in his depiction of the *circles* of Geneva in *Letter to d'Alembert*. In the circles, public speech is both deliberative and transparent, uniting listeners while simultaneously transcending the problems of division, artifice, and intrigue. This desire to produce conditions whereby public speech actually sustains identification is also present in movement politics. However, in movement discourse, transparency and public speech are reconciled through the performative practice of Chicano and Puerto Rican poetry.

Despite such attempts at reconciling speech and identification, both Rousseau and movement activists sought out nondeliberative forms of identification capable of transcending the dangerous and destabilizing force of agonistic speech. In Rousseau, such nondiscursive forms of civic identification are most fully embodied by the *festival*. The festival, or public spectacle, represents an ideal context for citizens to identify passionately with one another and experience themselves as a *moi commun* (a common self). A form of civic engagement capable of transcending self-interest, the Rousseauian festival represents a merging of the body politic that feels both mystical and intimate. This impulse toward intimacy and identification was equally essential to movement politics. The fiestas, *flor y cantos* (music and poetry events), rallies, and other mass gatherings of the late 1960s and early 1970s can be best understood as employing a Rousseauian conception of

---

*In making this move, I do not mean to imply that Latino activists were sitting in cafés discussing the theoretical and organizational implications of *Letter to d'Alembert* or *The Social Contract*. Chicanos and Puerto Ricans in the 1960s and 1970s neither explicitly nor intentionally invoked Rousseau. Yet it is my contention that a reconsideration of Rousseauian categories as seen through the lens of *Latinidad* allows us to see movement politics in a new and richer light.

political community, one that sought to bind the Latino body politic together by emphasizing unity and a conception of civic life as "an affair of the heart."[1]

This chapter is organized into four sections. In the first section, I explore Rousseau's concept of identification and its relationship to both pity and reason. Transposing Rousseau's concept of *identification* onto the field of movement politics, the section concludes by exploring the relationship between identification and the movement concept of *hermanidad*. The second section contrasts Rousseau's concept of the general will with the debates surrounding Chicana feminism at the National Chicano Liberation Conference. In both instances, civic health is equated with harmony and the absence of conflict, whereas agonistic debate is seen as a sign of corruption and civic decay. The third section considers the effort to reconcile transparency with healthy public speech through Rousseau's depictions of the circles of Geneva. I then put Rousseau's characterization of healthy public speech in conversation with the performative practice of Chicano and Puerto Rican poetry. The chapter concludes with a discussion of the Rousseauian festival and the democratic implications of movement events, including fiestas, *flor y cantos*, marches, rallies, sit-ins, takeovers, and other forms of participatory mass action.

Exploring the Rousseauian drive toward identification, we gain a better understanding of the power and attraction underlying identity politics—the promise of participatory civic spaces that offer familiarity, immediacy, mutual recognition, and the possibility of intimate public speech. Reading Rousseau, we come to understand the depth of this yearning not only in identity politics but in political life more generally; we come to recognize both the democratic and the antidemocratic implications of identification. Ultimately, by approaching these movements through Rousseau, we gain a better sense of how movements founded on a radical vision of participatory democracy can simultaneously display a desire to erase dissent and conflict.

"Not Our Minds but Our Feelings"

In order to grasp how subjectivity and community function in Rousseau's political theory, one must turn to his understanding of *identification*. In his open letter to the city of Geneva, Rousseau's dedication reveals the importance of identification in his depiction of the ideal political community:

> If I had to choose my birthplace, I would have chosen . . . a state where, all the individuals knowing one another, neither the obscure maneuvers of

vice nor the modesty of virtue could be hidden from the notice and judgment of the public, and where the sweet habit of seeing and knowing one
another turned love of the fatherland into love of the citizens rather than
love of the soil.[2]

In Rousseau's Geneva, citizenship and patriotism are characterized not by "love of
the soil" but by "love of the citizens." For him, political membership is at its best
when it emerges through such bonds of affection. As Lori Jo Marso notes, a "communitarian dream of the transparent and unified whole" permeates Rousseau's
writings.[3] In Rousseau's political thought, community is defined by authenticity
and the absence of duplicity; here we find no break between seeming and being.
Citizens continually appear before one another, yet the virtues and vices of its
citizens are not "hidden from the notice and judgment of the public." Instead,
Rousseau's subjects identify with their fellow citizens and the shared polity; such
identification produces well-ordered subjects capable of perceiving and enacting
the common good.

Rousseau's understanding of identification is related to his notion of *pitié*.
In the *Discourse on the Origin and Foundations of Inequality Among Men* (*Second
Discourse*), he characterizes primitive man as driven by two fundamental desires:
amour de soi (self-preservation) and *pitié* (pity or compassion). According to
Rousseau, it is *pitié* that forms the basis of man's goodness, what political theorist
Clifford Orwin describes as "the only pure natural morality."[4] Rousseau views
pitié, an emotional impulse based on identification rather than the "subtle arguments" of rational speech, as a virtue "all the more universal and useful to man
because it precedes in him the use of all reflection."[5] For him, *pitié*—this instinc-
tual aversion to the suffering of others—is what impels savage man to see outside
himself.

For Rousseau, the true self is not the rational self. *Pitié*, not reason, forms the
basis of our goodness: we are less our minds than our feelings.[6] In contrast to *pitié*,
which Rousseau characterizes as natural and innate, reason is recently acquired
and morally inconsistent. Reason "engenders vanity and reflection fortifies it;
reason turns man back upon himself, it separates him from all that bothers and
afflicts him."[7] In a well-known passage describing the philosopher's response to
witnessing a violent attack, Rousseau writes:

His fellow-man can be murdered with impunity right under his window;
he has only to put his hands over his ears and argue with himself a bit to
prevent nature, which revolts within him, from identifying him with the
man who is being assassinated. Savage man does not have this admirable

talent, and for want of reason he is always seen heedlessly yielding to the first sentiment of humanity.[8]

For Rousseau, "reason divides men; only sentiment reliably unites them."[9] The claim here is not that reason is negative or unnecessary; Rousseau is making a more subtle point, about the *limitations* of rationality.[10] In the *Discourse on the Origin and Foundations of Inequality* we are reminded that one of modernity's most distinguishing features has been its ability to justify and intellectualize war, inequality, and other forms of political violence.

For Rousseau, identification not only generates a sense of mutual recognition and affirmation—it is capable of becoming a form of *resistance*. In *The Government of Poland*, for example, identification becomes a strategy of opposition and self-determination. Pessimistic about the ability of the Polish people to resist Russian domination, Rousseau asks: How can the Poles remain "free" even under Russian occupation? His solution is that the Polish people "establish the republic in the Poles' own hearts" so that they can maintain a cohesive identity no matter what their oppressors may do.[11] "You cannot possibly keep them from swallowing you," writes Rousseau; "see to it, at least, that they shall not be able to digest you."[12]

In discourse in the Chicano and Puerto Rican movements, efforts to produce a similar sense of internal cohesion and collective identification can be seen in the rhetorical use of *familia* and *hermanidad*. Describing the proper role of Chicano student organizations, *El Plan de Santa Barbara* states: "It is important that every Chicano student on campus be made to feel that he has a place on that campus and that he has a feeling of *familia* with his Chicano brothers. . . . Above all the feeling of *hermanidad* must prevail so that the organization is more to the members than just a club or a clique."[13] Here, *hermanidad* means more than *brotherhood*—it signifies unalienated belonging, recognition, and internal harmony. As discussed in chapter 1, when romantic narratives of *familia* are dominant, political membership becomes constitutive of one's cultural identity; Chicano and Puerto Rican activists understood themselves as linked to their fellow Latinos through a sense of affection and familiarity. However, this sense of partiality and internal cohesion was defined by a nationalist critique of the dominant society as simultaneously hostile and homogenizing. Like Rousseau's claim in the *Poland* that the Polish people must construct a distinct and separate identity that sets them apart from their fellow Europeans, movement activists promoted a strategy of identity maintenance that stressed resistance to the political practices of the dominant citizenry.

Like *pitié*, identification is an emotive and participatory encounter between subjects that transcends the problems of intrigue and artifice.[14] Unlike *pitié*, however, identification is a form of authentic contact between subjects who share not simply a common humanity but a common *civic* membership. In this way, identification produces a sense of unity and fellow feeling among members of a polity, what political scientist Daniel Cullen describes as "a union of hearts."[15] For Rousseau, such a union of hearts represents civic life at its healthiest and most satisfying. This equation of harmony with civic health is most clearly seen in Rousseau's portrayal of the general will in *The Social Contract*, and it is to this concept that I now turn.

Generalizing the Will: Democratic Uncertainty and the Problem of Deliberative Speech

Notions of "will" and "general" are central to Rousseau's moral and political philosophy. As Patrick Riley notes, without will, "there is no self-determination, no moral causality, no obligation."[16] Without generality, the will may become "capricious, egoistic, self-loving"—in a word, "willful."[17] Unable to produce, perceive, or pursue a common good, subjects lacking a general will are able only to obey.[18]

Rather than the dominance of private and partial wills, Rousseau's general will exists when duty and interest converge. Characterized by unity and reciprocity, the general will is by definition a moral and collective body. Rousseau describes this process by invoking an image of almost mathematical efficiency:

> There is often a great difference between the will of all and the general will. The latter considers only the common interests; the former considers private interests, and is only a sum of private wills. But take away from these same wills the pluses and minuses that cancel each other out, and the remaining sum of the differences is the general will.[19]

The birth of a general will seems to mark a moment of collective recognition and communal identification whereby a people comes to recognize and understand itself. Such recognition, however, is far from natural—subjects must struggle to master their private desires in order to both produce and perceive the general will. Rousseau explains: "If there were no different interests, the common interest, which would never encounter any obstacle, would scarcely be felt. Everything would run smoothly by itself and politics would cease to be an art."[20]

For Rousseau, it is this ability to confront and overcome division that makes the general will a collective achievement, an "art." The general will exists only when the internal contradictions produced by "different interests" are able to be overcome, produced through the clash and contestation of partial and multiple wills. It is for this reason that Rousseau emphasizes a rigorous civic education—precisely because this ability to generalize must be *created*. Riley argues that because "men do not naturally or originally think of themselves as part of a greater whole, they must be brought to this non-natural belief."[21]

As Riley notes, the process of generalizing the will is difficult, "as difficult as squaring the circle."[22] This process is particularly complicated by Rousseau's emphasis on freedom. For Rousseau, the general will requires that one denature particularistic beings without destroying their autonomy.[23] As I discuss later in this chapter, the capacity to will the general is not produced through extended debate and deliberation. Instead, it is through participatory yet nondeliberative practices—including festivals and other forms of civic spectacle—that citizens learn to perceive the general will. Instead of contentious debate between citizens, the strength of the general will is visible through harmony and a lack of dissension.[24] As Rousseau describes the well-functioning assembly: "All the mechanisms of the State are vigorous and simple, its maxims are clear and luminous, it has no tangled contradictory interests; the common good is clearly apparent everywhere and requires only good sense to be perceived."[25] According to George Graham, Rousseau conceived of consensus—as expressed by the general will—as an "ideal type" of political discourse. "Rousseau did not expect to achieve full agreement in any society," Graham writes, "but he presents the ideal type as the proper goal for every society."[26]

As Rousseau's description makes clear, civic health in the assembly is expressed through unanimity. "Everything that disrupts the social bond of unity is useless," he writes. "All institutions which set a man in contradiction with himself are of no worth."[27] For Rousseau, the general will's dominance is threatened by tumultuous contestation and a multiplicity of views: "The more harmony there is in the assemblies, that is, the closer opinions come to obtaining unanimous support, the more dominant as well is the general will. But long debates, dissensions, and tumult indicate the ascendance of private interests and the decline of the state."[28]

In the Rousseauian assembly, it is the absence of both conflict and conversation that signifies civic health. In contrast to the quiet harmony displayed when the general will is dominant, excessive public speech (exhibited by "dissension," disagreement, and "long debates") characterizes the corrupt assembly. He writes:

> [W]hen the social tie begins to slacken and the State to grow weak; when private interests start to make themselves felt and small societies to influence the large one, the common interest changes and is faced with opponents; unanimity no longer prevails in the votes; the general will is no longer the will of all; contradictions and debates arise and the best advice is not accepted without disputes.[29]

For Rousseau, interactions between assembled subjects can all too easily devolve into inequality and lost virtue.[30] Nor is this simply a problem that emerges in modernity. Depicting the gatherings of early man in his *Discourse on the Origin and Foundations of Inequality*, Rousseau writes:

> People grew accustomed to assembling in front of the huts or around a large tree. . . . Each one began to look at the others and to want to be looked at himself, and public esteem had value. The one who sang or danced the best, the handsomest, the strongest, the most adroit, or the most eloquent became the most highly considered; and that was the first step toward inequality and, at the same time, toward vice.[31]

It is interesting to note that the inequalities that surround speech are characterized as particularly dangerous for Rousseau ("the most eloquent became the most highly considered; and that was the first step toward inequality and, at the same time, toward vice"). For him, corruption in the assembly is signified by an *excess* of speech, and such excess is linked to his critique of ornamentation. In the *Discourse on the Sciences and Arts* (*First Discourse*), ornamentation of dress and decor is posited against the virtue of simplicity:

> It is in the rustic clothes of a farmer and not beneath the gilt of a courtier that strength and vigor of the body will be found. . . . The good man is an athlete who likes to compete in the nude. He disdains all those vile ornaments which would hamper the use of his strength, most of which were invented only to hide some deformity.[32]

For Rousseau, eloquence represents a kind of verbal ornamentation—a form of deception as well as a kind of alienation.[33] And like ornamentation, eloquence seems to *produce* the very weaknesses and deformities it seeks to mask. Ornamentation increases the distance between seeming and being (appearance versus reality). And just as immorality and corruption are equated with the gilt of the courtier's clothes, so too is eloquence associated with "ambition, hate, flattery, and falsehood."[34]

Because deliberative practices between citizens expose difference, inequality, and disagreement, Rousseau's vision of the popular assembly is more about shared *presence* than about shared decision making. Once the general will comes into existence, the public assembly represents the civic site where this will is articulated and confirmed rather than produced. In this way, the assembly is envisioned as a political body that *expresses* rather than *produces* political agreement. For Rousseau, the general will is produced through education, mores, tradition, and civic rituals— not the dialogical struggle between citizens in the public realm. This is why in a healthy regime, the general will can be found even in silence. As Rousseau describes this process: "If, when an adequately informed people deliberates, the citizens were to have no communication among themselves, the general will would always result from the large number of small differences, and the deliberation would always be good."[35] As Danielle Allen notes in her discussion of the social-contract tradition, this idealization of oneness "brings with it a severely impoverished understanding of language as the medium of politics."[36] Rousseau's discussion of deliberation without communication involves "a peculiar conception of democratic deliberation" that reconceives deliberation as a "mutual exercise in silent examination," isolating each citizen from the influence of others.[37] Because the preconditions for general willing have been established *prior* to the convening of the assembly, dialogue *between* citizens is superfluous. In fact, because the healthy assembly is the site where previously socialized subjects gather, excessive and unnecessary public discourse could actually undermine and obscure the subjects' ability to distinguish the general will from self-interest or the will of all.

As political theorist Judith Shklar correctly notes, Rousseau's assemblies "do not govern and do not frame policies." Instead, "[t]he popular assemblies exist to preserve the republic, not to alter or adapt its laws." The primary purpose of the assemblies is to express confidence or dissatisfaction, to reconfirm original laws and to socialize the citizen by "identifying directly and constantly with the polity."[38] Instead of being the space where contending notions of the good are debated and fought out, the popular assembly of *The Social Contract* is a "defensive body in which the people do not so much forge their identity in the process of establishing consensus, as *preserve* it against the inevitable tendency of partial associations, and partial identities, to displace it." For Shklar, Rousseau's assembly *socializes* its citizens, encouraging them to identify "directly and constantly with the polity."[39]

The Rousseauian belief that contestation and a multiplicity of viewpoints represent a decline in the general will helps us make sense of the debates surrounding Latina feminists discussed in chapter 2, particularly the debates surrounding Latina feminism and the infamous resolution that emerged from the National

Chicano Liberation Conference stating that "it was the consensus of the group that the Chicana woman does *not* want to be liberated" (italics added).[40] Seen from a Rousseauian perspective, the resolution on Chicanas was more than merely antifeminist—it was a statement of the unanimity and civic health of the Chicano people. Instead of focusing on their own "narrow issues" that might potentially divide the community, Chicanas at the conference overcame their differences and recognized their larger interests and their shared fate with the Chicano people— hence the ascendancy of the general will. In their belief that a proper Chicano politics required this act of gendered renunciation, movement activists engaged in what political theorist Elizabeth Wingrove has described as "consensual nonconsensuality"—a form of Rousseauian consent in which "one wills the circumstances of one's own domination."[41] For Wingrove, Rousseau's political thought participates in a gendered logic whereby "republican identity is constructed through sexual identities and sexual identities, through political forms."[42] In a similar vein, a majority of movement activists also believed that a healthy Chicano political identity was necessarily constructed through the proper performance of masculine and feminine sexual identities. Such forms of identity and consent were critical to sustaining the general will of the community and its movement.

Despite this initial moment of "consensual nonconsensuality," in the months that followed the Denver conference, an increasing number of Chicanas began to speak out against the resolution, leading to increased debate regarding the status of women in the movement. From a Rousseauian perspective, we now see why movement activists generally interpreted this increase in debate and dissent as a sign of decline and civic decay. For many movement activists, the National Youth Liberation Conference marked the cultural and political rebirth of the Chicano people. For these activists, the collective will of the Chicano people was articulated at the Denver conference, and the movement's task was to enlarge and deepen its dominance. This goal, however, was threatened by the rising feminist presence in the movement. Despite the feminist claim that confronting sexism would ultimately *increase* unity and enlarge the sphere of agreement, many movement activists viewed the shift in gender relations and the concomitant rise in contentious speech as signifying corrosive division and the loss of civic agency. Put somewhat differently, the Rousseauian elements of the movement made it difficult for feminists to effectively argue their case for gender justice. Within movement discourse, the general will was understood as produced through identification and gendered forms of renunciation, while the debates with feminists involved new forms of rights-claiming, disagreement, and contentious debate. In the latter case, *speech* was paramount. However, in Rousseau's characterization of the public assembly, such speech is fraught with risk.

A Union of Hearts: The Power of Nondeliberative Speech

Because public speech in the popular assembly is so unstable and prone to faction-alism and inequality, Rousseau turns to civic practices capable of "filtering out" the conflict associated with political speech. In his desire to produce a sense of unity and fellow feeling among members of the civic body, he seeks deliberative practices that transcend the problems of intrigue and artifice. This desire is apparent in Rousseau whenever he speaks about the "heart" of the citizen.

The heart is important to Rousseau not as a signifier of merely private senti-ment but as something in need of civic education.[43] This view of the heart as the "engine" of civic life can be seen in the final chapter of book 1 of *The Social Con-tract*, when Rousseau concludes his delineation of the various types of law (polit-ical, civil, and criminal) by stating:

> To these three types of laws is added a fourth, the most important of all; which is not engraved on marble or bronze, but in the hearts of the citizens; which is the true constitution of the State; which gains fresh force each day; which . . . preserves a people in the spirit of its institution, and impercepti-bly substitutes the force of habit for that of authority.[44]

For Rousseau, public speech among members of the political body would succeed if it involved this sort of "union of hearts"—a space where deliberation and iden-tification could coexist. This belief in the possibility of communication without dissimulation represents his dream of *transparency*.[45] According to theorist Tracy Strong, Rousseau harbors a vision of relations among men in which "there is no possibility to take the speaker as other than that person is."[46] When public speech is transparent, "there is no disjuncture between emotion and expression, between weeping and words, between meaning and saying."[47] For Rousseau, transparency represents a mode of communication "without dissimulation."[48]

Rousseau's Circles: Speech without Intrigue

By linking deliberation to transparency, Rousseau was able to articulate a form of public speech that was both political and emotive—capable of uniting the listeners and transcending the problems so often produced by intrigue and eloquence.

In *Letter to d'Alembert*, Rousseau invokes the circles of Geneva as a civic institution that engages in public speech yet is capable of being both deliberative
and transparent.

For Rousseau, the circles are an example of public speech and face-to-face
deliberation that bind men together in a free and healthy polity. In describing this
institution, Rousseau writes:

> The *circles* are societies of twelve to fifteen persons who . . . meet and
> there each gives himself without restraint to the amusements of his
> taste; they gamble, chat, read, drink and smoke. . . . Also they often go
> walking together, and the amusements they provide for themselves are
> exercises fit to cause and maintain a robust body. . . . In a word, these decent
> and innocent institutions combine everything which can contribute to
> making friends, citizens, and soldiers out of the same men, and, in conse-
> quence, everything which is most appropriate to a free people.[49]

Theorist James Miller describes the circles as a form of "healthy interactions"
where men come to see themselves "not as anonymous neighbors, but as thoughtful
compatriots."[50] Most important, the circles are spaces in which transparency
and deliberation can coexist. Describing the deliberative practices of the circles,
Rousseau writes:

> Our *circles* still preserve some image of ancient morals [manners] among
> us . . . [T]he men . . . can devote themselves to grave and serious discourse
> without fear of ridicule. They dare to speak of country and virtue without
> passing for windbags; they even dare to be themselves without being
> enslaved to the maxims of a magpie. If the turn of conversation becomes
> less polished, reasons take on more weight; they are not satisfied by jokes or
> compliments. They cannot get away with fine phrases for answers. They do
> not humor one another in dispute; each, feeling himself attacked by all the
> forces of his adversary, is obliged to use all his own to defend himself; it is
> thus that the mind gains precision and vigor. If some licentious remarks are
> mixed in with all this, one ought not to take umbrage at it. The least
> vulgar are not always the most decent, and this language, a bit rustic, is still
> preferable to the more studied style.[51]

As Jean Starobinski argues, because the transparency of minds creates "the communication of souls," citizens in the circles "dare to be themselves," secure in the
knowledge that they can speak freely and "without fear of ridicule."[52] Yet within the
security of this setting, the circles also involve rigorous and occasionally contentious

debate. Because the circles are characterized by transparency, "compliments" and "fine phrases" will not suffice. Instead, attacks by one's adversaries must be fended off through the "precision and vigor" of one's argument.

Yet despite the intensity of the interactions, when analyzing the deliberative character of the circles, what becomes apparent is how safe, constrained, and familial the dialogue is. In Rousseau's characterization of the circles, language is innocent. Opinions are exchanged and defended, but deliberative dialogue never transforms one's view, never changes one's mind—because for Rousseau, to be transformed by another's speech is to be vulnerable to domination; it means one is no longer "everything for himself."[53] Instead of transformation, Rousseau offers transparency. In the circles, the discussion and debate may sometimes be heated, even vulgar—but it is also relaxed and intimate, "cordial and frank."[54] Speech is fraternal rather than formal, personal rather than public. This is no discourse between strangers. This is speech without subterfuge or hidden agendas, speech stripped of the contingencies and dangers of politics. In this state of transparent relations, the claims of each are recognized and taken seriously. "Here," Miller writes, "alienation is unknown."[55]

In his conception of democratic deliberation, Rousseau demands an exceptionally high level of intimacy in order to create the preconditions for transparency. In doing this, the democratic possibilities of deliberation are deeply constrained. Even at his most deliberative, Rousseau is unable to envision democratic dialogue capable of productive contestation among subjects who share membership but not affection.

In *Letter to d'Alembert*, Rousseau invokes the circles as a civic institution that engages in public speech yet is capable of being both deliberative and transparent. In Chicano and Puerto Rican discourse, transparency and public speech are reconciled through the use of Spanish and (even more effectively) through the performative practice of movement poetry.

Movement Poetry: Identification through Public Speech

It is said that MOTECUHZOMA ILHUICAMINA
Sent
An expedition
looking for the Northern
Mythical land
wherefrom the Aztecs came

la Tierra de Aztlán
mythical land for those
who dream of roses and
swallow thorns
or for those who swallow thorns
in powdered milk
feeling guilty about smelling flowers
about looking for Aztlán
—Alurista, "Poem in Lieu of Preface" (1970)[56]

As a cultural practice, movement poetry represents public speech at its most political and its most performative. According to Rafael Pérez-Torres, from its inception, movement poetry has been intimately linked to the political struggles of a people. As such, "its utterances mark a collective position."[57] Poetry—both the writing and the performing of it—was central to this process of identity production and identification.[58] Movement poetry is akin to Rousseau's circles; both operate from a civic agenda that wants its respective political membership to see themselves in terms that are familial and intimate. Like the circles, the poetic practices of the movement represent an expressive form of public speech capable of both uniting listeners and transcending divisive political disagreement.

Most important, poetry is a public speech act that is simultaneously political *and* nondeliberative. By this, I mean that it is emotive but not dialogical. Unlike the circles, poetry does not involve conversation (and possibly contestation) between its members. Instead, the practice of movement poetry required a listening subject and a speaking subject. But because both subjects are presumed to be united by culture and experience, it is a relationship based on identification rather than deliberation. The connection between movement poetry and the circles is most apparent in this context of affection and shared group membership.

Because it exists in the realm of rhetoric, movement poetry is an expressive form of discourse that seeks to transcend the disjuncture that Tracy Strong describes— between emotion and expression, weeping and words, meaning and saying. In this way, the Rousseauian ideal of transparency animates Chicano and Puerto Rican poetic practices. For those anxious about deliberation and disagreement, movement poetry was a particularly attractive form of discourse—political and participatory yet capable of avoiding divisive dialogue and debate. According to Ignacio García, movement poetic practices provided a general ethos "capable of meaning most things to most activists and their followers."[59] By operating within the realm of the symbolic, poetry can politicize its listeners while evading contradiction and conflict. Moreover, in its reliance upon mythic memory and legends, movement poetry locates itself outside the parameters of traditional history, thereby avoiding another site of potential disagreement.

Little attention has been paid to the fact that the most significant Chicano and Puerto Rican organizations turned to poetry to mark their entry into the public realm. In 1969, the Young Lords made their first public appearance, with Felipe Luciano speaking on the need for more revolutionary action and (accompanied by congas) performing his poem "Jíbaro, My Pretty Nigger."[60] Similarly, "Corky" Gonzales wrote his most famous poem, "Yo Soy Joaquín," for his organization, the Crusade for Justice, performing it at the National Chicano Youth Liberation Conference in 1969.

A great deal of "classic" movement poetry has a strong civic impulse—it seeks to be both educative and socializing.[61] Poets such as Gonzales, Alurista, and Pedro Pietri saw their poetry as an organizing tool that served an "agitprop function."[62] According to Gonzales, "Yo Soy Joaquín" was written "first and foremost for the Chicano Movement."[63] Written in 1967, "Joaquín" traces the Chicano struggle through a historical overview of Mexican/Chicano history.[64] Distributed by mimeographed copy and recited at conferences, fiestas, rallies, and strikes, "Yo Soy Joaquín" has been described as "an expression of Chicano political philosophy, self-discovery and the epic story of a people."[65]

One central characteristic of movement poetic practice was its commitment to public performance and public ritual. In *Chicano Poetry*, Cordelia Candelaria describes the significance of ritual for Chicano poetics: "Both in its overt replication of a communal rite through the poem/performance and in its recognition of an ethnopoetic tradition . . . Chicano poetry is most fully comprehensible within a context of ritual."[66] Because public ritual is linked to the performative, movement poetry "is often meant to be spoken rather than read."[67] For this reason, Chicano poetry was and is often performed as an event.[68] "Yo Soy Joaquín," for example, was recited for years before it found its way into book form.[69]

Because it was most often performed for community groups, movement poetry was not intended to be entertainment for strangers. Like Rousseau's circles, it was public speech understood to be fraternal and familial. The speaking of Spanish was yet another aspect of Chicano poetics that combined transparency and ritual; as noted in my earlier discussion of language and the Rousseauian "heart," reclaiming Spanish served to connect movement activists to both their politics and their people.[70] According to literary scholar Hector Calderón, movement artists and writers chose public forms of expression that could be enjoyed in an oral, communal setting: "A new pride in the language was reflected by writers who have continually returned to the lived speech act to capture in print the oral quality of Chicano Spanish and English vernaculars."[71]

Politically, movement poetry served as a way of constructing personal speech acts for public purposes—of unifying and inspiring its listeners. In its nondeliberative structure, poetry is capable of engaging in public, political speech without risking disagreement and divisiveness. Like the circles, movement poetry is a participatory form of civic speech as powerful as it was constrained.

Given Rousseau's hostility to the theater in *Letter to d'Alembert*, one might well assume that the performative aspect of movement poetry would be seen in a similarly negative light. As noted earlier, Rousseau had serious concerns regarding the risks posed by theatrical performance. In the theaters of Paris, the audience is moved, but for Rousseau, these emotions are premised on manipulation rather than authentic experience. Actors do not behave as citizens; instead of a display of brotherhood and authentic connection, they pretend and manipulate. Given the dissembling nature of the theater, how can movement poetic practices escape the Rousseauian critique of performance?

I would suggest that movement poetic practices are akin to a form of theater to which Rousseau gives qualified praise: the theater of ancient Greece. Like Greek theater, movement poetry "relies on political themes that invoke national traditions."[72] Like *corridos*, movement poetry often involves a retelling of a significant historical event or an ode to a Puerto Rican, Chicano, or Mexican leader (César Chavez, Pedro Albizu Campos, Emiliano Zapata, etc.). Like other forms of Chicano art (murals, music, *teatro*), movement poetry features tales of resistance and cultural affirmation. As Starobinski notes, such practices remind listeners of their own past, including nostalgic remembrances and shared suffering.[73] Rather than identifying with lovers, villains, and corrupt sophisticates—as they do in the theater of Paris—Latino subjects were more akin to Greek citizens in their engagement with forms of performance that encouraged identification with their fellow citizens and their shared civic history.

Equally important, both the poetic tradition of the movement and Greek theater sought to minimize the distance between audience and actor. *Flor y canto* events, for example, often involved a portion of the performance dedicated to audience participation: audience members were encouraged to perform a poem, tell a story, or sing a song. Movement poetic practices involved precisely the type of public performance that Rousseau celebrates—a form of performance in which the separation between spectator and actor came closest to being overcome.

Festival Politics: Rousseauian Spectacle and the Politics of Identification

Describing the founding of a people, Rousseau writes:

> In order for an emerging people to appreciate the healthy maxims of politics, and follow the fundamental rules of statecraft, the effect would have to become the cause; the social spirit, which should be the result of the institution, would have to preside over the founding of the institution itself; and men would have to be prior to laws what they ought to become by means of laws. Since the legislator is therefore unable to use either force or reasoning, he must necessarily have recourse to another order of authority, which can win over without violence and persuade without convincing.[74]

As Alan Keenan notes, "the very fact of the people's autonomy—that they themselves must form themselves into a people, yet without natural or external rules for what they share that makes them a people—renders their identity and legitimacy forever open to question."[75] Despite turning to the founding power of the Lawgiver, the democratic contradiction Rousseau identifies (yet cannot resolve) points to the fact that political communities are always in the process of calling themselves into being. One must necessarily "speak and act in the name of the people before receiving the people's own sanction."[76] In this passage, we see Rousseau grappling with the need for conditions of commonality (what he calls "the social spirit") that are not fully present. But prior to the creation of the civic institutions, how can such a spirit exist? This is the paradox. For Rousseau, this dilemma cannot be resolved by either "force or reasoning." Instead, he calls for an alternative form of authority, one that can "win over without violence" and "persuade without convincing." But what does this mean? What does such a form of "nonauthoritarian authority" look like?

For Rousseau, it is the *festival* that most successfully melds identification with autonomy. As a form of democratic socialization, the Rousseauian festival represents a form of civic education that holds the key to making men "what they ought to be."[77] As Patrick Riley notes, "It is no accident that education (domestic and civic) is everything in Rousseau."[78] "Public enlightenment," Rousseau writes, "results in the union of understanding and will in the social body."[79] In this way, the festival is his fundamental method of denaturing without domination. Capable of melding "abstract principles of political right with the enthusiasm of communal identification," the festival can "win over without violence" and "persuade without convincing."

Tracy Strong has described the Rousseauian festival as "the bacchanalia of the political," with public festivals, dances, and competitions representing the ideal context for subjects to identify passionately with one another.[80] "[L]et the spectators become an entertainment to themselves," Rousseau writes in *Letter to d'Alembert*, "make them actors themselves; do it so that each sees and loves himself in the others so that all will be better united."[81]

The Rousseauian festival also functions as a way of solving the problem of generality—of having citizens "perceive the general when they look at political questions and avoid being 'blinded' by their particular interests."[82] According to Starobinski, "The exaltation of the collective festival has the same structure as the general will of the *Social Contract*. . . . [T]he festival accomplishes on the level of feeling what the general will aims at on the level of political right."[83] The games and ceremonies of Rousseauian festival sought to transform the weak and divided subject into a citizen *animated* by an inner strength derived from his sense of being "part of a greater whole and of having a 'patria' that is genuinely his."[84] James Miller explains:

> For one glorious instant, the festival rebaptizes society as one "big family." In the collective euphoria, individual reserve is swept aside, "all live on the most intimate terms." . . . At the height of the celebration, differences momentarily melt, and the individual experiences the delicious sensation of abandoning himself to the collective spirit.[85]

Because it requires that every citizen feel the eyes of his fellow countrymen upon him, the festival is deeply participatory, as performative as it is democratic. At the festival, "no one is a mere spectator; each is an actor who identifies himself with all."[86] In a famous footnote to *Letter to d'Alembert*, Rousseau captures the power of public spectacle:

> I remember having been struck in my childhood by a rather simple entertainment, the impression of which has nevertheless always stayed with me in spite of time and variety of experience. The regiment of Saint-Gervais had done its exercises . . . gathered after supper in the St. Gervais square and started dancing all together, officers and soldiers, around the fountain, to the basin of which the drummers, the fifers and the torch bearers had mounted. A dance of men . . . five or six hundred men in uniform, holding one another by the hand and forming a long ribbon which wound around, serpent-like, in cadence and without confusion . . . the excellence of tunes which animated them, the sound of the drums, the glare of the torches, a

certain military pomp in the midst of pleasure, all this created a very lively sensation that could not be experienced coldly. It was late; the women were in bed; all of them got up. Soon the windows were full of female spectators who gave a new zeal to the actors; they could not long confine themselves to their windows and they came down; the wives came to their husbands, the servants brought wine; even the children, awakened by the noise, ran half-clothed amidst their fathers and mothers. The dance was suspended; now there were only embraces, laughs, health, and caresses. . . . My father, embracing me, was seized with trembling which I think I still feel and share. "Jean-Jacques," he said to me, "love your country. Do you see these good Genevans? They are all friends, they are all brothers; joy and concord reign in their midst. You are a Genevan; one day you will see other peoples; but even if you should travel as much as your father, you will not find their likes." . . . I am well aware that this entertainment, which moved me so, would be without appeal for countless others; one must have eyes made for seeing it and a heart made for feeling it. No, the only pure joy is public joy, and the true sentiments of nature reign only over the people.[87]

In contrast to the passivity of the Paris theater, Rousseau's civic festival requires participation. As Rousseau indicates in his story of "soldiers dancing," the audience is *part* of the spectacle. According to Strong, Rousseau's footnote in the *Letter* represents a "festival without invidiousness."[88] In Rousseau's idealized recollection, the dance is both "coordinated and formless," spontaneous yet cohesive. Strong rightly notes the significance of Rousseau's father embracing him and naming him as a citizen at the culmination of the dance ("You are a Genevan") and the way in which "unity"—a unity of both emotion and movement—represents the "paradigm of citizenship" in Rousseau's anecdote.[89] For Strong, the festival represents the civic space where "words, music and action together provide the model of what community is for Rousseau."[90]

The fiestas, *flor y cantos*, marches, rallies, sit-ins, takeovers, and other mass gatherings of the late 1960s and early 1970s can all be seen as employing a Rousseauian conception of political community that sought to meld abstract rights "with the enthusiasm of communal identification."[91] Both the Rousseauian festival and movement gatherings sought to overcome what was perceived as a weak and divided subjectivity, transforming it into a new civic consciousness that symbolized membership in part of a greater whole. For scholars of the Puerto Rican movement, it was "the dramatic actions, colorized by the Afros, dark glasses and dashikis dancing to the rhythm of Latin Soul" that most powerfully capture the movement's spirit of "popular power and liberation."[92] Like the Rousseauian festival, movement gatherings functioned as a civic space where, together, words, music, and action provide a model of community and authentic contact among its members.

An important aspect of the Rousseauian festival is its *inclusive* character: "[T]he festivals . . . encompass the entire community in one intoxicating bacchanalian whirl, breaking down the boundaries that define the particularity of each individual. It is here that the truth of the whole is forged and reaffirmed. Wives and children, domestic and foreign residents, all flock together in a civic communion celebrating events and institutions that define their life in common."[93] In the context of the festival, those who are traditionally outside the public sphere can enter and join in this "civic communion."[94] According to Latin Americanist Ilan Stavans, such inclusivity is characteristic of the festival in Latin American culture: "What characterizes the Latino fiesta is the possibility of dissolving racial, cultural, and social boundaries. The fiesta opens up the spirit and allows for alliances that otherwise could not take place."[95]

Like Rousseau's festival, the movement's massive rallies and demonstrations sought to make the community "into a sort of constant spectacle in which all the citizens are participants."[96] Describing her experience at one movement gathering, Chicana activist Marta Varela explains:

> "Conference" is a poor word to describe those five days. . . . It was in reality a fiesta: days of celebrating what sings in the blood of a people who, taught to believe they are ugly, discover the true beauty in their souls during years of occupation and intimidation. . . . [T]his affirmation grew into a *grito*, a roar among the people gathered in the auditorium of the Crusade's Center.[97]

By providing members of the community with the opportunity to *witness* one another politically, movement gatherings articulated a participatory ethos emphasizing the power of shared display in common public space. In Varela's characterization, participants of the conference were not gathering *for* something so much as they were gathering *as* something. In other words, these large-scale, grassroots gatherings reflected activists' desire to understand themselves as engaging in a politics of *presence*. By putting participants in the gaze of one another, subjects generated the unity of emotion and movement that characterizes the Rousseauian festival.

Describing Rousseau's depiction of the harvest feast in *La nouvelle Héloise*, Starobinski notes that within the festive atmosphere, "all veils have been lifted, and the characters live in trusting intimacy."[98] It is in this atmosphere that Rousseau presents his "charming spectacle" where duty and pleasure are reconciled through "Dionysiac rapture and careful organization. The holiday is also a day of work."[99] Similarly, movement gatherings were also events that combined political work alongside the pleasures of celebration. Like Rousseau's depiction of the harvest feast, "[t]he work of the harvest is scarcely distinguished from the day's amusements: 'in no other holiday has man been able to combine the agreeable with the useful.'"[100]

As an alternative form of democratic participation, the Rousseauian festival emphasizes group harmony and mass participation by reconciling civic harmony and participation through its capacity to transcend the confines of public speech. Like Rousseau's festivals, the movement's conferences, marches, and fiestas represent an attempt at "uniting the affections" so that political subjects would be more capable and more inclined toward "general willing" than they would otherwise be. And while some festivals are explicitly political while others are not, they are always powerfully *public* acts, for in every incarnation, the festival puts citizens into one another's gaze. For Rousseau and movement activists, the festival enacts alternate conceptions of democratic participation through practices that are passionate, performative, and familial. Its democratic impulse is implied in the belief that while not everyone deliberates over public policy, *everyone* is capable of meaningful contact between his or her fellow citizens. Nevertheless, a commitment to participatory democracy that is coexistent with an aversion toward political deliberation and public contestation has profound—and often troubling—implications for both the political theory of Jean-Jacques Rousseau and the theory and practice of movement politics more generally. For although the general will emerges through conflict, its maintenance is premised on a dream of collective agreement and harmony. Following its establishment, the popular assembly is no longer conceived as the space where contending notions of the good are debated and fought out. Instead, the assembly emerges as a "defensive body in which the people do not so much forge their identity in the process of establishing consensus, as *preserve* it against the inevitable tendency of partial associations, and partial identities, to displace it."[101] The festival and other forms of spontaneous unanimity produce an idealized notion of community without the risk of disagreement. Instead, the Rousseauian assembly *socializes* its citizens, encouraging them to identify "directly and constantly with the polity."[102]

In their tendency to conceive of the assembly as a Rousseauian space of confirmation rather than deliberation, movement activists understood public gatherings as the space where unity was both embodied and expressed. The power of these practices was their ability to create democratic spaces where participants came to feel themselves to be a people. But in making the assembly a site of preservation and confirmation, the movement denied itself a crucial space of democratic discourse. By demanding that the movement gatherings express their health and vibrancy primarily through expressions of unity, the civic practices of the movement shut down critical space for critique and conversation, limiting the movement's ability to develop politically.

Conclusion

This chapter began by asking if *Latinidad* is haunted by its movement past—whether its emotionally charged practices of identification inspired future political action or, conversely, left subjects in a state of political despair. The answer is complicated. In my reading, movement politics was driven by the longing for a passionate and participatory politics capable of generating a sense of unity and "peoplehood"—coupled with the desire to avoid political conflict and agonistic speech encounters. As I have suggested, such contradictory aspirations can productively be characterized as Rousseauian. Such practices have a profound effect on how subjects come to understand themselves politically. It is often the memory of such emotive encounters that sustains political actors through the tedious, frustrating, and disillusioning aspects of political involvement.

Yet reading Rousseau reminds us of just how fraught such practices are. In their capacity to "persuade without convincing," performative mass gatherings run the risk of making other civic practices appear insufficient and unsatisfying. If identification is understood as the "ideal type" of political discourse, the quotidian work of democratic citizenship becomes all the more difficult to sustain. Angry and disillusioned about the emergence of disagreement and agonistic speech within a political community, subjects envision and demand a civic life defined primarily in terms of unity, inspiration, and intensity. Rather than sustaining civic life, the memory of Rousseauian identification runs the risk of leaving citizens frustrated and dissatisfied.

Yet even here, there is much worth preserving in Rousseau's affective theories of democracy. More than most, Rousseau sought to grapple with the problem of political consent—he recognized that political agreement is often experienced as simultaneously natural and created. This process of simultaneously overcoming and coming into oneself is particularly powerful for those who understand themselves as having been transformed by their involvement in politics.

In *Justice and the Politics of Difference*, Iris Marion Young quotes Michel Foucault in criticizing "the Rousseauist dream." Envisioned as "unified and homogenous" and defined by "purity and security," in a Rousseauian state of immediacy, "we are transparent to one another, purely copresent in the same time and space, close enough to touch, and nothing comes between us to obstruct our vision of one another."[103] Young develops this critique in *Inclusion and Democracy*, arguing against privileging the idea of direct democracy and its emphasis on face-to-face interactions. Instead, large-scale multicultural societies require more expansive and inclusive forms of participation that Young characterizes as "communicative democracy"—a form of deliberative democracy that respects the "multiple, sometimes disorderly ways that citizens participate in political life."[104] Rather than depoliticizing democratic actions by excluding practices deemed uncivil, irrational, and/or inappropriate, she argues for including forms of political communication that go beyond rational-critical arguments. Such practices include greetings, stories, rhetoric, political art, and protest.[105]

Interestingly, Young's critique of deliberative democracy and the broadened theory she names "communicative democracy" relates to the "Rousseauist dream" in unanticipated ways. For although she disagrees with Rousseau in fetishizing a politics of presence, both theorists recognize the limits of rational-critical debate. For Rousseau, passion and identification were necessary preconditions for "general willing." Neither science nor rationality produces and undergirds the common good. Instead, "human understanding owes much to the passions . . . it is impossible to conceive why one who had neither desires nor fears would go to the trouble of reasoning."[106] Engaging Rousseau, we are reminded that spectacle, mass gatherings, and passionate identification are not simply markers of emotional excess or a threat to democratic rationality; to assume as much is to misunderstand Rousseau and democratic life more broadly. Rather, civic practices emphasizing sentiment, imagination, and identification are powerfully implicated in how subjects make democratic commitments, participate collectively, and resist inequality.

Reading Young alongside Rousseau reveals unexpected connections between two theorists of democracy who seem to exist on the opposite ends of the sameness/difference divide. Moreover, in seeking to expand the limits of democratic communication, Young proves less able to consider the Rousseauian risks of communicative democracy's more participatory practices. As I hope this chapter has shown, protest and other forms of communicative democracy are capable of comfortably existing alongside a Rousseauian aversion to contentious dialogue and debate. Communicative democracy may enact (rather than overcome) the very Rousseauist dream that Young criticizes.

The fact that identification is as necessary as it is dangerous brings us back to Keenan's claim that democracy must always remain a *question*, since no theory of democracy is ever adequate to the experience of democratic politics.[107] Such democratic openness means that the varied practices that are necessary for democracy are the same practices that can simultaneously turn against it. Simply put, the practices that enable and enrich democracy are also those that can undermine it. Turning to Rousseau reminds us that our capacity for collective action is always in question, always unstable. This loss of consensus was Rousseau's fear as well as that of movement activists. Neither was able to escape the possibility of failure—that what we hold as common can all too easily disappear.

4 From Identification to Representation
Civic Latinidad and the Making of the "Latino Vote"

By the late 1970s, the Chicano and Puerto Rican movements were in steep decline, with both scholars and activists noting the shift away from mass participation and the politics of protest.[1] And while the movements produced a significant socio-political class that helped establish and run a variety of political organizations, the emerging advocacy groups were far less reliant on the involvement of local, mass-based memberships.[2] Instead, as Isidro Ortiz has shown, organizations such as the Mexican American Legal Defense and Education Fund and the National Council of La Raza developed a "professionalized" rather than "participatory" approach to politics: political empowerment increasingly focused on political elites whose job it was to "carry out the organization's activities and rely upon corporate contributions for the resources necessary to maintain the organization."[3] In stark contrast to the movements' militant nationalism, civic leaders became increasingly engaged in this new strategy of corporate accommodation.[4] By the 1990s, scholars were characterizing Latino leaders as "politically moderate, knowledgeable of the dominant political system, relatively young, well educated, politically articulate and visible and accessible to the media."[5]

In the era of mass participation and protest, movement activists made demands and mobilized communities to support their efforts. Contemporary Latino politics has shifted toward the electoral realm, with advocacy groups and politicians focusing on electoral politics and questions of representation. In other words, when speaking of Latino political interests today, we are more likely to frame the discussion in terms of the "Latino vote" rather than social movements and grassroots activism.[6] This shift suggests that contemporary discussions of "Latino politics" often involve acts of translation and interpretation. Rather than analyzing the actions of a particular movement speaking on its own behalf, today's discussion of Latino politics often centers on deciphering election results and polling data in order to comprehend the inclinations and interests of this emerging electorate. In shifting our attention from participation to representation—from an activist minority to voting majorities—the questions nowadays are as follows: Why do Latinos vote the way they do? What role does Latino identity and/or ethnic identification play in their decisions as voters? What (we ask) do Latino voters "want"?

Complicating these postmovement efforts at translation and interpretation involves yet another shift in the discursive terrain of Latino identity. Latinos are now increasingly characterized in *pan-ethnic* terms—simply as Latinos—rather than as members of particular subgroups (Chicanos, Puerto Ricans, Cubans, etc.). This shift in terminology and political frame of reference has emerged as one of the most significant developments in contemporary American politics.

Initially, the rise of *Latinidad* appears to challenge the homogenizing tendencies so evident within the Chicano and Puerto Rican movements. Constructing a cohesive identity from a multiplicity of Spanish-origin subgroups requires an acceptance of internal diversity and dissimilarity that seemed unimaginable during the movement era. Overall, the rise of pan-ethnic politics would seem to imply that the movements' influence is on the wane and a less nationalistic and more pragmatic approach is in ascendance.

Yet despite the shift away from radicalism and toward a politics increasingly focused on diversity, professionalization, and descriptive representation, the political logic of pan-ethnicity continues to harbor its own homogenizing impulse. Advocates and politicians who claim to speak for or on behalf of Latinos continue to put forward theories of empowerment that rely on presumptions of Latinos as a cohesive electorate. This approach reflects a widespread investment among elites in sustaining the idea of "Latino interests" alongside political strategies capable of both explaining and mobilizing this emerging electorate.

Analyzing the rise of pan-ethnicity from its emergence in the 1980s to its political institutionalization in the 1990s and toward its more widespread use today, this chapter examines the theoretical and political assumptions that support the shift to pan-ethnicity. I argue that the commitment to civic *Latinidad* is ideological, emotive, and pragmatic: confronted by an interest-group paradigm that rewards national over regional interests and cohesive voting blocs that can be quickly mobilized around a recognizable set of issues, Latino elites have found it useful to present themselves as a politically cohesive national minority group equivalent to African Americans.

Beyond pragmatism, pan-ethnic unity is also ideologically and emotively linked to earlier efforts at racial justice and political empowerment. As discussed in chapter 1, the Chicano and Puerto Rican movements led to the development of institutions and produced a sociopolitical class that continues to work in a wide variety of organizations on behalf of various Latino communities. Beyond its own activism, this political generation has played a role in educating and training a younger generation of Latino advocates who now share certain assumptions regarding the importance of unity for Latino political empowerment.

In other words, while no longer defined by nationalist politics, the movement's ethos of unity and linked fate translates easily to the pan-ethnic terrain of contemporary Latino politics. This ethos—while no longer connected to radical forms of political critique—continues to permeate Latino politics. The unitary impulse behind pan-ethnic politics makes it not only strategic but ideological. Understood as a sign of political literacy, pan-ethnic identification is often characterized as a sign of proper political socialization: subjects who identify with their fellow Latinos are often characterized as displaying civic agency and voice, while those who lack such a perspective are depicted as disempowered and politically ineffectual. Precisely because it *is* ideological, *Latinidad* is a political concept central to the very project of Latino politics. Such a commitment does not yield easily to opposing or contradictory data.

Ultimately, the current discourse of civic *Latinidad* reflects an unresolved tension regarding the nature of Latino political consciousness. Within the pan-ethnic paradigm, group identification is characterized as both artificially produced and naturally preexistent. Enmeshed in a discourse whose tortured logic is never fully resolved, the concept of civic *Latinidad* highlights the complexities regarding how democratic community comes into being. In this way, the civic face of *Latinidad* is emblematic of the larger question of how subjects are made capable of collective action. And here again, Alan Keenan's language of democratic paradox proves insightful. As discussed in chapter 2, democracy is a self-constituting process whereby "a people must call themselves into being." The fundamental incompletion of this act means that one must "speak and act in the name of the people before receiving their sanction." Democracy inevitably involves subjects speaking from this "not-yet-fully-democratic" position."[7]

Given the inevitable ambiguity of all democratic claims, my goal is not to challenge the legitimacy of civic *Latinidad*. Instead, I seek to analyze *Latinidad* in terms of whether such unitary practices produce more or less space for democratic political action. What sort of political gains (and losses) are produced by characterizing Latinos as a cohesive electorate? Does this strategy of civic *Latinidad* lead to a more united and effective political community, capable of advancing Latinos onto the national stage? Or does this effort become the cause of increasingly bitter fragmentation? Is the dream of a national electorate productively shaping Latino political values, or is this unitary vision eclipsing our capacity to think creatively about alternative progressive formations?

In examining the theoretical and political assumptions that underlie the pan-ethnic vision, this chapter concludes by arguing that *Latinidad* should be understood as one strategy among many rather than the precondition for Latino political advancement. Such an approach requires approaching civic *Latinidad* not as the foundation for a particular politics but as the subject of permanent debate.

The chapter is divided into three sections. The first provides an overview of Latino pan-ethnicity, its history as a concept (including debates over terminology), and its recent emergence as popular "fact." The second provides an analysis of both quantitative and qualitative research concerning civic *Latinidad* at both the mass and elite levels during the 1990s. Focusing on the groundbreaking Latino National Political Survey and Maurilio Vigil's discussion of the Congressional Hispanic Caucus in his book *Hispanics in Congress*, this section discusses the uncertain reality of pan-ethnic political identification, analyzing the strategic and emotive reasons involved in efforts to present Latinos as a politically cohesive national minority group akin to African Americans. The third section looks at how the Latino electorate is being portrayed as both collectively conscious and internally heterogeneous. Using the 2006 Latino National Survey and the 2002 Pew Hispanic Center/Kaiser Family Foundation's National Survey of Latinos, this section explores the increase in pan-ethnic identification alongside claims that Latinos are "swing voters" by looking at debates regarding Latino support for George W. Bush in 2004 and Barack Obama in 2008.

The Name Game: "Hispanics," "Latinos," and the Rise of Pan-Ethnic Politics

The term *Latinidad* has been deployed and defined to characterize a whole host of practices involving the pan-ethnic representation of subjects who claim a national identity from and within Latin America. As an interpretive framework, *Latinidad* has emerged as a space of "contestatory and contested potential," signifying strategic possibility as well as homogenizing stereotype.* According to sociologist Juan Flores, such pan-ethnic identifiers are meant to refer to something "real or in the making," whether a demographic aggregate, a voting bloc, a market, a language, a cultural group, or a community.[8]

In large part, it was U.S. government resources defined in ethnic terms that led to the recent rise of pan-ethnicity.[9] In 1970, at the behest of the Nixon White House, the long-form U.S. census questionnaire added the Hispanic-origin question.[10] Six years later, Congress passed the Roybal Act, requiring the Census Bureau and other federal statistical agencies to produce separate counts of persons of Hispanic origin.[11] The production of Latinos as a pan-ethnic community was further reinforced in 1980, when a Hispanic-origin question was added to the short census form, the one mailed to every American household.[12] As with other marginalized groups seeking recognition (women, gays and lesbians, Asian Americans), the democratic and public-policy initiatives implemented in the aftermath of the civil rights movement became the strategic and legislative blueprint for Latino politics in the United States.

Beyond federal policy, there is also a history of various Spanish-origin subgroups organizing and identifying across national lines. This was particularly true in Chicago and New York, where the groups lived and worked in close proximity. According to Virginia Sánchez Korrol, Puerto Ricans residing in New York City were identifying themselves as Latinos or Hispanics at the turn of the twentieth century.[13] Describing the pan-ethnic atmosphere of New York City prior to World War II, Sánchez Korrol writes: "New York hispanos read Spanish-language newspapers, saw Mexican and Argentine films, listened to Spanish-language radio stations, formed associations that promoted language, culture, and civic concerns, and danced and listened to Latino music."[14]

Such pan-ethnic practices were often explicitly political as well. Revolutionary poet and activist José Martí, for example, founded the Partido Revolucionario

---

*The term *Latinidad* has come to refer to the process whereby various Latin American national-origin groups are understood as sharing a sense of collective identity and cultural consciousness. In previous years, this process was generally talked about in terms of pan-ethnicity. Borrowing from the work of David López and Yen Espiritu, Juan Flores defines pan-ethnicity as "a group formation that emerges out of the interaction or close historical congruence of two or more culturally related ethnicities." In this sense, Latinos are understood as an ethnicity, but one that does not exist "but for the existence of its constituent 'subgroups'" (*From Bomba to Hip-Hop*, p. 150). In this chapter, I use both terms interchangeably ("pan-ethnicity" and *Latinidad*) in order to refer to this process of collective identification.

Cubano (Cuban Revolutionary Party) in New York City in 1892. The Partido organized the Sección de Puerto Rico, which "united the two Caribbean nationalities
in a joint struggle against Spanish colonialism."[15] That such alliances were occur-
ring more than a century ago is a valuable reminder that pan-ethnic practices are
not altogether unfamiliar. What *is* new is the discursive context of contemporary
discussions surrounding pan-ethnicity. As Juan Flores notes, by the 1990s, the
terms "Hispanic" and "Latino" assumed "an emotive charge and connotative
complexity unknown in their previous historical usages."[16] Geoffrey Fox's depiction of Latino identity on the jacket flap of his 1996 book *Hispanic Nation* is typical
in this respect:

> A new ethnic identity is being constructed in the United States: the Hispanic
> nation. Overcoming age-old racial, regional, and political differences,
> Americans of Mexican, Puerto Rican, Cuban and other Spanish-language
> origins are beginning to imagine themselves as a single ethnic communi-
> ty—which by the turn of the century may become the largest and most
> influential minority.[17]

Over the past decade, such characterizations of the Latino population have
continued apace: Noticiero Univision anchor Jorge Ramos echoed Fox's depiction
in his book *The Latino Wave: How Hispanics Will Elect the Next American President*
(2004):

> The United States is becoming a Latino nation. . . . The growth and influ-
> ence of the Latino community will significantly change the power structure
> within the United States as well as the way in which we live on a day-to-day
> basis. Nothing—absolutely nothing—will remain untouched by this Latino
> presence.[18]

No longer an example of cross-cultural interaction or self-conscious political
solidarity, today's advocates of pan-ethnicity tend to depict such group identification as a mass-based internal phenomenon in which the vast majority of each
subgroup shares a common political and cultural consciousness. In other words,
regardless of whether they are Cubans living in Florida or Dominicans from New
York, according to Fox and Ramos, Latinos have developed a distinct cultural
perspective that includes a distinct political perspective based (at least in part) on
their shared sense of civic *Latinidad*.

The mass media consistently portray Latinos as a collective body with common
interests. "Latinos officially passed African Americans last year to become the
nation's largest minority," *BusinessWeek* noted in 2004. "[T]he Latino Generation

is becoming a driving force in the economy, politics, and culture."[19] According to Jorge Ramos, those who refuse to recognize the Latino community's "unprecedented growth and influence . . . do so at the risk of losing the vote of this country's largest minority block."[20]

Nowhere is the language of *Latinidad* more explicit than in the realm of electoral politics, where discussions of Latino emergence are most pronounced. Moreover, because several states with large Latino populations decided to move their presidential primaries to early 2008, candidates publicly courted these voters like never before. A year and a half before the 2008 election, U.S. senator Robert Menendez (D-N.J.) described the Latino electorate's potential power:

> We are approaching an election year in which the road to the presidency runs right through the Latino community. . . . Our numbers and our influence are no longer a hypothesis to be proved—they are a reality. And beginning in 2008, when one of the most important presidential elections in history will determine the direction of our nation at a critical moment, it is becoming clear that Latinos will hold the key to the White House. . . .
>
> February 5, which might as well be called Latino Tuesday. Consider New York: a delegate-rich state, 16 percent Latino. Illinois: another mega-state, 14.5 percent Latino. There's Arizona, 28.6 percent, Colorado, 19.5 percent, and New Mexico—which is more than 43 percent Latino. Oh, and I should probably also mention California—by far the most delegates at stake in both parties, and it also has an enormous Latino population: 35.5 percent. Let's not forget my home state of New Jersey and Connecticut, Rhode Island. All with sizable Latino populations. All holding primaries on February 5. . . . We are talking about the Latino population holding a key—holding *the* key—to the presidential nomination and, eventually, to the White House.
>
> And when we speak through our votes, our roar will be deafening.[21]

According to Senator Menendez, the 2008 election offered Latinos in the United States a crucial opportunity "to explain to the candidates—and by extension, the American public—our core values and issues."[22] Political parties got the message loud and clear: Republicans and Democrats both see courting Hispanic voters as a central part of their future electoral strategy. Reporting on presidential candidates' summer 2007 efforts to win Hispanic votes, *The New York Times* wrote:

Helped by the fight over immigration, Democratic presidential candidates are courting Hispanic voters like never before, prompted by a string of early primaries in states with sizable Hispanic voting blocs.

It has forced candidates to hire outreach consultants, to start Spanish-language Web sites and to campaign vigorously before Hispanic audiences. . . .

Earlier this month, Mr. Obama traveled to Nevada, a heavily Hispanic state that moved its caucus to Jan. 19, and sat down for interviews with Spanish-language television and newspaper reporters. . . .

Mr. Edwards, who hopes his populist appeal will draw support from Hispanics, is dispatching his political director, David Medina, to meet with members of [the] Democratic Hispanic Caucus of Florida. Mr. Richardson alternates between English and Spanish on the campaign trail. Senator Christopher J. Dodd, Democrat of Connecticut, also often likes to display his fluency in Spanish, including when he announced his candidacy on CNN en Español.

By contrast, the Clinton campaign has already put in place a driven Hispanic outreach team that, among other things, issues press releases in Spanish on a regular basis and has a stable of Spanish-speaking surrogates to fill in for Mrs. Clinton at events that focus on Hispanics. It has also assigned a prominent role to its campaign manager, Patti Solis Doyle, a woman of Mexican descent who has been one of Mrs. Clinton's most trusted advisers and friends since her days as first lady of Arkansas.[23]

In all these statements, civic *Latinidad* is characterized as a political reality and popular "fact," an assumption not worthy of comment. Moreover, throughout these discussions, the precondition for national emergence and influence is the idea of Latino *pan-ethnicity*. For advocates of pan-ethnicity, the assumption is that Latinos in the United States share not only cultural and linguistic characteristics but also a political perspective.

This conflation of cultural and linguistic characteristics with a shared political perspective is not simply a phenomenon of the mass media. In academic and political forums sympathetic to the concept of *Latinidad*, Latinos have long been characterized as a political community identifiable by a shared sense of mutual obligation, unity, and a commitment to the common good of the group. Writing almost twenty years ago in *Latinos and the Political System*, for example, political scientist Richard Santillan described the Latino community as "an excellent example of a constituency of common interests."[24] He wrote: "All in all, the political destiny of Latinos is inherently linked, regardless of geographic region, and this common bond only serves to underscore the present need for a national political agenda as Latinos enter soon into the twenty-first century."[25] Sixteen years later, Raul Yzaguirre, founder and former president of the National Council of La Raza (NCLR), a Washington, D.C.–based advocacy group and think tank, echoed Santillan's claim that Latinos represent "a constituency of common interests." Discussing the "State of Hispanic America" series (a report that seeks to highlight the major issues of concern to Hispanic families and voters) in 2004, Yzaguirre stated:

> Thirteen years ago, when NCLR created the State of Hispanic America series, many questioned whether in fact an Hispanic America truly existed. It is one of the most gratifying developments in my career to see that, in 2004, we are *closer than ever to a national Latino community with a shared past, a common agenda, and a united future.* . . . But if we are to be heard and, more importantly, be effective, we must *define* what we stand for. This task will not be accomplished in one day or perhaps even one generation, but we must be bold enough to begin the discussion [italics added].[26]

For many advocacy organizations such as the NCLR, the desire to depict America's 44 million Latinos as representing a constituency of common interests remains powerful—even as internal contradictions continue to complicate the logic of such assertions.

More significantly, in these statements, we see something larger than a demand for increased recognition. Instead, both Santillan and Yzaguirre depict pan-ethnic political consciousness as spontaneous yet undeveloped. In other words, both statements are as much *calls* for pan-ethnic unity as they are descriptions of it; both quotes speak to the *emergence* of a sense of shared interests and civic linked fate among Latinos. Nor is this unusual: such shifts often characterize the political discourse of *Latinidad*. Pan-ethnic collective consciousness is almost always portrayed as spontaneous *and* situational, inherent *and* strategic.

The shift from ethnic-specific labeling to pan-ethnicity has not escaped criticism. Many activists and scholars have questioned the federally established grouping of Spanish-speaking subgroups under the ethnic label "Hispanic."[27] For many scholars of the various ethnic-specific groups, the label is simply too vague to have any real descriptive power. According to sociologist Martha Giménez, the label "Hispanic" represents a flawed statistical construct that "has hardly any relation to the real world."[28] In an essay on Latino pan-ethnicity and public health,

Giménez asks, "What can this or any other 'umbrella' term identify? What is the meaning of the data gathered about this population?"[29] She writes:

> The problem facing social scientists and public health specialists in trying to make sense of the data collected by federal, state, and other agencies is the problem not only of comparability but of meaning. . . . To speak about "Hispanic" fertility, child-rearing habits, health, subculture, migration patterns, etc. is to engage in empty talk, at best, or in stereotyping. The heterogeneity of national origin groups, in turn, undermines generalizations about the entire group.[30]

Giménez's point is especially well taken as it applies to questions of politics. If pan-ethnicity is a flawed paradigm for analyzing public health issues such as reproductive and child-rearing habits, it becomes even more problematic when trying to assess something like "Latino political interests" or a "Hispanic political viewpoint."

Other scholars have echoed Giménez's concerns regarding the homogenizing effect of the term "Hispanic." As Candace Nelson and Marta Tienda note, "Hispanic" combines "colonized natives and their offspring, foreigners and political refugees under one ethnic umbrella."[31] Similarly, Suzanne Oboler argues that "the ethnic label Hispanic obscures rather than clarifies the varied social and political experiences in U.S. society of more than 23 million citizens, residents, refugees, and immigrants with ties to Caribbean and Central and South American countries."[32] Given this diversity, it is hardly surprising that scholars such as Giménez, Nelson, and Tienda criticize "Hispanic" for being merely a "heuristic device" that is "questionable on theoretical grounds."[33] For these academic researchers, "Hispanic" creates what Latin American scholar Edna Acosta-Belén describes as "a false image of homogeneity and unity" that "mystifies" the various cultural, racial, and class differences and disparities among individual groups.[34]

This erasure of specificity is not only descriptively and methodologically problematic—it has political implications. Oboler, for example, argues that the specificity of Chicanos and Puerto Ricans (their history and social movements) in the late 1960s and early 1970s was rendered invisible by the emergence of the label "Hispanic." According to Oboler, "following the 1960s movements by both [Puerto Ricans and Chicanos], their respective experiences as historical minorities in the United States were in fact thrown back into invisibility through the emergence of the label Hispanic in the early 1970s."[35] The historical and cultural legacies of Chicanos and Puerto Ricans were therefore "largely dissipated by the fusion of the two group into a newly created 'ethnic group' with a new notion of its heritage and identity in the United States." Rather than signifying a new national and public recognition of these populations and their particular histories and political struggles and issues, the creation of a Hispanic ethnic community in the United States "essentially erased the respective civil rights movements of Chicanos and Puerto Ricans."[36]

Oboler's critique regarding the political implications of the "Hispanic" label, as well as the timing of its emergence, points to another significant criticism—that "Hispanic" has been *externally* imposed, by federal agencies and governmental institutions whose motives and agenda are viewed as suspect by a significant number of Latino activists and academics. Anthropologist Jorge Klor de Alva, for example, is critical of the many institutions and individuals who lump together all Latinos. For de Alva, "The mass media, advertising firms, government agencies, and the non-Hispanic population attempt to simplify their responses to the bur-geoning Spanish-speaking population by obscuring their substantial differences through collective labels (like 'Hispanic') and stereotypical assumptions concern-ing their supposed common cultures and socioeconomic conditions."[37] In a similar vein, sociologist José Calderón criticizes "Hispanic" as a term that "has apparently been imposed from the outside, rather than developing from the cohe-sion of the groups themselves."[38] Historian Juan Gomez-Quiñones echoes Calderón's analysis when he describes the label "Hispanic" as a "transparent ploy, undercutting the ethnic revitalization movement. It quickly became the preferred term by bureaucrats, academics, business, and media."[39]

For critics such as Oboler, Calderón, and Gomez-Quiñones, "Hispanic" repre-sents another instance in which the various subgroups have been denied their history and the power to name themselves. "Chicano," "Boricua," and "Nuyorican" were ethnic labels that emerged out of radical social movements. To self-identify in these terms was to signal both racial pride and political consciousness. "Hispanic" has no such progressive connotations. In fact, among many former movement activists and sympathizers, to adopt "Hispanic" is viewed as a politi-cally conservative stance.[40] Calderón, for example, describes self-proclaimed Hispanics as often having "a stake in protecting their property and managerial positions and [being] unwilling to affiliate with a political identity that might jeopardize them."[41] For critics, "Hispanic" is problematic not so much for its conceptual limitations as for the perceived ideological agenda behind the term. Nevertheless, the conceptual and empirical problems surrounding pan-ethnicity are equally problematic regardless of the term one uses. Embracing notions of *Latinidad* does nothing to resolve the dissimilarities in attitude, region, and class that Giménez so rightly identifies. Claiming a collective identity rather than having one imposed by federal and state bureaucracy is an improvement, but the problems of political community remain unresolved. Yet critics such as Oboler, Calderón, and Gomez-Quiñones often embrace *Latinidad* as though it somehow transcends the political problematic produced by the pan-ethnic imperative.

Interestingly, many of the same scholars who powerfully criticize the grouping of Spanish-speaking subgroups under "Hispanic" express a simultaneous commitment to the pan-ethnic impulse. In his essay "Pan-Latino/Trans-Latino," Juan Flores expresses wariness at "catchall categories" such as "Hispanic" and "Latino" that have become the "stock-in-trade of most media, government, commercial, social science, and literary-cultural 'coverage'" of New York's diverse Spanish-speaking populations.[42] Of particular concern to Flores are the many ways in which the "pan-ethnic" rubric has failed to give "adequate analytical weight" to the particular conditions of Puerto Ricans in New York City and the United States more generally.[43] He explains:

> Puerto Ricans remain the "exception" among the New York groups. . . . This difference is marked off, in a formal sense, by U.S. citizenship, and in the practical social arena . . . by the second-class nature of that supposedly privileged status. Direct colonial relations, and an uninterrupted legacy and ever-present reality, govern the motives and outcomes of the whole migratory and settlement process, and fix a constantly low ceiling on the group's expectations and opportunities. For Puerto Ricans, the "blessings" of American citizenship have been even worse than mixed.[44]

Unable to address the colonial legacy of commonwealth status, the "new politics of Hispanic assimilation" often approach Puerto Ricans as the abject component of the Hispanic whole, the "stain" on *Latinidad* that must be cleansed.[45] For Flores, such efforts "put the lie to any too facile, wishful, or ominous image of Latinos as a seamlessly knitted tribe or horde."[46]

Given the force of his analysis, it is surprising that Flores concludes his essay by insisting that "practical disjunctures do not necessarily invalidate the strategic prospects and formative process of Latino unity. Rather, they point up the need for an eminently flexible, inclusive concept based on a clear understanding of historical differences and particularities."[47] The adequacy of the pan-ethnic rubric, Flores writes, "hinges on its inclusiveness towards the full range of social experiences and identities, and particularly its bridging of the divergence within the contemporary configuration between recent 'Latino immigrant' populations and, for want of a better term, the 'resident minority' Chicano and Puerto Rican communities."[48] Despite the weight and power of his own critique, Flores remains reluctant to give up the idea of unity, calling instead for the "pan-ethnic net" to be "cast wide enough across and along language, 'racial,' class, and geographic lines."[49] Struggling to embrace the very category he calls into question, Flores deploys notions of historical particularity and inclusivity in an attempt to resolve the political contradictions he so powerfully conjures. Despite its failings, visions of *Latinidad* continue to offer seductive narratives of community that seem central to uniting and empowering this disparate group of political subjects.

Despite the fact that pan-ethnic unity is often portrayed as a strategic possibility and necessary precondition for Latino political empowerment, the actual *existence* of a pan-ethnic Latino political community is far less certain. In the introduction to their book *Diversity in Democracy: Minority Representation in the United States* (2005), editors Shaun Bowler and Gary Segura refute the idea that Latinos constitute a homogeneous interest bloc:

> [T]he assumption of opinion homogeneity, even within minority groups, . . . may, at best, be overdrawn, and, at worst, be simply wrong. . . . For example, although we often distinguish Cubans from other Latinos, the remaining subpopulation still contains important distinctions. While most of those in the remaining Latino population might be directly concerned with the issues of immigration, Puerto Ricans, born U.S. citizens, face no immigration worries at all. Their interest, however, in the future status of the island of Puerto Rico is of little concern to Mexican Americans in Los Angeles. Cubans themselves are increasingly politically diverse, as second- and third-generation Cuban Americans are less and less identified with an anti-Castro, island-focused political agenda. To speak of Latino political interests as if they were monolithic is thus to misperceive the nature of the group.[50]

Such refutations of conventional wisdom are not new. In fact, the 1980s and 1990s marked the emergence of a particularly complex and contradictory discourse on the Latino electorate. At the conclusion of his book *Latinos and the Political System* (1988), for example, F. Chris Garcia expresses a sense of uncertainty in an intriguing disclaimer regarding his own claims concerning the existence of civic *Latinidad*:

> With regard to alliances, it is not entirely clear that the various nationality groups within the Latino rubric actually constitute a cohesive "community."

Certainly, Mexican-Americans, Cuban-Americans, Puerto Ricans and other Spanish ancestry groups have a great deal in common, including language and other cultural manifestations. . . . Yet it is also evident that there are significant differences between each of the groups' historical, demographic, and socioeconomic circumstances. *Indeed, although we have done so, one cannot speak with complete confidence about a unified Latino political community.* Much research is needed to clarify the precise parameters of political and cultural identifications within and among Latino groups, how these groups feel about themselves and other Latino groups, as well as their identification with the United States political community [italics added].[51]

Garcia's postbook research—the Latino National Political Survey—would give credence to some of his earlier concerns, highlighting the gap between the vision of a pan-ethnic political community versus the disparate viewpoints that characterized these populations in the 1990s.

Data, Strategy, and Ideology: Civic *Latinidad* in the 1990s

The 1992 publication of the Latino National Political Survey (LNPS) made explicit the contrast between presumptions of pan-ethnic identification and actual attitudes and perspectives. The survey's goal was to collect basic data describing "the political values, attitudes and behaviors of the Mexican-, Puerto Rican, and Cuban-origin populations in the United States."[52] Prior to the LNPS, the dearth of reliable national data meant that both Latinos and non-Latinos were often guilty of making unsubstantiated claims regarding these populations. Researchers sought to empower Latinos by providing information that more accurately and effectively addressed these groups' concerns.[53]

Many of the findings of the LNPS challenged the assumptions of both scholars and practitioners of Latino politics. According to Louis DeSipio (an LNPS researcher and author of *Counting on the Latino Vote: Latinos as a New Electorate*), the findings tell us that "[m]easuring ethnicity's meaning for Latinos has the added complexity of the possible irrelevance of the pan-ethnic identity to the national-origin groups that make up the pan-ethnic whole."[54] According to DeSipio, "Latinos did *not* view themselves as having common political concerns," with noncitizens being even *less* likely to report similarities between various pairs of Latino national-origin groups. No more than 14 percent of any group reported that another Latino group was "very similar" to themselves.[55] "Citizens and non-citizens alike reported that Latinos shared a 'somewhat' similar culture," but "Latinos themselves did not see common political or cultural bonds."[56] The LNPS showed that the three subgroups "overwhelmingly prefer to identify in national-origin terms" and that "more respondents prefer to be called 'American' than Latino."[57]

According to DeSipio, the absence of pan-ethnic bonds was due in part to the "low level of contact among the Latino national-origin groups." The LNPS showed that vast majorities of the three big groups did not interact with other Latinos other than their own national-origin group: 15 percent or less of each group reported "a lot" of contact with Latino groups other than their own.[58]

The lack of contact between Latino subgroups highlighted the continued regional concentration of ethnic-specific groups (Mexican Americans in the West and Southwest, Cubans in Florida, Puerto Ricans in the Northeast) and the theoretical and political insufficiency of "nationalizing" narratives that ignore or downplay this demographic reality. Moreover, even in regions where the various Latinos experience relatively high levels of cross-group contact, research prior to the LNPS continued to show significant differences in political behavior and attitude between subgroups.[59]

Interestingly, the affinities *between* Latino subgroups proved to be even lower than with other racial or ethnic groups: "Mexican-American citizens, for example, reported that they were personally closer to Anglos and African-Americans than they were to either Puerto Ricans or those of Cuban ancestry. Puerto Ricans were closer to Anglos than to those of Mexican or Cuban ancestry. They ranked African-Americans equally to those of Mexican ancestry in terms of closeness."[60] Significantly, none of the Latino groups reported negative perceptions of other Latinos; instead, neutrality was the most common response. According to DeSipio, "This neutrality . . . reflects the lack of awareness of other Latinos . . . and leads to a lack of perception of a common political or cultural agenda, thereby reducing the likelihood of a mass-based Latino identity, at least in the near future."[61] DeSipio notes that while more individuals might be identifying and describing themselves as "Latino," the use of this broad, common identifier does not currently denote "an overtly political manifestation."[62] Suzanne Oboler's research on Latino immigrants substantiated DeSipio's claim that "it cannot be assumed that all believe that they have to have a common identity in the U.S. public sphere with people of other nationalities who are labeled Hispanics."[63] Instead, "differences in social and racial backgrounds, personal life experiences, and political beliefs are key to understanding not only the meaning of the ethnic label Hispanic in people's lives but also Latinos' decisions to participate actively under an umbrella term in movements for social justice in the United States."[64]

Yet despite the fact that surveyed Latinos did not see themselves as having common political concerns, the LNPS *did* find that the three groups had significant shared views on some domestic policy issues. According to the authors:

> They [Latinos] favor increased government spending on health and crime and drug control; education; the environment; child services; and bilingual education. They also overwhelmingly look to government to solve the problems that most concern them. Thus, large majorities of each group support what may reasonably be called core elements of a liberal domestic agenda. . . . [E]xpanding this agenda beyond these issues would be problematic, however, because the groups differ regarding their attitudes toward most other domestic issues. . . . Mexicans, Puerto Ricans, and Cubans have a great deal in common, but they also differ in significant ways on important issues. Thus, there may be a Hispanic political community, but its parameters do not fit any existing presuppositions.[65]

> In order for pan-ethnicity numbers to be politically meaningful and successful, Latinos must understand themselves as a political community with shared values and interests. But ultimately, the authors and researchers of the LNPS conclude: "Overall, these groups do not constitute a political community. They clearly agree on some key questions, but they disagree on others. Indeed, sometimes a particular group more closely resembles Anglos than any of the other Latino populations."[66]

The results of the LNPS posed a data-based challenge to the claim that there existed a "Latino political community" with a preexisting and discernible political agenda. Whether these populations were described as "Hispanic" by governmental bureaucracies or "Latino" by progressives and/or former activists of the Chicano and Puerto Rican movements, in the early 1990s, neither term seemed to have captured their political hearts and minds.

LNPS scholars agreed that, overall, Latinos in the United States lack a shared sense of the common good. However, the researchers did not rule out the rise of pan-ethnic consciousness in the future. Instead, the LNPS portrayed Latinos as a *potential* community; subjects could come to believe themselves as having a shared fate:

> Mexicans, Puerto Ricans, and Cubans do not report high rates of involvement in activities related to their respective groups. They do not have much

knowledge about Latino leaders or organizations, but they express ethnic solidarity and support for co-ethnics. They also indicate a strong predisposition to vote for a co-ethnic if they have the opportunity to do so.[67]

As a form of mutual recognition, civic *Latinidad* was understood as requiring a certain level of collective overcoming in order to recognize one's pan-ethnic "Latino" identity by seeing outside any particular ethnic-specific subgroup (Mexican American, Puerto Rican, etc.). For LNPS scholars, this uncertainty was also a condition of possibility: Latinos in the United States might not see themselves as a common people *today*, but they might *tomorrow*.

As we have seen, the discourse on pan-ethnicity in the 1990s seemed to veer between popular presumptions of a common consciousness that was both natural and shared, despite the fact that scholars of Latino politics were simultaneously gathering data showing that Latinos could not be defined by a distinctively pan-ethnic consensus on political questions. Democratic and Republican Party officials, journalists, and Latino advocacy groups and their spokespersons continued to refer to a collective Hispanic consciousness that was unproblematically rooted in shared culture, experience, and condition. In part, this was due to the fact that scholars studying Latino political attitudes and behavior were sometimes themselves invested in depicting civic *Latinidad* not as mistaken so much as *premature*. Rather than characterizing civic *Latinidad* as a political fiction, scholars generally characterized group cohesion as existing more in the realm of potential and possibility than actual political reality. Interestingly, this depiction of Latino political consciousness as simultaneously artificial and incipient is one possible reason that the discourse surrounding the nature of Latino political empowerment remained so muddled throughout the 1990s: while LNPS scholars focused on the latent potential of Latinos as a pan-ethnic political community, other Latino elites continued to characterize pan-ethnic political unity as a political *reality*. Advocacy groups, political activists, and scholars all continued to be invested in the possibility of a unified and recognizable set of "Latino political interests" and the emergence of a united Latino political community to achieve its goals.[68] Despite the presence of contradictory data, why did this depiction of group identification among Latinos continue to persist?

One reason the pan-ethnic paradigm remained such a compelling interpretive framework is that in African Americans and the civil rights movement, Latino political elites saw an opportunity and a model. And like other marginalized groups in the United States, Latinos in the political system were confronting an interest-group paradigm that rewards national over regional interests and cohesive voting blocs that can be quickly mobilized around a recognizable set of issues. Because high levels of group cohesion and political unity are characteristic of black politics, Latino civic elites have put enormous political energy into developing a recognizable set of "Latino political interests" and stressing the necessity of a united Latino political community to achieve these goals. Portraying Latino voters as a potential bloc or swing vote in highly contested elections is a crucial element of echoing the African American paradigm.

Latino comparisons to the black community have often been quite explicit. In describing the rapid growth of Spanish-origin subgroups during the 1980s and 1990s, Latino civic elites have consistently contrasted the growth of the Latino electorate with that of African Americans, emphasizing how Latinos would soon overtake African Americans as the nation's largest minority (which they did in 2003). Such articulations of demographic displacement and political replacement reflect the varied and conflicting reactions that emerge when Latino civic elites confront the black political experience. Emotionally, the history of black politics has tended to produce a potent combination of envy, inspiration, and resentment among Latino civic elites.[69] Interestingly, Latino activists often counter such invisibility by constructing racial narratives that more closely approximate the very group they feel overshadowed by. In their efforts to gain recognition, Latino civic elites deploy African American racial narratives in order to expose the racial violence perpetuated upon Chicanos and Puerto Ricans. Describing the conditions of Mexican Americans in the Southwest, Ronnie Lopez, executive assistant to former Arizona governor Bruce Babbitt, asserted: "The Mexican-American has been the black man of the Southwest. . . . There have been rapings and lynchings. We couldn't use swimming pools. People's land was taken from them."[70]

For Lopez, drawing on widely understood narratives of the African American experience allowed him to explain and make intelligible the discrimination and racial violence experienced by Mexicans in the southwestern United States. Latinos and African Americans share the experience of racism and racialization; moreover, as Mary Hawkesworth has argued, prejudice and racial stereotyping are experienced at all class and professional levels. In her research on women of color who serve in the U.S. Congress, Hawkesworth shows how even at this elite level, Latina and African American congresswomen are treated as "less than equal in various ways that carry palpable consequences for their identities and their political priorities."[71] Not surprisingly, then, invoking analogous encounters with discrimination has been a powerful way for Latinos to frame their own experiences of marginalization and exclusion.

This desire for visibility and recognition is as organizational as it is historical. Discussing the NCLR's role in providing data and information to policymakers, for example, founder and former president Raul Yzaguirre states: "It is important that Hispanic groups become household names for Hispanics just as the NAACP and the Urban League are for blacks."[72] By invoking the NAACP and the Urban League, Yzaguirre articulates his desire that Latinos have the same moral claim on public consciousness that African Americans have. In their efforts to gain both community recognition and national standing, Latino civic elites such as Yzaguirre have regularly voiced this combination of competition and emulation, making it a persistent theme within contemporary Latino politics.

Given that African Americans have served as the racial prototype for how to demand power and resources at the federal level, the pan-ethnic impulse made strategic sense in the postmovement years.[73] As John Garcia wrote, uniting persons of Spanish origin under a "pan-ethnic" umbrella had the effect of expanding the population and geographical base for Hispanics/Latinos, thereby projecting Latinos into the national arena.[74] In the 1990s, defining Latinos as a "pan-ethnic" community "significantly increased the population base—from approximately fourteen million Chicanos to over twenty-two million Latinos."[75] Strategically, then, "pan-ethnic" identity functioned to legitimate Chicanos and other Spanish-origin subpopulations as part of a "larger, national minority group."[76] By defining themselves as a national minority group, Latinos were then better able to secure both federal resources and national exposure.[77] Strategically, then, a "pan-ethnic" identity allowed Latino civic elites to more easily present Latino voters as a potential bloc or swing vote in highly contested elections. A statement by the National Hispanic Leadership Agenda (NHLA), a coalition of national organizations, is typical in this regard:

> By the year 2050, Hispanics are projected to account for 25 percent of the U.S. population. The effects of this dramatic growth are being felt everywhere. In the political arena, Hispanics will be decisive voters in eleven key states with 217 of the 270 electoral votes needed to win the presidential election.[78]

Invoking pan-ethnicity allows the NHLA to portray Latino voters as a potentially ethnically unified body of voters.[79] Nevertheless, while the *political* logic of pan-ethnicity is clear, as the LNPS and other data showed, the actual existence of a collective consciousness among such a heterogeneous population was far less obvious.

The Congressional Hispanic Caucus (CHC) offers a particularly compelling example of the tensions produced when the discourses of empowerment, unity, and Latino heterogeneity came into contact. Latino politics scholar Maurilio Vigil delved into this dynamic in his book *Hispanics in Congress: A Historical and Political Survey* (1996). Vigil's analysis is a fascinating window into the CHC's political logic—as well as into the author's own assumptions regarding the nature of group unity and Latino political power. Using Vigil and his reading of CHC as an optic, we see how Latino elites have been engaged in a politics whose very heterogeneity authorized its claims yet simultaneously limited its political possibilities and potential. More important, the political assumptions articulated by both Vigil and the CHC were far from unique. In fact, they were common to those who participated in the political debates and discussions surrounding Latino empowerment in the 1990s.

The Congressional Hispanic Caucus: Community, Conflict, and Empowerment

In the preface to *Hispanics in Congress*, Vigil emphasizes that a significant element of the book is its examination of "the role and impact of the Congressional Hispanic Caucus."[80] Founded in December 1976 as a legislative service organization of the House of Representatives, the CHC describes itself as "members of Congress of Hispanic descent . . . dedicated to voicing and advancing, through the legislative process, issues affecting Hispanic Americans in the United States."[81] According to the group's Web site, the CHC seeks to address "national and international issues that have a particular impact on the Hispanic community." Given the existence of such issues, "[t]he function of the Caucus is to serve as a forum for the Hispanic Members of Congress to coalesce around a collective legislative agenda."[82]

Looking at Hispanic members of Congress in the early 1990s, Vigil characterizes them as "a microcosm, a reflection of the diversity of the Hispanic people of the United States. Mexican-Americans, Cubans and Puerto Ricans from different parts of the country and reflecting different partisan and ideological orientations are represented."[83] Vigil's acknowledgment of the ideological and regional diversity of the Latino congressional delegation makes his analysis of the CHC all the more intriguing. As he describes the CHC's organizational intent:

> The objectives of the caucus were to advance the interests of Hispanics
> through public policies and to enhance public awareness of Hispanic issues

and problems. It was envisioned as a bipartisan group of Congressmen with a common commitment to developing a united Congressional effort on behalf of Hispanic Americans.[84]

In Vigil's writings regarding the CHC, a series of assumptions about politics and identity go unexamined. In each statement, there exists the presumption that a "collective legislative agenda" can be constructed that will favor *all* Hispanics, regardless of class, region, ideology, or ethnic origin. Neither Vigil nor the CHC clearly or coherently articulates what "Hispanic issues" are or what constitute "the interests of Hispanics." Both assume that these interests are already known, understood, and agreed upon.[85] The belief and desire for a panethnic political agenda that will serve all Latinos equally well echo repeatedly in Vigil's analysis of the CHC. For both him and the CHC itself, Latinos are understood to share a common political perspective capable of being mobilized in the electoral arena.

The CHC's nonpartisan status is also meaningful. Within Latino political discourse, nonpartisanship has been understood as allowing for a broader community base to be built, thus allowing more Latinos to "unite" around an agenda. Nonpartisanship has also been part of a strategic effort to remain politically relevant and influential during both Democratic and Republican administrations. For Vigil and the CHC, however, nonpartisanship goes beyond the tactical: in their analysis, Latino interests somehow *transcend* ideology and party. Furthermore, this belief that "Latino interests" somehow "exceed" ideology and party politics is characteristic of the vast majority of Latino advocacy groups. The CHC, NCLR, NHLA, Mexican American Political Association, and National Association of Latino Elected and Appointed Officials all emphasize their nonpartisan political status. For the CHC, bringing together the full range of Latino institutional and ideological forces is treated as a central requirement for Latino political and legislative advancement. Put somewhat differently: the politics of both nonpartisanship and bipartisanship are related to the politics of unity and the tendency to speak of "Latino interests and issues" as transparent terms that require neither articulation nor clarification.

Like other nonpartisan and pan-ethnic organizations, the CHC is driven by a belief that evading ideological debates increases the potential for unified action and flexibility. In reality, Latino elites are embracing a form of unexamined multiplicity that ultimately has led to political conflict and paralysis. Because "Hispanic interests" have never been adequately articulated and agreed upon, the CHC is often unable to achieve its pragmatic agenda.

The Congressional Hispanic Caucus: Disunity in Action

In his analysis, Vigil often focuses on the *difficulty* the CHC has had in functioning as a cohesive and united body. He discusses the various significant pieces of legislation on which the caucus worked (including the Simpson-Mazzoli Immigration Bill in 1983, the Immigration Reform and Control Act of 1986, and NAFTA in 1993) and the legislators' consistent inability to achieve consensus:

> Historically, the greatest difficulty of the Caucus has been that its members have pursued their own individual agendas whether based on constituency interests, personal goals, ideological or other interests, rather than pursuing a common agenda on Hispanic concerns.[86]
>
> [T]he Caucus had difficulty in achieving agreement [in the 1980s] as to priorities, programs and policies that affect Hispanics. The Caucus had been unable to arrive at a coherent national Hispanic policy or to develop the necessary legislative agenda and the unity to carry it out . . . [b]ecause of the different personalities, backgrounds and philosophies of the members.[87]
>
> It is apparent that the CHC presently lacks a decision-making mechanism to develop a specific and coherent program of legislation for Hispanics, for presentation to the Congress.[88]

For Vigil, unity is a marker of political commitment and proper political socialization: Latino members of Congress behave like active representatives when trying to unify themselves. In this way, a shared sense of *Latinidad* is understood as somehow more "fundamental" than ideology. For Vigil, underneath the "personalities, backgrounds and philosophies" of Latino members of Congress there exists a unity based on common cultural characteristics capable of grounding a "coherent program of legislation for Hispanics." Like the logic of the caucus he sought to analyze, he assumed that, deep down, identity would produce the nugget of agreement that can (and must) be "dug out" if Latinos are to have political agency and power.

Vigil notes that "the CHC has not yet achieved the desired visibility as a collective spokesman for Hispanic Americans." But he finds encouragement in recent elections of Hispanic representatives who have then joined the CHC. He notes that the new members have provided a "greater ideological and regional mix that more accurately reflects the diversity of America's Hispanic population."[89]

At this point, Vigil's critique of the CHC harbors two contradictory impulses: the desire for a unified agenda that can claim to speak for the entire Latino body politic, and the desire to represent the diversity of Latinos as a group. What Vigil seems unable to confront is that to truly represent Latino political diversity is to undermine the unity of the CHC and the dream of a single "Hispanic agenda."

It is here—where the desire for comprehensive representation meets the contending demand for group unity—that the fundamental tension at the heart of civic *Latinidad* is revealed. In the case of the CHC, diversity is a necessary component of representative authority. Members of the congressional caucus were understood to be engaged in a process of internal and collective struggle, whereby participants would work to overcome disagreement and individual differences. Even more important, ideological diversity was figured as the necessary obstacle required for the "unity of the community" to emerge. Participant diversity *gave* the caucus its politics: empowerment could be produced only through the transformation of heterogeneous subjects into a political collective capable of seeing itself as acting with one mind and one agenda. In other words, for civic *Latinidad* to be legitimate, internal contradictions and a multiplicity of interests were necessary at its inception. In order for the output to be truly legitimate, diversity was required at its starting point, for only then could Latino political elites invoke the power and authority of the representative "we." Diversity was celebrated as its starting point (the caucus includes "Republicans from Florida" as well as "liberal to moderate Democrats"), but Latino unity was the necessary end point. A multiplicity of political viewpoints comes in, but a unifying "national Hispanic policy" that represents "Hispanic interests" is what must emerge.

At the conclusion of *Hispanics in Congress*, Vigil offers recommendations regarding how the CHC should function and how the group could be most effective:

> [I]t is vital that the Caucus present a united front on any issue it addresses. Even the slightest hint of internal dissent will greatly diminish its effectiveness in persuading other congressmen that the Caucus position truly represents the Hispanic position.
>
> The inability of the CHC to present a united front on a variety of issues deprives it of a very important strategic tool. . . . [U]nity is important because of its potential influence on the other 418 Congressmen, some of whom have sizable Hispanic constituencies or who may be sensitive to Hispanic concerns.
>
> It is unlikely that all the members of the Hispanic Caucus will achieve consensus on all or even the most important issues to Hispanics. It is more

likely that the different personalities, partisanship and political ideologies, constituency interests and personal agendas of the individual members, will undermine the unity of the Hispanic Caucus. However, the extent to which the individual members can rise above these differences and come together, on the basis of common, cultural, linguistic and surname characteristics, will determine the collective future of Hispanics in American politics.[90]

What is striking about Vigil's analysis is the way in which he puts "partisanship . . . political ideologies [and] constituency interests" on a par with "personalities" and "personal agendas." Here, Vigil's analysis echoes claims made by Chicano movement leader Rodolfo "Corky" Gonzáles and his characterization of partisanship as "tremendous words of intellectualism" and "a bunch of garbage" that fade in the face of Chicano identity and experience.[91] For both Gonzáles and Vigil, the commitment to racial consensus and group identification means that "[e]ven the slightest hint of internal dissent" represents political failure. Profound differences in political viewpoints are characterized as recalcitrant pettiness. In the end, Vigil can only hope that Latino members of Congress will be big enough to "rise above" their differences and "come together, on the basis of common, cultural, linguistic and surname characteristics."

Electorate or Aggregate? *Latinidad* and the Politics of Divergence

In recent years, the discourse surrounding civic *Latinidad* has moved in two directions. On the one hand, Latinos are characterized as increasingly diverse and (somewhat paradoxically) defined by a growing tendency to identity collectively. Recent publications by both advocacy groups and scholars of Latino politics are now often quite explicit about the sociopolitical diversity within various Latino communities.[92] For example, in the 2002 Pew/Kaiser survey, respondents continue to demonstrate "a very strong association with their countries of origin—identifying themselves as 'Mexicans,' 'Cubans' etc."[93] Respondents in the 2002 poll "indicate very clearly that they believe Latinos of different countries of origin have separate and distinct cultures rather than one unified Hispanic/Latino culture."[94] Despite an increase in pan-ethnic identification, the tie to one's home country still proved much more salient than the category "Latino." According to the poll, "Latinos who were born in the United States continue to be more likely to describe themselves as American than as anything else. . . . Latinos whose families have been in the United States for multiple generations and among those who say English is their primary language . . . select the term 'American' as their primary identification."[95]

Yet despite the existence of such complex statements of identity and identification, in much of the current literature, Latino diversity is acknowledged only to be quickly sidestepped through a renewed emphasis on the growing size and potential influence of the Latino electorate. This tendency to declare pan-ethnic heterogeneity while highlighting displays of collective identification can be seen in the 2006 Latino National Survey (LNS). Hosted by the University of Washington Institute for the Study of Ethnicity, Race and Sexuality, the LNS project was a major "national" telephone survey of 8,600 Latino residents of the United States undertaken from November 2005 to August 2006. The 2006 survey, which included respondents from fifteen states, was the first such national study since the Latino National Political Survey and indicated a number of significant changes in the Latino community since 1989.

The LNS also sought a broad understanding of the qualitative nature of Latino political and social life in America. All Latinos, not just citizens or voters, were sampled to be interviewed for approximately forty minutes on a wide range of political questions, conducted in English and Spanish. A major part of the project included the Latino National Contextual Database, which offered census, economic, and demographic data, as well as political and educational data.[96]

One of the featured findings of the LNS was that 67.2 percent of the respondents identified themselves as of "some other race" rather than white or black, with 51 percent saying that Latino/Hispanic is an entirely separate race.[97] LNS researchers also found that while two-thirds of the survey's respondents identified with the United States, high percentages also thought of themselves in a pan-ethnic context (with 63 percent of respondents answering "very strongly" when asked if they thought of themselves as Hispanic or Latino).[98] While the tendency to identify in national-origin terms remained strong, the growth in pan-ethnic identification marked a shift from the findings in the earlier LNPS as well as the 2002 Pew/Kaiser survey. In highlighting this finding, researchers involved with the LNS argued that the doubling of pan-ethnic identification since 1989 "holds implications for the possibility of Latinos as a political force."[99]

What is intriguing about this claim is how LNS researchers interpreted pan-ethnic identification as a form of proper political socialization. In their analysis, enhanced political power is conflated with enhanced group identification. In this view, Latinos represent a potential electorate whose developing group identity holds the potential for increasingly cohesive political action. Yet the political meaning behind enhanced pan-ethnic identification remains unclear. For example, during the same period that Latinos in the United States were increasing their tendency to identify pan-ethnically, more Latinos were voting for Republican candidates. The primary example of this was in 2004, when an estimated 40 percent of Latinos voted to reelect President George W. Bush.[100] Such voting patterns make clear that increased levels of pan-ethnic identification did not produce a more cohesive or "united" Latino electorate. Instead, increased pan-ethnic identification appears to tell us very little about partisanship and/or voter choice.

Even more significantly, pan-ethnicity has proved to be a discourse whose logic can easily be put in the service of both conservative and liberal ends. As Gary Segura has written, it was the newly elected Cuban American Mel Martinez (a Republican senator from Florida) who in 2005 "shattered a 216-year tradition of the U.S. Senate . . . when he used the ceremonial occasion of his first floor speech to speak three sentences in Spanish." While the event marked the first time a language other than English was entered into the *Congressional Record*, it was done in support of Mexican American Alberto Gonzales's nomination to the post of attorney general. In this moment of conservative *Latinidad*, Cuban American Martinez described Mexican American Bush appointee Gonzales as "*uno de nosotros*" (one of us).[101] As Segura's anecdote makes clear, pan-ethnic identification has no natural relationship to a particular ideological stance. It is a form of identity that moves comfortably across party lines and political agendas.

In recent years, the increasing visibility of ideological diversity among Latinos has been managed through characterizations of Latinos as the new "swing vote." In these accounts, Latinos are portrayed as a rapidly growing electorate whose loyalty is available to either political party. For example, in a 2007 brief discussing the profile and trends of the Latino electorate, the NCLR continually portrays Latinos as subjects whose political allegiances are up for grabs. While noting that the majority of Latinos continue to vote Democrat, the NCLR report highlights that "the percentage of Latinos voting for the Democratic candidate has decreased relatively steadily since 1988," that "Hispanics have shown a willingness to split the ticket," and that they "support candidates based on their records and positions, not party affiliation alone."[102]

Yet when it comes to electoral prognostication, Latino voters can be counted on to confound. Much of this has to do with journalists' ignorance of Latinos and commentators' readiness to make simplistic arguments based on simplistic and often fallacious views regarding "Latino culture."[103] During the 2008 Democratic primaries, for example, some pundits initially hypothesized that Latino voters might be too patriarchal and "macho" to vote for Hillary Clinton, a woman they viewed as emotionally "cold" and forbidding.[104] Once Latino voters began showing support for Clinton, it was characterized as the "Evita effect," since, as one Clinton adviser put it, "There's a whole long tradition in Latin America of strong women whose political careers are built on the backs of their husbands, who ran the country first" (this despite the fact that the majority of Latinos are Mexican American and—as one Latino politician noted—Mexico has no tradition of Eva Perón–like leaders).[105] Then, some characterized Latino support for Clinton over Barack Obama during the primaries as racist, portraying Latinos as unwilling to support a black candidate.[106] Of course, as Matt Barreto has argued, this slander ignores the long history of Latino voters supporting African American candidates.[107]

After the primaries, Latino voters supported Obama in the general election by a two-to-one margin over John McCain.[108] Nationwide, Hispanics voted 67 percent for Obama and 31 percent for McCain, leading progressive pundits to characterize Latinos as the leading edge of a long-term center-left political realignment based on a "black/brown coalition."[109] Yet in the end, while Latino voters grew in number and were thus able to play an important role in swing states like Colorado, New Mexico, and Florida, Latino voters voted largely in line with their past record. According to ABC/*Washington Post* data, Obama's Latino support was "essentially the same as their House vote in '06, and within a point or two of the tallies racked up by Clinton nationally in '96 and Michael Dukakis in '88." Ultimately, it appears that on average, in presidential elections, roughly 30 to 35 percent of Latinos vote for the Republican candidate while 65 to 70 percent vote for the Democrat.[110]

Nevertheless, as Arlene Dávila has written, advocacy groups continue to struggle with how to best characterize the Latino electorate. As one of her interviewees (Clarissa Martinez, a researcher for the NCLR and coauthor of the 2007 brief) put it: "We walk a fine line because when we maintain that the Latino population is not a monolith, people assume that Latinos are all over the place, that you can't have a Latino strategy and be easily dismissed."[111] Martinez's stated concern that a Latino political strategy might be "easily dismissed" if the idea of a monolithic community is challenged is significant. Such a concern reveals a fundamental tension that exists within the very project of civic *Latinidad*. On the one hand, the NCLR claims that "more research and polling is needed to deepen understanding of Latino issue perspectives."[112] Yet the NCLR and other voices of Latino political advocacy have a complex relationship to specificity and disaggregating the Latino vote, for it is precisely *Latinidad*'s ideological obscurity that makes it so politically potent. More specific data would likely undermine the logic of Latinos as a swing vote, since (as the ABC/*Washington Post* data show) many portions of the Latino electorate have not swung much at all. As Michael Alvarez and Lisa García Bedolla and have shown, Latino partisanship has not changed dramatically over the past decade.[113] In terms of Republican and Democratic identification, "both national origin and education continue to be statistically significant: Cubans are more likely to be Republican than Democratic, while Mexicans are more likely to be Democratic than Republican, controlling for all other social, economic, and political factors."[114] In other words, a more thorough breakdown of the data might show that this electorate is not so much swinging as growing and diverging. Rather than a "swing vote" that shifts across party lines, the Latino electorate may actually consist of segments that are growing and dispersing in different directions.

Perhaps, then, this is not a "political force" to be reckoned with so much as a variegated—sometime even disparate—collection of racialized subjects whose allegiances go in different directions and who require local and state-specific strategies of mobilization to get them to the polls. Put somewhat differently: perhaps Latinos are not so much an *electorate* as an *aggregate*. If this is the case, then as this population grows, terms such as "Latino interests" and "Latino issues" will become increasingly meaningless. When it comes to analyzing this growing portion of the electorate results, the language of civic *Latinidad* may obscure more than it reveals.

Even more important, the excessive hype regarding the growth of the Latino electorate obscures the ongoing reality of Latinos' widespread political disenfranchisement.[115] Fascination with the "Latino vote" displaces larger questions of power and the fact that most Latinos remain alienated spectators to America's political system. In other words, conflating democracy with voting allows us to ignore a more uncomfortable truth: that Latino voters (like the majority of all citizens) generally experience civic life as bystanders rather than as democratically engaged participants.

Conclusion

In recent years, *Latinidad* has become a mainstream concept whose political meaning is increasingly opaque. Yet my analysis suggests that the opacity and heterogeneity of the "Latino vote" is not only a problem—it is a central part of the concept's appeal. The unifying logic of *Latinidad* means that both liberals and conservatives can invoke the "Latino vote" to mean almost anything. Across the ideological divide, *Latinidad* can be invoked in ways that promote a particular policy agenda while engaging in selective erasures of particular forms of Latino subjectivity. Such erasures allow *Latinidad* to speak on behalf of both the left and the right.

At its best, the impulse toward civic *Latinidad* is based on the belief that racism, racial identity, and class create ties and obligations that exceed and challenge the language of self-interest. In this way, the drive toward pan-ethnicity represents the belief that Latino subjects are marked and constituted by historical circumstance. This form of civic *Latinidad* is drawn to a cross-class form of linked fate wherein the Cuban businesswoman, the Salvadorean gang member, the Chicana physician, the Puerto Rican hospital worker, and the Mexican immigrant recognize each other as part of a shared political community. In this vision of unity, no one is forgotten, demonized, or denied. This desire to create an inclusive Latino political community recognizes that too many communities are still struggling for political and social equality. Framed in this way, one can clearly recognize that the dream of "pan-ethnic unity" has attractive elements embedded within it, particularly its implicit critique of the narrow individualism and social atomism that often dominate American politics.

Yet this ethos of civic *Latinidad* is ideological, not preexistent. It represents a vision of political solidarity that is less *found* than *forged*. Accepting the political and ideological elements of group identification would mean forsaking the solace that comes with envisioning Latinos as a natural political community. Rather than seeing Latinos as ideologically akin to one another, this approach requires coming to terms with the fact that Latino interests are not only varied but actively in competition and conflict with one another. A good example of this can be seen in the needs of small business versus the working poor. Increases in the minimum wage and providing health care both serve the interests of the Latino working class but would create new economic burdens on Latino small-business owners. But because Latino advocacy and civic groups have felt compelled to stress unity and common interests, they have been ill equipped to discuss this internal tension. Instead, Latino organizations often voice broad platitudes about "economic empowerment" rather than explicitly addressing such contradictions. Not surprisingly, it is the working poor who are most hurt by these evasions and the inability to seriously debate policy.

By approaching Latino interests as ideologically heterogeneous, Latino civic elites could abandon the struggle to produce a single "Latino agenda" based on "Hispanic interests." And by emphasizing policy agreement over pan-ethnic inclusion, Latino civic elites would gain the freedom to forge coalitions based primarily on ideas and beliefs rather than similar "cultural, linguistic and surname characteristics."[116]

Such a move will not be easy. For some, rethinking the political efficacy of the pan-ethnic "we" may feel like a retreat into invisibility, a loss of collective agency. Yet as Wendy Brown argues, by resisting the tendency to equate one's social position with one's moral position, we shift the focus from what "I am" toward the more *political* language of "I want this for us." In making such a move, Brown encourages an emphasis on desired futures rather than "the formulation of identity politics as fixed position."[117] As I discuss in the following chapter, the recent immigrant-rights marches are just one example of how new forms of democratic action can sometimes resist the politics of fixed position and engage (rather than evade) the diversity and multiplicity we have long sought to transcend.

5 Labor, Action, and the Space of Appearance
Immigrant Embodiment and the Problem of Freedom

The undocumented live out their lives in the shadows. Their masks of anonymity conceal their hopes and aspirations to be members of society. Their role as political actors for the most part remains as subterranean as their lives, hidden from public view.

—William Flores[1]

The art of politics teaches men how to bring forth what is great and radiant. . . . Greatness, therefore, or the specific meaning of each deed, can lie only in the performance itself and neither in its motivation nor its achievement.

—Hannah Arendt[2]

As noted in the previous chapter, most citizens generally experience civic life as spectators rather than participants. And as Benjamin Barber argues, democracy falters when politics is no longer something we *do*: when politics becomes overly defined by representation and passively maintained rights, "citizens, like spectators everywhere, may find themselves falling asleep."[3] Yet in 2006, action replaced spectatorship as millions of immigrants and their allies took to the streets in some of the largest demonstrations for any cause in recent U.S. history, campaigning against harsh new anti-immigrant legislation. Americans were witness to the improbable, as immigrants claimed participatory rights not only for citizens but for all those who lacked such sanction.

Several months earlier, the U.S. House of Representatives had passed H.R. 4437, dubbed the Border Protection, Antiterrorism, and Illegal Immigration

Control Act of 2005, which contained several notably harsh provisions: the bill declared that simply being undocumented constituted a felony and criminalized any offer of nonemergency assistance to undocumented workers and their families.[4] Facing a government more interested in criminalization than reform, immigrants across the United States, both legal and undocumented, responded not by retreating into further isolation but by participating in hundreds of marches, rallies, and school and labor walkouts.[5] The sheer magnitude of the 2006 protests was remarkable: 20,000 to 40,000 rallied in Washington, D.C., on March 7; 100,000 to 300,000 marched in the streets of Chicago on March 10. On March 25, a turnout estimated at 1 *million* participated in "La Gran Marcha" in Los Angeles. On April 9, between 350,000 and 500,000 marched in Dallas; 300,000 rallied in New York City the following day; and hundreds of thousands more participated in 170-plus events across the country.[6] The vast majority of these demonstrators had never before engaged in protest politics. Yet in state after state and city after city, immigrants and their allies made the unprecedented decision to choose public action over fear and concealment. That many of the participants were themselves noncitizens living in the United States illegally made their participation all the more significant.[7] Dressed in white and carrying multilingual signs reading, "I Am a Worker, Not a Criminal," "Justice for All," and "Let Us Be a Part of the American Dream," immigrants sang the national anthem in both English and Spanish and waved the flags of their home countries alongside American flags.

Supporters saw the demonstrations as an attempt to claim rights and express membership. For some Latino activists and academics, the marches of 2006 represented an extension of the mass demonstrations that punctuated the Chicano and Puerto Rican movements.[8] For example, Alfonso Gonzales argues that the success of the 2006 marches can be traced to the nuclei of leadership developed during the Chicano movement a generation earlier. For Gonzales, it was "the Chicano struggle for self-determination" that set the ideological groundwork and organizational infrastructure crucial to defeating H.R. 4437.[9] For the American left, the marches of 2006 proved the radical potential of Latino politics in the United States. The marches were a display of progressive resistance: protesters were demanding citizenship and economic justice while claiming solidarity with other immigrants across lines of race, region, gender, and class. Liberal supporters saw the marches somewhat differently: rather than linking them to the Chicano or Puerto Rican movements or other forms of radical protest, liberal advocates highlighted the "traditional values" of immigrants—emphasizing their strong work ethic, deep religious faith, and commitment to family—as proof that noncitizens sought to join and strengthen the United States rather than subvert its identity and institutions. Emphasizing the marches' peaceful and exuberant atmosphere, advocates characterized them in terms less of protest than of the participants' desire for national belonging. Many characterized the marches as emblematic of the "sleeping giant" waking—as a precursor to what would eventually be a large and influential voting bloc, with the popular chant "Today we march, tomorrow we vote" capturing this sentiment.

Overall, pro-immigration forces understood the protests as a moment of revelation—a display of communities and status populations whose concerns and desires had previously been hidden and unknown.

Anti-immigrant forces saw the marches in a very different light. For law-and-order conservatives, the 2006 marches were the actions of an illegitimate mob shamelessly demanding rights and benefits that were not theirs to have; the spectacle of protesters singing and chanting in Spanish and waving the flags of their home countries was another example of immigrants showing contempt and defiance toward the United States and its laws. In an ironic misinterpretation of Chicano radicalism, some of the marches' more xenophobic critics saw the protests as proof of a burgeoning anti-American secessionist movement wherein Latino nationalists seek to "reconquer" the American Southwest.[10]

In other words, while progressives and liberals generally saw the marches as part of an established narrative of immigrants as hardworking subjects seeking rights and membership, critics countered by characterizing noncitizens as a destructive force—lawbreakers who pose an ever-growing economic and cultural threat and whose willingness to work for low wages threatens Americans' economic survival.

Lacking from each of these accounts is virtually any recognition of the profoundly *political* character of the events of 2006. When faced with the extraordinary and unanticipated fact of noncitizen mass protest, both pro- and anti-immigrant forces tended to shift the focus away from the unexpected quality of these activities, instead reverting to discussions of economics, naturalization, and public policy. Across the United States, noncitizens were actualizing a power they did not yet have, yet the implication of these actions was overshadowed by discussions of legal status and debates over the impact of low-wage labor. In this chapter, I suggest that too much is lost by viewing the events of 2006 in such narrow terms.

This chapter offers an alternative account of immigrant political action. More specifically, I want to suggest that measuring the success of immigrant action in terms of future participation in the electoral process, xenophobic backlash, replicability (i.e., the ability to recapture and re-create previous demonstrations), or immediate legislative "results" drastically limits our understanding of the demonstrations' significance. Such circumscribed analysis misses much of what was democratically distinctive and politically consequential about noncitizens laying claim to the public realm. What remains underappreciated is the question of political freedom—what Hannah Arendt describes as the capacity for new beginnings. In this chapter, I take up the political thought of Arendt in order to construct an alternate account of the 2006 demonstrations. Arendt's analysis of politics as the space of appearance and her focus on action as the uniquely human capacity to do the unexpected help to foreground what I take to be one of the demonstrations' most significant aspects: their power as a moment of *initiation* and an inaugural performance of the political. By taking to the streets and claiming space and rights, immigrants and their allies created relational spaces of freedom and common appearance where none existed previously.

Bringing Michael Warner's conception of counterpublics to bear on the immigrant-rights marches, I approach the demonstrations as scenes of public disclosure and self-making akin to Arendt's language of world-building. In contrast to the common perception of the marchers as a political community just waiting to come out from the shadows, the 2006 demonstrations should be understood as the emergence of an immigrant counterpublic. As a crowd witnessing itself through shared physical space, this counterpublic can be understood as a relation of strangers defined by active participation rather than ascriptive belonging.[11] While such initiatory action remains far from certain, by constituting themselves as a public, immigrants and their allies created self-organized sites of transformation that came to exist by virtue of their address. By elaborating new citizenships, new privacies, and new critical languages, this plurality of counterpublics challenged familiar scripts regarding the undocumented, unsettling traditional notions of sovereignty and blurring the boundaries between legal and illegal, assimilation and resistance, civic joy and public outrage.

In turning to Arendt and Warner, I seek to expand on chapter 2's discussion of "fugitive democracy." Here, my analysis of immigrant action is inspired by Sheldon Wolin's characterization of democracy as "a crystallized response to deeply felt grievances or needs on the part of those whose main preoccupation—demanding of time and energy—is to scratch out a decent existence."[12] Understood as episodic, unpredictable, and rare, such fugitive moments can be understood as "responsive to grievances on the part of those who have no means

of redress other than to risk collectivizing their small bits of power."[13] "In protesting actualities and revealing possibilities," Wolin's notion of democracy focuses
on "the needs and aspirations of the Many" rather than a vision of unity that sees
the people as a "pre-existent, continuous entity."[14] Most important, Wolin's
analysis highlights the importance of refusing to make sustainability the standard
by which we define successful democratic action. Rather than defining democracy
in terms of the legislative assembly, democracy might best be understood as "an
ephemeral phenomenon rather than a settled system"—an *experience* as opposed
to a mode of government.

By considering notions of the "fugitive" through the categories of Arendtian
action and counterpublics, we are better able to appreciate the events of 2006.
Such a reading allows us to appreciate the protests as events in which noncitizens
experienced a richer and more expressive instance of citizenship than the vast
majority of their legally sanctioned counterparts. In other words, Arendt's performative vocabulary of enactment shifts our attention toward present-day acts of
freedom rather than questions of nationalization, administration, and instrumen-
tality; the marches represented far more than a prelude to citizenship. Drawing on
the democratic and transgressive elements of "public joy" and the "passion for
distinction," I characterize the immigrant counterpublics of 2006 as practicing
forms of "festive anger" that challenged the dehumanizing effects of anonymity
and illegality. An appreciation of such agonistic enactments offers an alternative
to the more limited conception of the undocumented as either "givers to" or
"takers from" the nation-state.[15] Challenging the dichotomous logic of immigrants as either grateful subjects or dangerous lawbreakers allows us to consider
the more radical possibilities inherent in action and other acts of unauthorized
"taking."

Against the Grain: The Challenge of Reading the Undocumented into Arendt

In turning to Arendt to consider noncitizen mass protest, we are immediately
confronted with several shortcomings in her own political thinking. As many
have noted, Arendt's conceptions of labor, the body, the private realm, and "the
social question" mark her as a rather vexed figure in democratic theory.[16] In her
desire to privilege freedom and action, she often problematically denies political
status to questions of necessity and economics (what Mark Reinhardt refers to in
The Art of Being Free as "the problem of human needs").[17] We see this side of

Arendt in a famous passage in *On Revolution*, in which she describes the impoverished French peasantry as follows: "[W]hat urged them on was the quest for bread . . . and the cry for bread will always be uttered with one voice. In so far as we all need bread, we are indeed all the same and may as well unite into one body."[18]

Because they live in a regime of enforced invisibility, the undocumented are often linked to privation, their political aspirations conflated with questions of economic survival, material need, and bodily necessity. Given this tendency to portray the undocumented as the personification of poverty, Arendt's critique of the social and the related issues of bodily necessity and social inequality would seem to make her a theorist particularly ill suited to address the concerns of those protesting for immigrant rights.[19] From her perspective, the undocumented would seem akin to the starving peasants of France—the social question incarnate.

Yet despite her tendency to presume definite and impermeable distinctions between public and private, political and social, and between labor, work, and action, notable scholars continue to engage Arendt's political theory, often in counterintuitive ways. Such efforts at confounding her categorical distinctions involve acts of appropriation and amendment—what Seyla Benhabib has described as "thinking with Arendt against Arendt."[20] My analysis is particularly indebted to Warner's suggestion that we read the slogan "'the personal is political' with an Arendtian understanding of the political."[21] Building on Bonnie Honig's reading of Arendt as a theorist of "agonistic and performative politics," Warner reads Arendt against herself by denaturalizing notions of privacy and approaching private-realm identities such as gender, race, and sexuality as sites for politicization. By recognizing how "privacy is publicly constructed," Warner both draws on and challenges Arendt's political thought in order to provide a necessary corrective to her more limited conception of how social and group identities relate to the categories of public and private.

Given that *The Origins of Totalitarianism* is Arendt's most explicit work regarding noncitizens, it may surprise some that my reading draws most extensively on *The Human Condition* and (to a slightly lesser extent) *On Revolution*. While other theorists have productively turned to Arendt's analysis of statelessness in order to consider refugees, displaced persons, human rights, and "the right to have rights," it is my contention that Arendt's nonconsequentialist account of action offers the richer optic for considering undocumented politics in the United States.[22] Even more significantly, my reading of *The Human Condition* reveals unexpected conceptual resources in Arendt's concept of labor and her depiction of *animal laborans*—one that bears a striking resemblance to contemporary depictions of the undocumented, defined by their close relationship to the practices that minister to human beings' material life and comfort. The menial and physical labors that immigrants typically perform (farmwork, domestic work, construction, food production and processing) are activities that have become constitutive of undocumented subjectivity. In other words, to be undocumented is to be a subject *made* for arduous labor, a subject whose very existence is understood in terms of his or her willingness to engage in toilsome practices that allow for the maintenance of life itself.

In turning to Arendt's account of *animal laborans*, my point is not to argue that this depiction is "correct." Instead, Arendt's account of labor captures a particular set of political dynamics currently in play. As Bhikhu Parekh has noted, by disjoining freedom and necessity, Arendt is unable to invest labor with political significance.[23] She understands labor as inescapably meaningless—endless and incapable of revealing singularity. It is my contention that contemporary depictions of undocumented labor betray a similar lack of imagination. The ongoing failure to rethink the relationship between freedom and necessity provides a deeper understanding of why it remains so difficult for the undocumented to appear as individuals engaged in acts of political freedom. Arendt's problematic account of labor helps us understand why certain subjects continue to be viewed as interchangeable and indistinct.

As Linda Martín Alcoff has argued, race and gender represent "epidemically salient and ontologically real" identities that affect not only one's public status "but one's experienced selfhood as well." Despite the fact that racial and gender identities are produced socially, they continue to have political, sociological, and economic salience.[24] Given that practices of labor are inevitably intertwined with questions of race and gender, my reading is necessarily supplemented by a wide range of scholars concerned with issues of immigration, race, citizenship, and embodiment. Such intersectional interventions into Arendt expose the limitations of the undocumented invoking their capacity to labor as a way to gain political visibility and standing. Because the politics of race complicates the view of wage labor as constitutive of American citizenship, Latino immigrants face a double bind when emphasizing their willingness to engage in hard work. Rather than emphasizing wage labor as constitutive of citizenship, my analysis suggests that Latino immigrant action would be better served by emphasizing counterpublic practices of freedom, initiation, individuation, and transformation.

Discerning Undocumented Action: The Limits of Statelessness

> Once they had left their homeland they remained homeless; once they had left their state they became stateless; once they had been deprived of their human rights they were rightless, the scum of the earth.
>
> —Hannah Arendt[25]

> [M]en, though they must die, are not born in order to die but in order to begin.
>
> —Hannah Arendt[26]

Arendt characterizes the power of beginnings as "the freedom to call some-thing into being, which did not exist before, which was not given, not even as an object of cognition or imagination, and which therefore, strictly speaking, could not be known."[27] Deeply attentive to the significance of natality, *The Human Condition* draws our attention to that ordinary yet awesome recognition that "nobody is ever the same as anyone else who ever lived, lives, or will live."[28]Because new people are constantly entering our common world, action is defined by the "plurality" of human beings, each capable of initiating the unforeseen.

In an Arendtian framework, it is through participation in the polis that man is most able to distinguish himself.[29] For Arendt, the polis is less an actual physical location than it is "an organized way to remember great deeds"—the "space of appearance" rather than a legislative locale where laws get passed.[30] Linda Zerilli refers to this as Arendt's "action-centered" conception of politics, citing "coffee-houses, street corners, living rooms, and kitchens" as exemplifying "how any physical space can be transformed into a political one and, indeed, how it is that things become public."[31]

Speech and action are closely related in *The Human Condition*, which is why, for Arendt, "the doer of deeds" must also be a "speaker of words."[32] Moreover, because speech and action require the presence of others, our very appearance depends upon the attention of others whose perceptions we do control.[33] Because action entangles us in the world and in the lives of others, our actions will inevi-tably be interpreted in ways we do not intend.

Notions of beginning are central to Arendt. As Patchen Markell has written, "[W]hat makes a beginning a beginning for Arendt, what lends it its eruptiveness, is not its degree of departure from what preceded it, but rather our attunement to its character as an irrevocable event, which also means: as an occasion for response."[34] The eruptive power of beginning can be seen in the formation of the 2006 demonstrations, as immigrant advocates and organizers consistently found themselves surprised by the spontaneous participation of so many who had not demonstrated previously. The protests were exceptional in both their size and their intensity, often leaving organizers scrambling to keep up with the popular momentum of each subsequent event.[35] While years of labor and community organizing helped produce "viable mobilizing structures" that laid the ground-work for the protests, the events' size and intensity nevertheless surprised orga-nizers, pundits, and the general public.[36] In this way, the spring protests can be read in Arendtian terms as a moment of "infinite improbability."[37] Beyond their sheer scale, the unforeseen quality of the marches was apparent in their reach outside states with long-standing Latino populations, such as California and Texas. Large-scale marches and protests occurred in a number of southern and midwestern states with new and growing Latino immigrant populations, including Tennessee, Wisconsin, Kansas, and Iowa.[38]

Arendt's insights regarding the longing for renown gives new meaning to the marches' escalating size and proliferation throughout the spring of 2006. The growth and success of each march generated further energy, attracting addi-tional individuals and leading to more and more participation (what the *New York Latino Journal* described as "a growing tsunami of immigrant protest across the nation").[39] Seen in this light, the impulse to join in the demonstrations can be read as an attempt at collective presence—an "an organized way to remember great deeds."[40]

In contrast to *The Human Condition*, Arendt's account of statelessness in *The Origins of Totalitarianism* is a terrifying depiction of what it means to render human beings "superfluous" to the social and political order in which they live. Explicating this process in the context of displaced populations in Europe following both world wars, her account involves the migrations of groups who, unlike their predecessors, "were welcomed nowhere and could be assimilated nowhere."[41] Echoing Burke's critique of the Declaration of the Rights of Man and of the Citizen, Arendt cites the traumatic history of subjects who have lost the protection of a sovereign legal body and have instead sought refuge in the idea of universal and inalienable human rights.[42] For Arendt, a man who is "nothing but a man" has lost the very qualities that make it possible for others to treat him as a fellow man.[43] As Seyla Benhabib notes, it is for these reasons that Arendt believed that only the restoration of their national rights could guarantee disempowered minorities their rights of membership.[44]

Emerging as a powerful weapon of totalitarian politics, denationalization cre-ated conditions of "illegality" through circumstances beyond victims' control: "The stateless person, without right to residence and without the right to work, had of course constantly to transgress the law. He was liable to jail sentences without ever committing a crime."[45] Forced outside the pale of law, stateless subjects suffered the loss of a "distinct place in the world." In Arendt's account, the calamity of rightlessness is not belonging to *any* community: "Their plight is not that they are not equal before the law, but that no law exists for them; not that they are oppressed but that nobody wants even to oppress them."[46] Arendt characterizes man as no longer in a state of political equality but, rather, thrown back on "the dark background of mere givenness"—"human and nothing but human."[47] It is here, when human beings become "perfectly superfluous" and "nobody can be found to 'claim' them," that the right to live is truly challenged.[48]

Arendt's account of statelessness and superfluity appears particularly valuable when considering genocidal regimes or the political impact of legal dispossession; consider the "rightless" subjects imprisoned at the detention camp at Guantánamo Bay Naval Base. Yet the political challenges faced by today's Latino immigrant populations (including the undocumented) differ from the condition of statelessness and superfluousness that European minorities, particularly Jews, faced during both world wars and the postwar period. As Richard J. Bernstein notes, Arendt's depiction of the "absolutely superfluous" is powerfully linked to her analysis of totalitarian evil and its attempts at total domination and annihilation.[49] By contrast, while the undocumented struggle with having their human plurality recognized, their struggle occurs on very different political terrain. As Lázaro Lima argues, Latinos have a long history of being constructed as "extranationals in the public sphere." Such practices of racialization have sustained and implicitly sanctioned a "tiered democracy of bodies" where certain bodies matter more than others.[50] In this way, Arendt's analysis of superfluousness is distinct from the language of denigrated *excess* that typifies depictions of the undocumented. As I discuss later, this language of massification and inexhaustibility is critically linked to undocumented labor and the critical role such labor plays in U.S. and global economies.

In *The Origins of Totalitarianism*, Arendt addresses statelessness primarily in terms of denationalization. Yet such a reading fails to address the question of how the stateless sometimes serve to *renationalize* the state. As Bonnie Honig has noted, the U.S. government has often viewed the foreigner as a reinforcing supplement to the nation. By choosing "us," the foreigner makes us feel good about who "we" are—a people worthy of being chosen. In the case of the undocumented, their willingness to break the law in order to live and work in the United States both unsettles Americans and confirms our status as a choice-worthy regime.[51] Moreover, while the undocumented *do* live under conditions of acute vulnerability—subject to deportation and lacking the range of political rights that come with full national membership—they are not permanently barred from citizenship. In the

United States, personhood does in fact offer a form of civic standing, limited though it may be. As Linda Bosniak notes:

> [P]ossession of citizenship status is not always a prerequisite for the enjoyment of substantive citizenship. In the United States, as in most other liberal democratic states, a great many of the rights commonly associated with equal citizenship and economic citizenship are not confined to status citizens at all but are available to territorially present persons. . . . [A]ll aliens in the United States, including the undocumented, formally enjoy most fundamental rights, including due process rights in criminal proceedings, expressive and associational rights, basic economic liberties such as contract and property rights, and even the right to attend public school. Citizenship, it turns out, is not actually "the right to have rights," despite the conventional wisdom. In many situations, only personhood is required.[52]

According to Bosniak, when it comes to the enjoyment or practice of rights, the status of citizenship is neither a necessary nor a sufficient condition for enactment. It is for these reasons that she suggests it is not necessarily incoherent to speak of the "noncitizenship of citizens" and the "citizenship of aliens."[53]

Beyond Bosniak's insights regarding the status of liberal personhood in liberal democracies, a more significant concern regarding *The Origins of Totalitarianism* has to do with Arendt's homogenizing depiction of the stateless. In her recognition that "the world found nothing sacred in the abstract nakedness of being human," she highlights the vulnerability of the stateless but not their capacity for action.[54] Such depoliticizing depictions of "bare life" create an ontological trap whereby the stateless are condemned to their status as those without rights.[55] By contrast, *The Human Condition*'s emphasis on "new beginnings" puts forward a valuable vocabulary for thinking about the aspirational and agonistic actions of the undocumented.

Focusing on the discontinuities inherent in plurality, this approach emphasizes the political character of immigrant action—what Jacques Rancière has termed "dissensus," the power exercised by those who have no qualifications for exercising power. Rancière describes such democratic enactments as "the count of the uncounted—or the part of those who have no part."[56] For Rancière, dissensus is not simply a conflict of interests or opinions—it is a dispute about the very frame within which we see something as given, "putting two worlds in one and the same world."[57] Throughout the spring of 2006, Americans witnessed an improbable staging of dissensus, as noncitizens sacrificed their already-uncertain safety in order to demand dignity and public recognition. Taking a cue from Rancière, let us turn our attention to a related aspect of Arendt's political thought: what she describes as the human desire for distinction.

The Passion for Distinction:
Protest, Public Happiness, and Festive Anger

> This is a movement. . . . We're sending a message that we are people of dignity.
>
> —Jaime Contreras, president of the National Capital Immigration Coalition[58]

> We want to be legal. . . . We want to live without hiding, without fear. We have to speak so that our voices are listened to and we are taken into account.
>
> —Ruben Arita, an illegal immigrant who joined the 2006 demonstration in Washington, D.C.[59]

> If you think I'm "illegal" because I'm a Mexican, learn the true history because I'm in my HOMELAND
>
> —Sign displayed by a demonstrator at La Gran Marcha, Los Angeles[60]

Arendt's interest in questions of individuation and distinction can best be seen in her appreciative reading of John Adams's *Discourses on Davila*, particularly his analysis of the political invisibility of America's poor. For Arendt, Adams is praise-worthy because he recognizes that the poor lack more than bread—they lack voice and visibility. As Arendt notes in *On Revolution*, next to self-preservation, the human "passion for distinction . . . will forever be the great spring of human actions," a passion Adams described as "more essential and remarkable" than any other human faculty.[61] According to Adams, "Wherever men, women, or children, are to be found, whether they be old or young, rich or poor, high or low, wise or foolish, ignorant or learned, every individual is seen to be strongly actu-ated by a desire to be seen, heard, talked of, approved and respected by the people about him, and within his knowledge."[62] Given Adams's belief in the human desire to excel and be recognized, to be overlooked becomes "intolerable."[63] In his 1790 *Discourses*, Adams writes:

> The poor man . . . feels himself out of the sight of others, groping in the dark. Mankind takes no notice of him. He rambles and wanders unheeded. In the midst of a crowd, at church, in the market . . . he is in as much obscurity as he would be in a garret or a cellar. He is not disapproved, cen-sured, or reproached; *he is only not seen.*[64]

What Arendt identifies as the desire for distinction—the struggle for individuation through "action in concert"—lies at the heart of the immigrant-rights marches. In making themselves present en masse, marchers sought to counteract the feeling of being faceless and unknown. Sick of living in fear, the undocumented were attempting a collective response to the dehumanizing and intolerable effects of illegality. Moreover, immigrants made it clear that their concerns went beyond the economic realm. Instead, the demonstrations focused on the issues of *dignity* and *recognition*. The ubiquitous signs "I'm a Worker, Not a Criminal," "Human Beings Are Never Illegal," "Justice and Dignity for Everyone," and "We Are Not Terrorists" reflected this effort to gain recognition as subjects who contribute to (rather than harm) the larger society. Signs such as "We Build Your Homes" and "Got Food? Thank a Farmworker" attempted to expose the chain of labor, consumption, and desire that authorizes the immigrants' presence while simultaneously demanding that their contributions be publicly acknowledged and valued. Such practices displace comfortable notions of mutual consent with a more complex reality of sacrifice and unequal loss. As Danielle Allen argues, Americans rarely grapple with the uncomfortable reality that "our benefits derive not merely from our own hard work or even luck but also from the sacrifices of strangers." By posing a political challenge, marchers staged a collective refusal to ignore how strangers bring us benefit.[65]

Moreover, by protesting an act of government, the marchers were attempting to gain new rights through a collective display of resistance. Yet by entering the public realm, the demonstrations immediately exceeded their instrumentalist goal. In the act of marching, the undocumented defeated their fugitive status by enacting a visibility they lacked prior to the event. As Paul Apostolidis writes, "For a brief time, people normally driven into the shadows to protect themselves from surveillance and deportation . . . created an array of sites where they could begin to develop their own style of opposition and visions of an altered 'American' future."[66]

As Apostolidis's depiction makes clear, such actions require enormous courage. As such, they resonate powerfully with Arendt's definition of heroism and citizen excellence. In Arendtian terms, the original goal of the polis was to multiply the occasions for individuals to win "immortal fame" and distinguish themselves. Yet as Hanna Pitkin notes, "heroic excellence" must be understood as more than the trivial urge for fame. Instead, "reality itself is at stake here."[67] In other words, Arendt's definition of a "heroic sensibility" can be understood as the refusal to endure a partial or limited existence:

[T]he word "hero" originally, that is, in Homer, was no more than a name given each free man who participated in the Trojan enterprise and about whom a story could be told. The connotation of courage, which we now feel to be an indispensable quality of the hero, is in fact already present in the willingness to act and speak at all. . . . And this courage is not necessarily or even primarily related to a willingness to suffer the consequences; courage and even boldness are already present in leaving one's private hiding place and showing who one is, in disclosing and exposing one's self.[68]

Ironically, Arendt's language of "leaving one's private hiding place" and being willing "to suffer the consequences" of action and speech is especially apt when applied to the political activism of the undocumented. As Holloway Sparks notes in her discussion of courage and feminist practices of dissident citizenship, courage has often been constructed as a "quintessentially masculine trait," long associated with conceptions of manhood and the performance of violence.[69] Yet political courage means far more than masculinist attempts at honor and personal glory.[70] According to Sparks, to act courageously involves the broader commitment to acting in the face of risk, uncertainty, or fear—"even when the outcome is uncertain."[71] Such was the courage of immigrant marchers: by appearing in public, protesters risked being photographed, arrested, and even deported. The dangers of violence and anti-immigrant backlash are a stark reminder that political courage is a central element of action, since such acts of public disclosure necessarily set in motion a chain of unpredictable events in ways both inspiring and hazardous.

While it is clear that what compelled individuals to join in the marches went beyond opposition to H.R. 4437, thinking alongside Arendt helps us consider the simultaneous (and at times almost incongruous) sense of both urgency *and* delight displayed at the marches. According to Arendt, individuals assemble in the public realm not only out of a sense of duty and self-interest but because "having a share in public business" involves a set of activities that give citizens "a feeling of happiness they could acquire nowhere else."[72] Such "public happiness" was a quality much commented on by journalists, who repeatedly remarked that the mood of the marches was "festive rather than angry."[73] Describing the May 1, 2006, protest in San Francisco, *Mother Jones* editor Russ Rymer noted that "'protest' seems the wrong word for such triumphant expression":

The crowds were whistling and cheering in a festival of American and Latin American flags; the cops were spectating from the sidelines, relaxed and laughing; and some among the office workers caught in the frenzy only because they were headed out to lunch found themselves unaccountably moved by what they saw. May Day had transmogrified into the Fourth of July.[74]

While the marches were undoubtedly a compelling combination of courage, theatricality, and public joy, the dynamic of action and affect was far more complex than the media's oversimplified depiction of the marches. In numerous press accounts of the marches, the audacity of immigrant action was softened by assurances regarding the demonstrations' orderly, happy, and peaceful character. By invoking the marchers' familial and festive mood, allies and advocates continually sought to characterize the demonstrations in ways that purged them of negative affect.[75]

A fuller understanding of immigrant action requires a willingness to consider the more complex emotive and political terrain I characterize as "festive anger." Emerging out of conditions of exploitation, hostility, and state-sanctioned violence against immigrants, "festive anger" involves a complex (and interconnected) set of civic emotions, including indignation, determination, irony, outrage, and joy. Such incongruous forms of expressivity complicate the reassuring words claimed by immigrant-rights advocates: that protesters desired only to "participate in the system, not to undermine it." For while the marchers were hardly the hostile, anti-American presence that some anti-immigrant advocates claimed, neither were they the merry and nonthreatening presence that liberal advocates and sympathizers depicted. By simultaneously cheering while brandishing slogans such as "This Is Stolen Land" and "Who's the Real Illegal Alien? . . . Pilgrim!" marchers challenged traditional narratives of immigration through displays of anger, pleasure, and irony—producing a counterdiscourse that demanded an acknowledgment of U.S. conquest and colonialism.

In its tendency to transgress the boundaries between acceptable and unacceptable expressions of membership and rights-claiming, festive anger can be read as an affective expression of Honig's discussion of "taking" in *Democracy and the Foreigner*. Building on James Madison's assertion that democracy is a form of politics in which power is not received by grateful subjects but, rather, is "taken, redistributed, reenacted, and recirculated" by way of popular political action, Honig argues that the iconic "taking foreigner" stretches the boundaries of citizenship, modeling transgressive forms of agency and possessing "potentially inaugural powers."[76] Festive anger can be read as this type of initial transgression—the taking of an agonistic pleasure. An understanding of festive anger would suggest that marchers were not simply enacting the desire to belong but were simultaneously taking pleasure in acts of defiance and public provocation. Appreciating the logic of festive anger gives new meaning to the expression "Today we march, tomorrow we vote." Viewed from this more agonistic angle, the marchers were making a promise that was itself an inaugural act of democratic taking: pledging an allegiance while issuing a threat.

Such attempts to combine democratic assurances with subversive critique are reminiscent of Danielle Allen's discussion of Ralph Ellison and his use of the term "agree 'em to death and destruction" in *Invisible Man*.[77] Highlighting the "subversive power of apparent agreement," Allen writes:

> The way to engage the issue of racism in the United States is to begin by agreeing—to the rights of humanity; that way leads to cultural self-contradictions and so, in the ideal, to political transformation. But [Ellison's grandfather character's] second insight is more subtle. He realizes that those who agree, in the face of violence and domination, cast aggressive acts into the starkest relief. . . . Those who are agreeable in this way show up violent citizens for what they are, and force witnesses to the spectacle to make a choice about whether to embrace or disavow the violence.[78]

During the protests, marchers were engaged in acts of reassurance (that they were peaceful and desirous to be a part of the polity) alongside disruptive expressions of outrage, frustration, and anger. Throughout the protests, marchers— encouraged to enact joy but criticized for expressing rage or indignation—straddled the line between the subversive power of agreement and the politics of direct confrontation. In this way, the language of festive anger can be read as a deeply complex and paradoxical political display; it highlights the tensions that characterize this emotive political terrain.

From Illegality to Action: Oppositional Publicity and Immigrant Counterpublics

As Susan Bickford notes, "Arendtian plurality has two characteristics: equality and distinctiveness. It is our distinctiveness that impels us into politics."[79] But what if the effort to gain equality is itself the subject of action? As a racialized population, Latino immigrants (particularly the undocumented) struggle with being perceived only in terms of the group and never as "a person with a unique story and singular opinions."[80] This is the challenge Arendt addresses in her discussion of the who/what distinction: the problem of getting entangled in "what" someone is (undocumented, Latino, an immigrant) versus "who" he is (an individual with a specific and distinct capacity to enact freedom). For Arendt, the emphasis on the "what" misdirects our attention and "actively distracts us from human plurality—from who-ness."[81] As Bickford makes clear, Arendt's clearly defined border between the "who" and the "what" needs to be reconsidered, particularly when seeking to understand the relationship between racial and political identities:

> Our group identities may subject us to stereotyped attention, but they are often also where we "draw our strength to live and reasons for acting." Our color, ethnicity, gender, class, or religion may be a constitutive part of our public identity because they are the contexts in which we learned to speak and think the languages that shape us and enable us to give voice to our unique selves. And it is within particular social groups that we first are paid attention to, and learn to attend to others—the very capacities necessary for an Arendtian politics.[82]

Like Bickford, Michael Warner seeks to theorize (rather than police) the Arendtian border between *who* we are and *what* we are. Warner's analysis of counterpublics echoes Bickford in his refusal to "bracket" questions of embodiment or status.

In his effort to move beyond Jürgen Habermas's model of "rational-critical debate," Warner's work on counterpublics begins with the assertion that movements around gender and sexuality do not always conform to the model of the bourgeois public.[83] Moreover, while publics are always plural, a counterpublic can be distinguished as a particular *type* of public.[84] What makes counterpublics distinct is that they are "defined by their tension with the larger public."[85] As Samuel Chambers notes, counterpublics not only produce alternative discourses—they are aware "that those discourses will be rejected or denigrated by the dominant public."[86] A counterpublic is *aware* of its subordinate status.[87] Drawing on Nancy Fraser's analysis of "subaltern counterpublics," Warner suggests that such alternative publics are distinctive in part because of "the odd social imaginary" established by this "ethic of estrangement."[88] He cites reading a gay-identified publication, attending a black church, and, in some contexts, "the code-switching of bilingualism" as examples of counterpublic discourse whose parameters continue to have a larger social salience.[89]

Aware of their marginalization, the 2006 marchers often displayed the counterpublic tendency to see themselves in opposition to the dominant public.

By identifying with "illegal aliens" (a socially marked population if there ever was one), participants challenged the stigma of illegality by producing new forms of community with noncitizens. In forming such a public, the marchers were enacting what Kevin Bruyneel has described as a "third space of sovereignty." Drawn from indigenous political thought, Bruyneel's third space marks a form of resistance wherein subjects fight to reimagine and enact a space of "sovereignty and/ or citizenship that is inassimilable to the modern liberal democratic settler-state and nation."[90] This claim "refuses to accommodate itself to the political choices framed by the imperial binary: assimilation or secession, inside or outside, modern or traditional, and so on." In enacting a version of this "third space," Latinos recalled their own complex relationship to the United States—articulating a common world in which membership and recognition are not contingent on citizenship. Such alliances are informed by the fact that a significant number of Latinos who are now either citizens or legal residents entered the country without papers or have family members who are neither native nor naturalized.[91] These multiple understandings of membership create the potential (though not the guarantee) that Latinos who are legally recognized subjects will develop a sense of linked fate with the undocumented. This sense of linked fate was prevalent throughout the marches, as Latino participants invoked their shared racialization in ways that blurred the line between citizens and noncitizens.

As Warner notes, the protocols of "discourse and debate remain open to affective and expressive dimensions of language . . . members make their embodiment and status at least partly relevant in a public way by their very participation."[92] Similarly, by wearing white and chanting slogans in Spanish, demonstrators made it difficult for onlookers to distinguish citizen from noncitizen. Such action can be characterized as "protection through collective action."[93] Drawing on the work of Renato Rosaldo, William Flores has termed such alliance activism "Latino cultural citizenship"—a process of claiming rights that includes "how groups form, define themselves, define their membership, claim rights, and develop a vision of the type of society that they want to live in."[94]

In advocating for more expansive notions of political community, Flores is *not* arguing that immigrants are not in need of the formal rights that come with citizenship. Instead, like Warner, Flores claims that by "acting upon and changing power relationships," excluded groups "not only demand existing rights, but create new ones."[95] Of course, as he notes, the civic border that divides legal from illegal can be crossed in both directions. This same combination of citizenship and racialization produces a complex dynamic of "other-ness" capable of undermining the political possibilities of Latinos more generally. In the context of the immigrant counterpublic, the enhanced visibility of illegal immigrants sometimes combines with the homogenizing effects of being racialized, resulting in the erasure of Latino diversity, rendering *all* Latinos homogeneously "foreign" regardless of citizenship status.[96]

As Warner notes, feelings of shame and marginalization are difficult (if not impossible) to overcome in isolation: "Visceral private meaning is not easy to alter by oneself, by a free act of will. It can only be altered through exchanges that go beyond self-expression to the making of a collective scene of disclosure."[97] The demonstrations can be thought of as such a moment of disclosure—as a space in which participants publicly celebrated and legitimated the presence of the undocumented in American society. According to Warner, such scenes of association and identity transform the private lives they mediate: "Homosexuals can exist in isolation; but gay people or queers exist by virtue of the world they elaborate together, and gay or queer identity is always fundamentally inflected by the nature of that world."[98] Similarly, one is "illegal" in isolation, but in elaborating a common world, marchers challenged the state's ability to define the parameters of membership.

As scenes of self-activity, publics are scenes of historical rather than timeless belonging. This emphasis on the performative denaturalizes presumptions of *either* intragroup hostility or homogeneity. For example, in looking at the mass gatherings of 2006, what quickly becomes apparent is that the power of these events was based in part on the fact that they involved broadly defined issues that had widespread support—namely, opposition to legislation that threatened to criminalize immigrants and those who assist them. Beyond this, demonstrators and the various organizations and activists who sponsored these rallies often disagreed strongly on what "justice" for immigrants would entail. Demonstrators held a wide array of views when it came to supporting or opposing policies such as a new guest-worker program, amnesty for the undocumented, and enhanced border control. Such views were both expressed and transformed during the protests. Moreover, while the mass gatherings of 2006 were a space of appearance that involved "the sharing of words and deeds," the marchers' speech tended to emphasize the unitary and collective aspects of public address. Chanting in unison and waving placards and flags, the marchers advanced a style of collective address whose structure was more participatory than deliberative. And while the demonstrations no doubt produced acts of revelatory speech (through both individual discussions and the speeches made at the rallies), on the whole, the protesters were not always in a position to distinguish themselves as unique individuals. Instead, by emphasizing the *mass* elements of participation (marching, chanting, sign waving), the gatherings risked downplaying the participants' diverse social locations. In other words, the very practices that promoted inclusive participation and collective visibility risked subjecting the marchers to a dehumanizing discourse of massification—as a seemingly inexhaustible flood of foreigners, dangerous lawbreakers, or an ignorant and easily manipulated group of political pawns.[99]

This combination of erased difference and internal heterogeneity highlights the fact that the 2006 protests were *not* an expression of organic Latino community simply waiting to be uncovered but, rather, an example of diverse and mediated publics. In this way, Warner's language of counterpublics can be read as an Arendtian form of world-building—a relation between the self and others instantiated through action. Because subjectivity was produced and transformed *through* these civic encounters, the marches can best be understood by emphasizing their capacity to produce the *new*—"not only new shared worlds and critical languages but also new privacies, new individuals, new bodies, new intimacies, and new citizenships."[100]

Of course, by putting on public display practices that were previously understood as private, counterpublics often produce intense reactions among nonmembers. As Warner notes, "Counterpublics are, by definition, formed by their conflict with the norms and contexts of their cultural environment, and this context of domination inevitably entails distortion." Such "public displays of private matters," he writes, are often seen as a debased form of narcissism, "a collapse of decorum, expressivity gone amok, the erosion of any distinction between public and private."[101] During the 2006 marches, the hostile reaction and controversy regarding participants' decision to wave their native countries' flags are an example of the sort of overheated reaction to which Warner is referring. Criticism aimed at the presence of foreign flags was heard almost immediately in conservative publications, on talk radio, and on the cable news networks. *National Review* editor Rich Lowry described marchers' waving of foreign flags as "ominous" in their hint of "a large, unassimilated population existing outside America's laws and exhibiting absolutely no sheepishness about it." A similar reaction occurred when marchers began to sing a new, Spanish-language version of "The Star-Spangled Banner" ("Nuestro Himno," or "Our Anthem").[102] President George W. Bush commented, "I think people who want to be a citizen of this country ought to learn English. And they ought to learn to sing the anthem in English."[103] In claiming the anthem as "ours," "Nuestro Himno" both asserts equality and demands an act of translation from its listeners. As Judith Butler notes, such acts of singing display how "the nation is being reiterated, but in ways that are not authorized—or not yet."[104] Interestingly, it was the stories of such unauthorized displays of both song and flags that seemed to most upset and unsettle viewers.

From Singing Our Freedom to Disposability: Action or *Animal Laborans*?

As Patchen Markell has argued, whether your action is recognized as a form of beginning is "never wholly under your control." Instead, it is "a matter of the character of the responses and reactions it provokes (or fails to provoke) in you and others."[105] In this way, Arendt's depiction of the "boundlessness" and "unpredictability" of action "applies to the very status of action as action."[106] In their efforts to "go public," subjects struggle to create a context in which forms of publicness can occur. During the 2006 demonstrations, one of the most common ways immigrants established themselves as worthy of membership was by emphasizing their role as laborers—as "hardworking" individuals. As part of the demonstrations, immigrants and their allies often stressed the undocumented's contributions to the U.S. economy. In this final section, I argue that emphasizing labor as the way to gain political standing is, simply put, a bad idea, for in identifying immigrants in terms of the jobs they do, the discourse of labor frames undocumented subjectivity in terms of economics and survival rather than of democratic action.

Because the undocumented already struggle with a public identity still powerfully enmeshed in their capacity to labor, emphasizing labor promotes the tendency to see the undocumented as subjects of *necessity* rather than *natality*. To explore this dynamic, I turn to Arendt's treatment of labor and *animal laborans*, supplemented by Nicholas de Genova's discussion of migrant "deportability" and Melissa Wright's discussion of labor and the politics of "disposability" along the U.S.-Mexican border. I suggest that such an intersectional analysis highlights the political challenges faced by those invoking labor in the service of noncitizen rights.

Arendt's account of labor is related to her critique of the modern condition and its tendency to reduce "freedom to necessity, and politics to economics."[107] For her, *animal laborans* is a subject condemned to a life of consumption—"procuring the necessities of life and providing for their abundance."[108] In this way, *animal laborans* refers not to a social class but to "a relationship to the world."[109] (In Arendtian terms, Paris Hilton is also *animal laborans*.) Nevertheless, while it is true that *animal laborans* is not a sociological category, Arendt's depiction of labor

as repetitive and interchangeable offers unexpected resources for thinking politically about the undocumented.

Unlike action—a practice that occurs in the public realm, involves speech,
and reveals human individuality and distinctiveness—labor is associated with
the private realm and related to human necessity. Forced upon human beings by
our biological condition, labor is defined as the necessary practices that humans
share with all living animals. According to Arendt, human beings have long sought
to escape the relentless repetition of menial labor. This evasion has meant that
since ancient times, specific segments of the population have often had the
weight of labor placed on them either exclusively or excessively, such as in the
cases of slaves, women, serfs—and foreigners. By forcing particular subjects to
commit their bodies to labor, free men were then relieved of such tasks and able
to focus on activities that went beyond the maintenance of bare life—particularly
the active engagement in politics that was once seen as a critical requirement for
citizenship.

Instead of the public display of uniqueness among free and equal subjects,
labor exists in the realm of necessity, involving the cyclical quality of nature and
survival. "It is indeed the mark of laboring," Arendt writes, "that it leaves nothing
behind, that the result of its effort is almost as quickly consumed as the effort is
spent."[110] Instead of revealing each individual's uniqueness, labor highlights the
interchangeability of activities done in the private realm. Because menial work
does not display our individual distinctiveness, others can do this work for us. The
activities of labor are characterized by "relentless repetition" and the cyclical
process of growth and decay "through which nature forever invades the human
artifice, threatening the durability of the world and its fitness for human use."[111]
For Arendt, the practices of labor require not speech but only the ability to engage
in the repetitive tasks of human maintenance. Such activities do not reveal human
uniqueness—instead, labor is defined by interchangeability.

In *Disposable Women and Other Myths of Global Capitalism*, Melissa Wright
describes how the Mexican women working in U.S.-owned *maquiladora* factories
come to personify the meaning of human disposability, "subjects who eventually
evolve into a living state of worthlessness."[112] Operating in the free-trade zone
along the U.S.-Mexico border, these labor-intensive assembly plants have developed systemic hiring practices that assume high levels of turnover among the
predominantly young and female workforce, often dismissed as "untrainable"
and "unskillable." This depiction of *maquila* workers as defined by high turnover
rates allows employers to characterize them as members of the "permanent labor
force of the temporarily employed."[113] Described as a story of capitalist turnover,

the Mexican *maquila* women are defined by the companies that hire them as "waste in the making . . . permanently and ineluctably headed towards decline . . . eventually worthless even as she creates value."[114] Linking her own critique of labor turnover in the *maquiladoras* with Uma Narayan's discussion of "death by culture," Wright connects the murders of women in Ciudad Juárez to this myth of capitalist disposability, claiming that the very logic of depicting some people as "eventually worthless" leads to a condition of violence wherein "female bodies have been dumped like trash in the desert."[115] In his discussion of Mexican meat-packers working in the western United States, Paul Apostolidis echoes Wright in his depictions of workers being told by management that they "aren't worth more than a bunch of disposable cups" that the company can use and then "toss in the garbage."[116] The prevalence of this discourse of disposability can even be seen in how workers themselves characterize the conditions of their labor. Describing the high rates of injury inside the plant, one meatpacker asserted that they were being treated like "tools that are no good anymore, so you just toss them, you throw them out."[117]

Defined by a cyclical and unending process of nondistinctiveness and inter-changeability, Arendt's vocabulary of labor can be considered here in relation to the bodies of Mexican *maquila* workers and the Latino undocumented in the United States. Just as Arendtian labor is meant to be "used up" in a cycle of pro-duction and consumption, so too is the labor of the undocumented. In a similar vein, Nicholas de Genova argues that "it is *deportability* and not deportation per se" that has historically rendered undocumented labor a distinctly disposable commodity.[118] As Ali Behdad has shown, the Border Patrol's "machinery of obser-vation" is significant "not so much for its capacity to 'catch' aliens" as for its ability to make subjects "watchful and insecure about the perils of illegal crossing."[119] In each instance, the qualities of disposability, deportability, and replaceability are the very characteristics that make this labor both denigrated and valuable. The value of undocumented labor, defined by workers' temporary status, is critically linked to the fact that it is understood to be impermanent and interchangeable. In this way, the value of undocumented labor is based less on long-term investment and its growing value over time than on its *endlessness*. It is here that the language of surplus and oversaturation becomes important. As Otto Santa Ana suggests in his work on metaphor and massification, Latinos in the United States have a long history of being characterized as dangerous figures of excess.[120] Depicted as an inexhaustible flood, the undocumented are enmeshed in a dehumanizing dis-course of superfluousness that is distinct from Arendt's discussion of superfluity in *The Origins of Totalitarianism*. Unlike Arendt's vision of making human beings

as human beings superfluous, here the undocumented are still being used as a
means to an (economic) end.[121] It is this vision of excess that gives the undocumented their economic value. They are essential precisely because there are too
many of them.

Arendt's account of labor shows us how the logic of interchangeability, use,
and disposability continues to impact how we think politically about subjects
defined by their labor. If undocumented subjectivity is indeed excessively defined
by labor, then the marchers of 2006 were fighting an uphill battle against a logic
that treated them as subjects of little worth or individuation. The depiction of the
undocumented as subjects whose value lies in their willingness to pick crops, clean
houses, mow laws, care for children, cook food, and so on, produces subjects
whose value lies not in their distinctiveness but, rather, in their collective existence
as an always-available mass. Individuality, intellect, judgment, reason, and insight
remain invisible, as the discourse of labor tends to overshadow acts of freedom
performed in the political realm.

Arendt's account of labor is symptomatic of the dangerous logic that emerges
when one's humanity is conflated with necessity. Yet this dynamic—whereby
efforts to honor the contributions of noncitizens lead to the conflation of *who*
they are with *what* they do—is the double bind of immigrant action. In making
labor visible, immigrants and their allies seek to invest it with political significance. Yet such visibility runs the risk of simultaneously mobilizing the more
problematic accounts of labor, those that emphasize necessity over freedom.
Such are the contradictions of all publics—including the immigrant counterpublic. As Warner reminds us, because they are formed by their conflict with the
dominant public, counterpublics are "damaged forms of publicness, just as gender and sexuality are, in this culture, damaged forms of privacy."[122] Despite their
capacity for transformation and reevaluation, counterpublics are also always
embedded in the larger public. This reality means that we must not simply reject
or celebrate labor—instead, this discourse needs to be questioned, resisted, and
renegotiated.

Claiming rights by invoking labor clearly has a certain logic. In the United
States, for example, the discourse of labor is often mobilized for nationalist
ends. Judith Shklar, for example, reminds us that labor and the right to earn
function as a central foundation of American citizenship. According to Shklar,
part of America's exceptionalism has involved the right to earn and the right to
vote.[123] Citing the Jacksonian belief in the dignity of work, she argues that
earning and the value of labor are constitutive of American citizenship. Dis-
missing ancient associations between leisure and citizenship, Americans have

often expressed a wariness of the idle rich, emphasizing the link between democracy and work. Given this history of conferring civic standing through a focus on suffrage and employment, it is unsurprising that pro-immigration advocates would seize on the idea of the undocumented as hardworking economic contributors. However, as Shklar's discussion of America also notes, the question of race remains a "core dilemma" in America's political history. The existence of chattel slavery both complicated and racialized the model of the independent citizen-earner: while wage labor conferred independence and autonomy, slavery "did more than any other institution to bring labor into contempt."[124] This sometimes led white workers to detest slavery "but hate the slave as well."[125]

Both pro- and anti-immigrant voices characterize Latino immigrants as not only willing but desirous of the dirtiest, most difficult forms of labor, eager to do the work that no else will do. Describing his proposal for a temporary-worker program in August 2006, President Bush described the undocumented in these terms when he stated, "There are people who have come across this border to do work Americans are not doing."[126] Karl Rove, Bush's then deputy chief of staff, articulated a more unvarnished version of this logic. Explaining the rationale behind the president's call for immigration reform, Rove told a Republican women's luncheon group: "I don't want my 17-year-old son to have to pick tomatoes or make beds in Las Vegas."[127] Implicit in Rove's quip is the undocumented's presumed willingness to accept toilsome, low-status work. Eagerness for such labor is what renders immigrants a necessary, beneficial, and nonthreatening presence in the American economy: since the undocumented take only the "worst jobs," American citizens can partake of the consumer benefits of a low-paid, unskilled workforce while not having to worry about competing for the same positions. By contrast, for critics of immigration, the undocumented's willingness to engage in such burdensome labor is precisely what makes them a threat to American workers and their higher standard of living. In this characterization, immigrants not only take jobs from Americans by driving down wages but leave a residue of exploitation and alienation in their wake. In an interview with *The New York Times*, for example, a construction worker from Scottsdale, Arizona, voiced his opposition to immigration reform: "They should all be ejected out of the country. They are in my country and they are on my job, and they are driving down wages."[128]Regardless of whether their labor serves to denationalize or renationalize the state, in both narratives the undocumented occupy a subject position defined by their willingness to engage in punishing, tedious, and dangerous labor.

In trying to make sense of this double bind, I want to suggest that in trying to claim one "central foundation" of American political thought (the civic standing conferred by work), immigrant-rights advocates have failed to comprehend the second "core dilemma": the history of race in America and the question of how the civic status conferred by work is complicated by racialization. While distinct from the question of slavery, Shklar's analysis highlights the way race can undermine the relationship between work and civic standing in the United States. Today's nativist voices often depict American workers as threatened by greedy corporate interests on the one hand and low-wage undocumented labor on the other. In this way, the labor of the undocumented is characterized not as a marker of value but as a threat to the polity. In both cases, the capacity to work hard and earn confers little or no civic standing on raced subjects. Instead, the undocumented occupy a subject position defined by their willingness to engage in undesirable labor. Moreover, deploying this discourse of labor often results in pro-immigrant forces offering incoherent arguments regarding justice and the value of the undocumented while failing to address central questions of equality and power. How immigrant counterpublics engage this difficult political landscape remains a central question for the emerging immigrant-rights movement. In *Who Sings the Nation-State?* Butler alludes to this tension by contrasting the singing of the national anthem in Spanish with invocations of one's capacity to labor:

> Some people chose that anthem as a way to go; there are other people who chose very different ways to go. The discourse of equality or the discourse of labor—we are the labor you need, we are the labor you rely on, watch what happens to your stores when we don't go to work; we are part of the system of production and circulation and distribution and your economy is not functioning without us and that gives us a certain kind of power. . . . We are the invisible disenfranchised underpaid labor that allows your economy to work. . . . [T]hat strikes me as very different from the national anthem moment and it may well be a different kind of we as well.[129]

For Butler, this discourse of labor stands in contrast to singing—which she reads as an incipient act of freedom that involved a "reworking of power, since those who sing are without entitlement"; the singing of "Nuestro Himno" by the undocumented alters not only the language of the nation "but its public space as well."[130] The question remains whether the discourse of labor can offer noncitizens and their allies anything equally compelling or politically potent.

Conclusion

Sheldon Wolin characterizes democracy, born in transgressive acts, less as a form of government than as a mode of being in which ordinary individuals contest forms of unequal power and, in doing so, create new patterns of commonality.[131] Wolin's emphasis on the uncertainty of action, echoing Arendt's, reminds us that while the marches inspire, these moments of initiation make no political promises. In their appropriation of patriotic symbols and songs, undocumented immigrants can be regarded as subjects engaged in nonsovereign practices of freedom that challenge established narratives of membership and consent. Yet by emphasizing their loyalty to the nation-state, their commitment to traditional notions of family, and their value as labor, this emerging immigrant-rights movement is equally capable of producing forms of nationalism that refetishize citizenship—drawing new yet equally problematic distinctions between subjects "deserving and undeserving" of rights and standing.

   In considering such variability, Michael Warner's insight that publics are always plural and contextually contingent becomes particularly relevant, for ultimately, this immigrant counterpublic represents just one form of the emerging Latino publics and counterpublics that seek to claim space and rights in the United States. Moreover, given that publics are always emerging and disappearing, the emerging immigrant counterpublic is best read as a politically contingent display of diversity and possibility. Rather than viewing the marches as an expression of collective agreement, perhaps we can best understand them as a display of ideological diversity in which differences are both expressed and concealed through mass action. Because the demonstrations generated a kind of collective status among participants, this embodied action made the protests appear more agenda-driven and united than they really were. Put another way, while the marches *were* profoundly political in their capacity to generate new possibilities, their outcome remains multifarious and far from certain.

   "Greatness," Arendt reminds us, "can lie only in the performance itself and neither in its motivation nor its achievement."[132] Appreciating both the fragility and the boundlessness of the 2006 protests requires a reconsideration of immigrant action attentive to just this sort of greatness. By appearing again and again, participants of this emerging counterpublic engaged in forms of display that emphasized social transformation rather than merely liberal inclusion—what Jacques Rancière has described as "the rights of those who have not the rights that they have and have the rights that they do not have."[133] In creating a space of appearance where noncitizens became present to themselves and others, counter-public practices remind us that when subjects enter the public realm, they are not simply enacting their already-existing commitments. Instead, subjectivity is produced and transformed through these civic encounters. The person who enters the public realm is not the same as the person who leaves. Regardless of their immediate results, the ongoing power of action involves the self-realization of a not-yet-completed person: the "making actual what is potential in the person and coming to realize who one really is."[134]

As one scholar of Arendtian action has rightly noted, "the most fundamental threat to democratic political activity lies in the loss of responsiveness to events: the erosion of the contexts in which action makes sense."[135] The actions of 2006 are a hopeful reminder that despite such erosions, sites of responsiveness continue to emerge. In thinking about beginnings, as the undocumented continue to engage the public realm, advocates should seek not to replicate the events of spring 2006 but to think creatively about new opportunities for immigrants and their allies to enact what always seems, prior to its performance, politically improbable.

Conclusion: Latino Is a Verb

Democracy, Latinidad, and the Creation of the Political

The immigrant-rights demonstrations of 2006 exemplify one of this book's fundamental claims: that in the United States, subjects marked "Latino" do *not* represent a preexisting community just waiting to emerge from the shadows. Instead, "Latino politics" is best understood as a form of enactment, a democratic moment in which subjects create new patterns of commonality and contest unequal forms of power.

The appearance of such a politics has often been generated by transgressive and evanescent moments of collective identification. Such participatory enactments sit uneasily alongside more static depictions of Latinos as an already-cohesive segment of the American electorate. In other words, rather than approaching Latino politics as something subjects *do*, we have too often understood Latino politics as the result of attitudes and interests that subjects already share. As previous chapters have shown, both grassroots activists and civic elites share this tendency to naturalize Latino political identity—characterizing *Latinidad* as rooted in common experiences and animated by a shared sense of linked fate. Yet such presumptions of shared political consciousness are continually challenged by the reality of Latino ideological diversity, both within its constituent subgroups and in larger notions of a pan-ethnic whole. That such political diversity has been seen as something to manage, justify, or explain speaks volumes about the anxiety and defensiveness that often surround Latino heterogeneity.

I conclude *The Trouble with Unity* by reflecting on how scholars might continue the process of theorizing *Latinidad*. In making this call, I want to push back against the prescriptive logic that often characterizes the study of Latino politics. Such pragmatics are understandable—in many Latino communities, majorities struggle against poverty, crime, exploitation, discrimination, political disenfranchisement, and a host of other conditions rightly recognized as unjust and untenable. Yet too often, depictions of Latinos as subjects existing in a state of "crisis" give rise to the tendency to displace and defer efforts to seriously theorize contemporary practices of political *Latinidad*. Rather than reimagine the content and parameters of a contemporary Latino identity and its attendant politics, political science all too often "brackets" these questions in an effort to address these populations' pressing issues. Such theoretical postponements lead to an overreliance on arguments for "strategic essentialism" and other claims that "Latino" is a "necessary fiction" when engaging questions of power and politics.[1]

While recognizing the urgency felt by those committed to the political future of these populations, I contend that now is the time to seriously reconsider the logics and categories that have thus far defined the Latino political project. The political and socioeconomic challenges that majorities of Latinos face today make it more, not less, necessary to give increased attention to theoretical alternatives—including efforts to reconceive concepts such as *Latinidad*. Moreover, as the category of Latino becomes the focus of increasing political attention and policy efforts, there is an acute need to more fully "think what we are doing."[2]

In pushing back against the pragmatics of crisis within Latino politics, I also want to resist the prescriptive standards that often bedevil democratic theorists of identity. Political theorists interested in questions of race, gender, and sexuality often face the added burden of being prescriptive. It is not enough that our theoretical efforts be penetrating or insightful—they must also be emancipatory. Failure to adhere to this standard can lead to criticisms of "abstraction" as well as accusations—from both outside and within—that intellectual privilege has left academics divorced from reality and "the real world." This stipulation reflects the assumption that such theorizing be evaluated primarily in terms of its potential to "solve" problems of race, gender, and sexuality, thus leading to more successful forms of political agency for these populations. By contrast, political theorists engaged in historical studies, aesthetics, and critical theory face far fewer disciplinary injunctions; in their efforts to grapple with complexities and contradictions that resist resolution, these scholars face a very different intellectual climate.

Throughout this work, I have sought to resist these disciplinary voices and instead consider what it might mean to develop a democratic ethos of *Latinidad* capable of negotiating the ongoing contingency that characterizes democratic action. In that spirit, my closing remarks here consider three possible approaches to reimagining the political contours of Latino pan-ethnicity: reconsidering the category "Latino" through feminist and queer theory, reassessing the practice of "Latino interests," and reimagining *Latinidad* as a rhizomatic form of resonance. I offer these theoretical interventions in the spirit of encouraging further efforts at creatively reconceptualizing *Latinidad* as a political category.

Feminist Challenges: Rethinking the Category "Latino"

In many ways, theorists of Latino identity face a challenge similar to that of feminists during the "category of woman" debates of the 1980s and 1990s. Like movement activists in the 1960s and 1970s, second-wave feminists were animated by dreams of unity. Yet these dreams of sisterhood and community were challenged by working-class women, women of color, and lesbians, all of whom criticized feminists for practicing a form of politics they experienced as alienating and oppressive rather than liberating and emancipatory. In response to such criticisms, 1980s feminism focused on questions of *difference* and making the category of woman more inclusive. Such efforts, however, only highlighted the inability of any definition to fully capture the deep diversity of women's experience and political needs. The possibility of forging a collective agenda seemed to run up against a feminism unable to speak of anything other than its own never-ending specificity.

It was postmodern feminists in the 1990s and beyond who shifted the debate away from the search for the category or practice that would unite all women and toward analysis of the political construction of the category itself. Recognizing that political communities are always implicated in dynamics of power, Judith Butler insists that "[i]dentity categories are never merely descriptive, but always normative, and as such, exclusionary."[3] Challenging the political assumption that "there must be a universal basis for feminism, one which must be found in an identity assumed to exist cross-culturally," Butler argues against the presumption that "the oppression of women has some singular form discernable in the universal or hegemonic structure of patriarchy or masculine domination."[4] Such insistence on a stable subject of feminism "inevitably generates multiple refusals to accept the category. These domains of exclusion reveal the coercive and regulatory consequences of that construction, even when the construction has been elaborated for emancipatory purposes."[5] Yet Butler's goal is not to "refuse representational politics—as if we could."[6] Instead, postmodern feminism seeks to reconceive the category of woman as "permanently open, permanently contested, permanently contingent, in order not to foreclose in advance future claims for inclusion."[7] Writes Butler:

> To take the construction of the subject as a political problematic is not the same as doing away with the subject; to deconstruct the subject is not to negate or throw away the concept; on the contrary, deconstruction implies only that we suspend all commitments . . . and that we consider the linguistic functions it serves in the consolidation and concealment of authority. To deconstruct is not to negate or dismiss, but to call into question and, perhaps most importantly, to open up a term, like the subject, to a reusage or redeployment that previously has not been authorized.[8]

For Butler, "The deconstruction of identity is not the deconstruction of politics; rather, it establishes as political the very terms through which identity is articulated." Such a critique "brings into question the foundationalist frame in which feminism as an identity politics has been articulated.[9]

Like Butler, Kathy Ferguson makes an argument for "multiplicity and undecidability in feminist discourses on subjectivity."[10] According to Ferguson, thematizing the subject as mobile "suggests a way to harness respect for difference with attention to the concrete, without eliminating either the desire for or the recognition of commonalities."[11] Such subjectivities are not "utterly groundless, but their grounds are shifting, provisional, passionately felt yet unreliable."[12] In a similar vein, Shane Phelan argues that a postmodern approach to identity politics requires a focus on *becoming* rather than on seeing identities as natural and fixed. In her call for a radical and democratic lesbian politics, Phelan argues that lesbians must rethink their assumptions regarding coalition and its relationship to identity. For her, this notion of coalition "enables us to join with others to fight our oppression and theirs without having to find the thread of the grand theory that connects us."[13] Such a stance involves recognizing that conflict within a coalition is not "cause for despair but grounds for continued rearticulation, new narratives of political structure and change." This definition of alliance "requires rethinking our assumptions about *everyone's* identity and sexuality, and also about politics."[14] Phelan explains:

[T]he problem for coalition politics is not, "What identities do we share?" but rather "What *might* we share as we develop our identities through the process of coalition?" Coalition cannot be simply the strategic alignment of diverse groups over a single issue, nor can coalition mean finding the real unity behind our apparently diverse struggles. Our politics must be informed by affinity rather than identity, not simply because we are not all alike, but because we each embody multiple, often conflicting, identities and locations. . . . . [W]e cannot assume that the people we work with will remain the same (or that we will, for that matter). I do not mean by this that we will work with "different" people, but that identities will change as a result of our politics.[15]

Like Butler and Ferguson, Phelan does not seek to find the "best definition of our identities so as to eliminate problems of membership and goals." Instead, she calls for a "shuffling between the need for categories and recognition of their incompleteness."[16] Jodi Dean characterizes this "we" that is continually "in process" in terms of "reflective solidarity." For Dean, such an approach replaces ascribed identities with "achieved ones," substituting "an enforced commonality of oppression with communities of those who have chosen to work and fight together."[17]

Building on the insights of feminist and queer theory, I argue that Latino identity must also be reconceived in a similar manner—as a site of permanent political contest. Rather than striving to uncover the unitary core that binds Latinos, scholars and advocates should embrace, rather than resist or deny, the instability and incompleteness of the category "Latino." This approach bears important similarities to Alan Keenan's understanding of democracy and the creation of "a people." As Keenan notes, "the people form not so much a clear ground as the open site and object of permanent debate and contestation."[18] Such an approach recognizes the persistent tension between democracy's constitutive incompleteness and its simultaneous desire to secure its accomplishments. Highlighting the ephemeral and contingent aspects of democracy shows democratic action to be both less (and more) than a form of government. Similarly, Latino political identity can also be understood in terms of collective creation and fugitive enactments. Paraphrasing the approach taken by radical democrats to popular rule, I want to suggest that we approach *Latinidad* in a similar vein: as "fragile, but no mere illusion."[19]

If taken seriously, this approach takes issue with efforts to answer the question of what Latinos actually *are* politically. Trying to settle the issue of whether

Latinos are culturally disruptive or easily assimilable, liberal or conservative, is fundamentally misguided, since such questions presume a single answer. Instead, to paraphrase Keenan, "*Latinidad* must always remain a question."[20] Understanding Latino identity as productively incomplete—a heterogeneous form of process rather than resolution—allows us to analyze and evaluate the various political formations that emerge from such provisional subject positions.

Such an approach does not mean abandoning the pragmatic political needs of subjects positioned as Latino in our society. Nor does it mean denying the racism and discrimination that Latinos have experienced as a group. As Butler reminds us, to deconstruct the subject does not mean to negate the subject. Problematizing the category "Latino" does not mean that subjects lose the ability to engage in political issues of particular concern to Latino majorities. However, by no longer grounding Latino politics within some undertheorized notions of identity, subjects will be better able to speak in terms of meaningful cultural and ideological specificity. Such specificity allows us to more fully consider the contending notions of *Latinidad* currently in play in U.S. politics. This approach to identity helps balance, as Ferguson puts it, the "desire for a stable and simple home in the world with recognition that neither stability nor simplicity is available."[21] Rather than trying to invoke *Latinidad* to secure a particular politics, scholars and advocates should confront *Latinidad*'s multifarious political possibilities, from its ability to consolidate forms of corporate power to its capacity to support progressive movements for immigration and worker's rights.

Reconsidering "Latino Interests"

By acknowledging that "Latino politics" is itself a site of contentious debate and ideological diversity, subjects who claim the category "Latino" are better able to articulate themselves as the subject of politics. This focus on the political helps displace the tendency to depict Latinos as figures of homogeneity characterized through oversimplified notions of culture, community, and tradition. By contrast, an attentiveness to the political nature of *Latinidad* exposes the ideological competition inherent in all forms of identification.

For example, while we might still speak of the "political interests of Latinos," such a claim requires a more critical theory of *interests*. Dean Mathiowetz, for example, offers a reconsideration of interest as "an activity of provoking political identity and agency."[22] Rereading Arthur Bentley and his seminal work *The Process of Government*, Mathiowetz argues that Bentley's signal contribution to the study of politics was his distinctive reading of interest and the dynamic nature of interest groups. For Bentley, it was "interest, rather than the group" that was central to his understanding of the political process.[23] Describing Bentley's approach to "interest groups," Mathiowetz writes: "[T]he groups and persons who act and are acted on in political life—do not 'have' interests that are prior to, and represented in, the political process. Rather their constitution, their being interested, is politics itself."[24] Understood as a form of activity and contestation, Bentley's reading of interest "emphasizes politics as an activity of constitution rather than representation; it reveals interest as the *manifestation* of politics, not its foundation" (italics added).[25] By contrast, later scholars of interest have characterized interest groups in more self-evident and static terms. In *The Governmental Process*, David B. Truman defines interest groups by their shared attitudes—attitudes that correspond to interests.[26] According to Mathiowetz, such an approach "turns interest into a thing, not an activity, rendering it an attribute of being to be observed rather than a moment of becoming to be described."[27] As Mathiowetz rightly notes, this shift from interaction to attitude—from something you *do* to something you *have*—makes it easier for such groups to become the proper object of social science. Pollsters and scholars of political behavior are better able to assert their claims regarding beliefs and attitudes when notions of interest are "objectified and reified."[28]

As seen in chapter 4, discussions of "Latino political interests" have often been guilty of the sort of static attitudinal approach that Mathiowetz criticizes. It is for these reasons that his effort to draw on Bentley's earlier, more "action-oriented ontology" of interest—"to see interest as a verb rather than a noun"—is so valuable. Mathiowetz's reconsideration of interest as "an activity of conjuring identity from complex and contested phenomena" allows us to reconfigure Latinos as persons and groups engaged in the process of becoming politically *interested*—as subjects whose group identities are formed through active contestation and action.[29] This approach not only suggests that "interests" be understood as an ongoing form of activity—it implies that Latino interests are multiple, crosscutting, and periodically opposed to one another.

Reconfiguring the language of interest as the process by which political identities are "contested and provoked to action" complicates political scientists' efforts to quantify and accurately measure "Latino interests." Yet the challenge of rethinking interest also applies to more qualitative theories of interest. For example, as discussed in chapter 2, democratic theorist Iris Marion Young argues for a politics of difference that involves the "specific representation of oppressed or disadvantaged groups." In *Justice and the Politics of Difference*,

Young insists that "[o]nly if oppressed groups are able to express their interests and experience in public on an equal basis with other groups can group domination through formally equal processes of participation be avoided."[30] In calling for the specific representation of social groups, she differentiates her theory from that of liberalism by claiming that her approach involves "social groups" rather than "interest groups or ideological groups." Young argues that social groups are distinct from interest or ideological groups because a social group is "a collective of persons differentiated from at least one other group by cultural forms, practices, or way of life."[31]

Yet despite her effort to transcend ideology while still giving voice and representation to the desires and concerns of oppressed groups, Young's more radical democratic ethos bears marked similarities to the more liberal notions of interest she seeks to reject. Like David Truman, Young characterizes the interests and shared attitudes of social groups as somehow prior to politics. Here, as in *The Governmental Process*, Young turns interests into something that can be observed, a *thing* that social groups possess rather than an activity in which subjects engage. In sum, scholars and advocates thinking critically and politically about interest—about how groups come to identify and create political formations—is something that needs to occur across the quantitative and qualitative divide.

Identity as Resonance: Rhizomatic versus Arboreal Readings of *Latinidad*

> We should stop believing in trees. . . . They've made us suffer too much. . . . Nothing is beautiful or loving or political aside from underground stems and aerial roots, adventitious growths and rhizomes.
>
> —Gilles Deleuze and Félix Guattari[32]

While Mathiowetz's reconsideration of interest is of enormous value, the dynamics of racial identification and the shared sensibilities that characterize *Latinidad* are not fully captured in the language of interest—even interest at its most political. In this way, Young is correct in her desire to indicate a distinction between traditional notions of ideology and interest and that which binds together the marginalized social groups she seeks to include. In the case of *Latinidad*, there *is* something about the dynamics of identification that exceeds more narrow forms of explanatory logic. In looking at the dynamics of identification at play throughout this book—during the Chicano and Puerto Rican movements, within current discussions of the "Latino vote," and exhibited during the immigrant-rights marches—it is clear that none of these moments of collective identification can be wholly understood through traditional arguments regarding self-interest, shared ideology, or linked fate. Instead, we remain in need of a political vocabulary more attentive to how the pan-ethnic impulse is produced through affinities of identity and sensibility.

In this final section, I want to offer a brief meditation on *Latinidad*'s capacity to hold together disparate elements, as well as what it might mean to approach *Latinidad* as a site of contested and constitutive political activity—as "fragile, but no mere illusion."[33] To do this, I turn to William Connolly's discussion of *resonance* alongside Gilles Deleuze and his discussion of *rhizomatic* versus *arboreal* approaches to identity. In doing this, I want to suggest that *Latinidad* might be productively understood as a practice of identity and involves forms of resonance that are rhizomatic in nature.[34]

In *A Thousand Plateaus*, Deleuze and coauthor Félix Guattari endorse a rhizomatic style of thinking, acting, and writing; they define a *rhizome*—a term taken from botany—as a continuously growing horizontal underground stem that puts out lateral shoots and adventitious roots at intervals. For Deleuze, the image of the rhizome represents that which has no fixed center but is characterized instead by multiplicities, unexpected assemblages, and directions in motion. Deleuze and Guattari write:

> A rhizome . . . is absolutely different from roots and radicles; bulbs and tubers are rhizomes. . . . A rhizome may be broken, shattered at a given spot, but it will start up again on one of its old lines, or on new lines. . . . There is rupture in the rhizome whenever segmentary lines explode into a line of flight, but the line of flight is part of the rhizome. . . . [A]ny point of a rhizome can be connected to anything other, and must be. This is very different from the tree or root, which plots a point, fixes an order. . . . Perhaps one of the most important characteristics of the rhizome is that it always has multiple entryways.[35]

Rhizomes, like all forms of life, are largely defined by connections. Such connections also enable what Deleuze describes as "lines of flight," forms of change and transformation that break away from preexisting forces of stratification and standardization. Lines of flight are an always-existing possibility; they can occur at any time and lead in any direction.

The logic of the rhizome stands in contrast to what Deleuze characterizes as forms and practices that are more "tree-like" or arboreal. For Deleuze, "rigid segmentarity is always expressed by the Tree. The Tree is the knot of arborescence or principle of dichotomy; it is the axis of rotation guaranteeing concentricity."[36]

Arboreal structures involve radicles, trunks, and taproots, all of which imply order, origins, unities, and entireties. Deleuze equates binary logic with the arboreal—that which is unbroken, primary, and whole. Calling binary logic "the spiritual reality of the root-tree," he argues that this system of thought assumes a strong principal unity and lacks an understanding of multiplicity."[37]

Unlike the tree, a rhizome is not an object of origins and reproduction but, rather, random, proliferating, and decentered. That which is rhizomatic operates by "variation, expansion, conquest, capture, offshoots":

> [U]nlike trees or their roots, the rhizome connects to any point to any other point, and its traits are not necessarily linked to traits of the same nature; it brings into play very different regimes of signs. . . . The rhizome is reducible neither to the One nor the multiple. . . . It is composed not of units but of dimensions or rather directions in motion. It has neither beginning nor end, but always a middle (milieu) from which it grows and which it overspills.[38]

For Deleuze, the rhizomatic and the arborescent "aren't opposites per se; they can infiltrate each other." There sometimes exist tree or root structures in rhizomes, and "A new rhizome may form in the heart of a tree, the hollow of a root, the crook of a branch."[39] Yet ultimately, "[t]he tree is filiation, but the rhizome is alliance, uniquely, alliance." The rhizome represents principles of connections and heterogeneity. Always in the middle, the rhizome has no beginning and no end; it is always between things, "interbeing *intermezzo*."[40]

Thinking with Deleuze, I suggest that the practice of *Latinidad* is rhizomatic in nature. More often than not, Latino pan-ethnicity has been conceptualized in arboreal terms; in other words, anxiety about that which is rhizomatic has often led to its displacement in the politics of *Latinidad*. For example, both the Chicano movement and the Puerto Rican movement involved lines of flight: they both mark moments of transformation that broke away from preexisting forces of stratification and oppression. Yet these moments of connection and transformation, which I previously described in terms of democratic openness, also produced moments of closure as lines of flight were captured and reterritorialized through the more confining logic of group unity. I understand such moments of democratic closure as being arboreal in nature. Certainly the movements' nationalism can be understood as a kind of tree logic, a logic based on the presumption of a strong principal unity. Moreover, with its emphasis on roots and origins, nationalism's related language of cultural authenticity can be read as what Deleuze characterizes as the logic of "tracing and reproduction."[41] Animated by commitments to hierarchy, repetition, and familiarity, nationalism's emphasis on cultural maintenance and preestablished paths made it difficult for participants to embrace the contingency, modifications, and unexpected displays of agonism that define politics.

Latino pan-ethnicity has also been understood in arboreal terms, with advocates of *Latinidad*'s political possibilities often conceptualizing pan-ethnic identity with some fundamental unity in mind. *Latinidad*'s "trunk"—its essential woody stem—has been identified as (among other things) the Spanish language, religion, class consciousness, and/or the shared experience of discrimination. In each instance, Latino pan-ethnicity's vertical logic has presumed an identifiable taproot.

But *Latinidad* is much more fruitfully conceptualized as rhizomatic. Rather than presuming the existence of a taproot, we should understand Latino pan-ethnicity as a process of connections and interactions, what Deleuze describes as "collective assemblages of enunciation."[42] *Latinidad*'s multiplicity is rhizomatic, a practice of identity capable of proliferating in unexpected places. Understood as a form of action, *Latinidad* has no fixed center—it can start up new lines from where it was once broken or shattered. Random and proliferating, a rhizomatic reading of Latino pan-ethnicity finds value in its capacity to be decentered, opportunistic, and expansive.

Most intriguingly, conceptualizing *Latinidad* as rhizomatic suggests that Latino identity has no telos. Rather than being defined in terms of some particular end, *Latinidad* "is always in the middle, between things . . . *intermezzo*." This definition helps to highlight Latino pan-ethnicity as a practice of becoming that understands itself in terms of circulation rather than arrival or completion. Since rhizomes "connect any point to any other point," this reading of *Latinidad* emphasizes the unexpected assemblages that are created from its connections.

Likewise, the 2006 immigrant-rights marches can be read in rhizomatic terms. Despite some advocates' tendency to describe the marches in terms of what Deleuze might characterize as a tracing or reproduction of earlier movements, the marches can be read as what Deleuze describes as "a map and not a tracing." In contrast to a tracing, a map is:

> detachable, reversible, susceptible to constant modification. It can be torn, reversed, adapted to any kind of mounting, reworked by an individual, group, or social formation. It can be drawn on a wall, conceived of as a work of art, constructed as a political action or as a meditation. . . . The coordinates are determined not by theoretical analyses implying universals but by a pragmatics composing multiplicities or aggregates of intensities.[43]

Understood in terms of the map, the marches were "open and connectable in all of [their] dimensions." In this way, the 2006 marches can be productively conceived as lines of flight.

Thinking of *Latinidad* as rhizomatic provides us with a dynamic imagery that is multiple through and through. Such an understanding of Latino pan-ethnicity is amenable to unexpected connections and semiotic chains. Rhizomatic readings move us away from a politics emphasizing that which is mimetic and duplicative. Instead, this reading of *Latinidad* imagines transformational multiplicities, off-shoots, and unexpected alliances. Instead of foundations, the rhizome proceeds from that which is already in process, in the middle of things.

I acknowledge that such claims sound both poetic and abstract. But such depictions seem to capture the current proliferation of Latino politics and political identities emerging across the country: undocumented Guatemalan labor activists living in North Carolina; Puerto Rican Libertarians attending college in New Jersey; young Chicano environmentalists attending Morrissey concerts in Los Angeles and supporting Hillary Clinton in the 2008 Democratic primary; Nicaraguan evangelicals supporting conservative ballot initiatives in Florida; Mexican American senior citizens registering voters in Colorado; queer Cuban radicals campaigning for Barack Obama in New York. *This is rhizomatic Latinidad.* Who knows what sort of ideological stems and shoots might emerge, what sorts of multiplicities, ideological infiltrations, and political alliances might be created by such subjects?

Affinities of Identity: Identification and the Politics of Resonance

Throughout this book, I have tried to approach *Latinidad* as a moment when diverse and even disparate subjects claim identification with one another. Such affiliations do not necessarily imply deep structure—they can be drawn from coordinates that are sometimes more cultural than ideological, more regional than partisan. Such connections might involve an emphasis on physiognomy and language rather than policy preferences.

In "The Evangelical-Capitalist Resonance Machine," William Connolly discusses the politics of resonance and the ways in which affinities of identity and latent intensities often inform our politics. Drawing on Deleuze, Connolly argues that the alliance between "cowboy capitalism" and evangelical Christianity in the United States cannot be understood solely through the categories of causality or ideology. Instead, similar spiritual dispositions of various constituencies are folded into different ideologies and creeds. These dispositions are then amplified through what Connolly describes as "the media politics of resonance." For Connolly, "causation as resonance" helps elucidate the logic of certain political and cultural alliances:

[C]ausality morphs into energized complexities of mutual imbrication and interinvolvement, in which heretofore unconnected or loosely associated elements fold, blend, emulsify, and dissolve into the other, forging a qualitative assemblage resistant to classical models of explanation. . . .

Identities are composed of a mixture of faith, doctrine, and sensibility. The affect-imbued ideas that compose them are installed in the soft tissue of affect, emotion, habit, and posture as well as the upper reaches of the intellect. These sensibilities trigger the responses of those imbued with them even before they begin to think about this or that event. This is particularly so when complementary dispositions loop back and forth in a large political machine, with each constituency helping to crystallize, amplify, and legitimize the dispositions of the whole.[44]

According to Connolly, the ethos of the "resonance machine" can be understood as an "unsung melody" that "reverberates back and forth between leaders and followers, until it becomes uncertain who directs and who sings the chorus."[45] In this way, the ethos of the resonance machine is capable of being "expressed without being articulated."[46]

While Connolly's analysis examines the evangelical-capitalist resonance machine of the Bush-Cheney era, he acknowledges that other doctrines and movements "are not immune to this sort of contagion."[47] And while Connolly focuses on the resonance machine's more antidemocratic capacities (the will to revenge, its resentment of cultural diversity and economic egalitarianism, etc.), this language of resonance is equally compelling when thinking about the elements of sensibility and ethos that often characterize Latino identity. Put somewhat differently, *Latinidad* is also a practice characterized by affinities of identity and shaped by incomplete and uncertain correlations between "economic interest, class position, formal religious doctrine, educational level, and age."[48]

Appreciating *Latinidad* as resonance recognizes that political identification is not just ideological but rhizomatic, driven not only by interest but by sensibility and other "affect-imbued ideas." Such affinities of identity are capable of creating intensities and assemblages that often *feel* foundational. This is particularly true when subjects are uncertain about their interests.

Connolly's depiction of the resonance machine reminds us that what Sheldon Wolin describes as "evanescent homogeneity"—the experience of commonality that is "forever possible, yet never guaranteed"—is enriched by a Deleuzean appreciation of resonance. In invoking an "unsung melody" whose ethos can be "expressed without being articulated," Connolly recalls how seductive affinities of identity can be. Further thinking about the political and theoretical possibilities of Latino pan-ethnicity demands more attention to such affective practices. Considering such rhizomatic encounters, though, highlights the fact that practices of identification are not limited to a politics defined by unity or homogeneity. In fact, *Latinidad*'s capacity for democratic assemblages and lines of flight requires leaving behind such unitary impulses.

Yet dreams of unity remain enormously seductive. In the realm of Latino politics, unity has implied political power and recognition—the emergence of that long-awaited "sleeping giant" whose will and agency cannot be ignored. But as I hope these pages have shown, such aspirations leave too little room for legitimate difference—and for democracy. This work suggests a different approach. Leaving the giant behind, let us consider a more explicitly political understanding of identity: one that celebrates specificity, the political capacities of engaged localities, and the possibility that human beings can be transformed through the shared practice of acting and speaking together.

Notes

Introduction

1. Waldron, "Farm Workers End Texas March for Wage Bill."
2. Godsell, "Hispanics in the US."
3. Johnson, "Vasquez Tells Latinos Their Time Has Come."
4. Ramos, *The Latino Wave*, pp. xvii–xviii.
5. Aizenman, "Immigration Debate Wakes a 'Sleeping Latino Giant.'"
6. See DeSipio and de la Garza, "Forever Seen as New," pp. 398–409.
7. U.S. Census Bureau, http://www.census.gov.
8. As Lisa J. Montoya notes, the metaphor of a giant was first used to describe the *national* pan-ethnic Latino electorate even before it was used to describe any ethnic-specific state electorate. See Montoya, "The Sleeping Giant in Latino Electoral Politics," p. 41.
9. Montoya, "The Sleeping Giant in Latino Electoral Politics," p. 42.
10. At the March 10, 2006, demonstration for immigrant rights in Chicago, for example, an estimated 100,000 to 300,000 rallied with the cry "El gigante despierta" (The giant wakes). See Wang and Winn, *Groundswell Meets Groundwork*, p. 6.
11. Bosse, a French artist, created the frontispiece etching for *Leviathan*'s 1651 publication with input from Hobbes.
12. Garcia, "The Chicano Movement," p. 92.
13. Oboler, *Ethnic Labels, Latino Lives*, pp. 17–18. This type of racist homogenization also occurred prior to the pan-ethnic experience. In his seminal book *North from Mexico: The Spanish-Speaking People of the United States*, Carey McWilliams discusses the ways in which Mexican Americans, regardless of their socioeconomic class, regional history, or citizenship status, were discriminated against as a generalized foreign Other. Describing the California gold rush of 1849, McWilliams writes: "[W]hether residents of twenty years' standing or immigrants of one week, all the Spanish-speaking were lumped together as interlopers and greasers" (*North from Mexico*, p. 132).
14. Latinos are not the only multi-ethnic group in the United States to recognize the emotional power of pan-ethnicity. Eric Liu, discussing Asian Americans, describes

pan-Asian identity as a form of "self-defense." Pan-Asian solidarity "is an affirming coun-ter-statement to the narrative in which yellow people are either foreigners or footnotes. It is a bulwark against bigotry" (*The Accidental Asian*, p. 63).

15. Huntington, *Who Are We?* p. 324.

16. See chapter 9 of *Who Are We?*

17. Dávila, *Latino Spin*, p. 1.

18. Butler, "Contingent Foundations," p. 17.

19. Butler, "Contingent Foundations," p. 8.

20. By "Latino political elites," I am referring primarily to those Latinos who advocate for the political empowerment of Latinos in the United States at the state, national, and local levels. This definition of "political elites" includes elected officials, grassroots activists, administrative professionals/bureaucrats, and scholars of Latino politics.

21. Cubans and Central and South American subgroups constitute a much smaller por-tion of the national population, with Cubans making up 3.4 percent, Salvadorans 3 percent, and Dominicans 2.8 percent (the remaining Latinos are of other Central American, South American, or other Hispanic or Latino origin). These smaller populations also continue to be concentrated in a relatively small number of cities. For example, roughly half of the nation's Dominicans live in New York City, and more than half of the nation's Cubans are in Miami–Dade County, Florida (U.S. Census Bureau).

22. Hero, *Latinos and the U.S. Political System*, p. 1. For more recent discussions of the Latinos as underresearched populations, see Espino, Leal, and Meier, *Latino Politics*; Garcia, *Latino Politics in America*; Garcia, "Symposium."

23. Some of the most recent and significant texts in this category include Oropeza, *¡Raza Sí! ¡Guerra No!*; Mariscal, *Brown-Eyed Children of the Sun*; Pulido, *Black, Brown, Yellow, and Left*; Melendez, *We Took the Streets*; Chávez, *¡Mi Raza Primero! (My People First!)*; Garcia, *Chicana Feminist Thought*; García, *Chicanismo*; Gutiérrez, *The Making of a Chicano Militant*; Rosales, *Chicano!*; Torres and Katsiaficas, *Latino Social Movements*; Torres and Velázquez, *The Puerto Rican Movement*; Marquez, *LULAC*; Anaya and Lomeli, *Aztlán*; and Muñoz, *Youth, Identity, Power*.

24. An exception to this tendency is Ernesto Chávez's book *¡Mi Raza Primero! (My People First!)*. One of the first nonparticipants to write seriously about the Chicano move-ment, Chávez argues that one major reason the movement failed to achieve its goals was "because of its essentialist imaginings of a community driven by an ideologically bankrupt cultural nationalism." See *¡Mi Raza Primero!*, p. 120. Yet as I discuss later in this chapter, Chávez's critique suffers from an excessive pessimism regarding the "failure" of the move-ment due to its conflicting ideologies.

25. For examples of this tendency to criticize the movement for its ideological and stra-tegic diversity, see García, *Chicanismo*, pp. 86–87, 142–43; Gómez-Quiñones, *Chicano Poli-tics*, pp. 5, 213; and Torres and Velázquez, *The Puerto Rican Movement*, p. 215.

26. Significant texts that deal with these aspects of Latino politics include Espino, Leal, and Meier, *Latino Politics*; a number of works by de la Garza and DeSipio, *Muted Voices*; *Awash in the Mainstream*; *Ethnic Ironies*; *Barrio Ballots*; *From Rhetoric to Reality*; and *Latino Voices*; DeSipio, *Counting on the Latino Vote*; Garcia, *Pursuing Power*; and Hero, *Latinos and the U.S. Political System*.

27. Examples of this research include García Bedolla, *Fluid Borders* and *Latino Politics*; Rosales, *The Illusion of Inclusion*; Marquez, *Constructing Identities in Mexican American Political Organizations* and *LULAC*; Jones-Correa, *Between Two Nations*; Flores and Benmayor, *Latino Cultural Citizenship*; de Genova and Ramos-Zayas, *Latino Crossings*; Gómez-Quiñones, *Chicano Politics*; Hardy-Fanta, *Latina Politics, Latino Politics*; Hardy-Fanta and Gerson, *Latino Politics in Massachusetts*; Garcia, *Latino Politics in America*; Laó-Montes and Dávila, *Mambo Montage*; Maciel and Ortiz, *Chicanas/Chicanos at the Crossroads*; Romero, Hondagneu-Sotelo, and Ortiz, *Challenging Fronteras*; Schmidt, *Language Policy and Identity Politics in the United States*; Vélez-Ibáñez and Sampaio, *Transnational Latina/o Communities*; Vigil, *Hispanics in Congress*; Villarreal and Hernandez, *Latinos and Political Coalitions*.

28. It is significant that there are almost no book-length manuscripts focusing on political theory in relation to Latino politics in the United States. One of the few books in the field is Edwina Barvosa's *Wealth of Selves: Multiple Identities, Mestiza Consciousness, and the Subject of Politics*.

29. One of the few works at the intersection of Latino studies and philosophy is Linda Martín Alcoff's *Visible Identities: Race, Gender, and the Self*. A major and much-needed contribution to the fields of both philosophy and Latino studies, *Visible Identities* draws on both philosophical sources and empirical studies in the social sciences to argue against critics of identity who presume that attachments to particular social identities are innately pathological or inescapably essentialist and conformist. Instead, by arguing that identities are historical formations whose political implications are always open to interpretation, Alcoff is able to draw on phenomenological approaches to embodiment that highlight the visual and material aspects of racialized and gendered identities. In *Visible Identities*, Alcoff seeks to engage the long-standing "culture wars" over identity politics, arguing against those who seek to simply repudiate any and all political claims grounded in racial or gendered identities. By contrast, my project is less a defense of identity politics than a work of democratic theory seeking to analyze contemporary Latino political thought and practice.

30. Some of the best examples of this scholarship include Wright, *Disposable Women and Other Myths of Global Capitalism*; Dávila, *Latino Spin, Barrio Dreams*, and *Latinos, Inc.*; Behdad, *A Forgetful Nation*; Lima, *The Latino Body*; Dorsey, *Pachangas*; Rodriguez, *Queer Latinidad*; Poblete, *Critical Latin American and Latino Studies*; Vila, *Ethnography at the Border*; Habell-Pallán and Romero, *Latino/a Popular Culture*; Sarlo, *Scenes from Postmodern Life*; Flores, *From Bomba to Hip-Hop*; García Canclini, *Hybrid Cultures* and *Consumers and Citizens*; Muñoz, *Disidentifications*; Joseph and Fink, *Performing Hybridity*; Gómez-Peña, *The New World Border* and *Warriors for Gringostroika*; Michaelsen and Johnson, *Border Theory*; Arteaga, *An Other Tongue*; Fusco, *English Is Broken Here*; Noriega, *Chicanos and Film*; Yúdice, Franco, and Flores, *On Edge*.

31. At times, these practices were related. During the movement era, for example, rallies, marches, and other forms of embodied public action were crucial to creating conditions of community while simultaneously avoiding the political differences that would have emerged had participants engaged in deliberative public speech.

32. Brown, "At the Edge," in *Edgework*, p. 74.

33. Ibid.

34. Brown, "At the Edge," in *Edgework*, pp. 74–75.

35. My approach here is indebted to Seyla Benhabib's discussion of Arendt and the need to confound her sometimes-impermeable categorical distinctions. See Benhabib, "Kantian Questions, Arendtian Answers," p. 173.

Chapter 1

1. See Pulido, *Black, Brown, Yellow, and Left*; Melendez, *We Took the Streets*; García, *Chicanismo*; Muñoz, *Youth, Identity, Power*; and de la Garza, "The Political Socialization of Chicano Elites."

2. According to de la Garza, a "political generation" is shaped by a shared experience of social upheaval that leads to a collective reevaluation of social norms and values. See de la Garza, "Chicano Elites and National Policymaking," p. 315.

3. Torres and Velázquez, *The Puerto Rican Movement*, p. xiii.

4. Gosse, "Postmodern America," in Gosse and Moser, *The World the Sixties Made*, p. 25.

5. As José Ramón Sánchez notes, "Many of the institutions and leaders that emerged after the Lords, like the Puerto Rican Legal Defense and Education Fund and El Museo, had ex-Lords or associates as leaders and founders." See Sánchez, *Boricua Power*, p. 209.

6. See "Bustamante Won't Renounce Ties to Chicano Student Group," August 28, 2003, Foxnews.com; and John Leo, "Ignoring Radical Racialism," *U.S. News & World Report*, September 15, 2003.

7. Sotomayor was a member of National Council of La Raza and, from 1980 until 1992, a board member of the Puerto Rican Legal Defense and Education Fund. She resigned from the PRLDEF when she became a federal judge. See Charlie Savage, "Republicans Question Sotomayor's Role in Puerto Rican Group's Legal Battles," *New York Times*, July 2, 2009; Krissah Thompson, "Latino Groups Step Up Support of Sotomayor," *Washington Post*, June 1, 2009.

8. Pulido, *Black, Brown, Yellow, and Left*, p. 216.

9. García, *Chicanismo*, p. 3.

10. Mariscal, *Brown-Eyed Children of the Sun*, p. 3.

11. Barrera, "The Historical Evolution of Chicano Ethnic Goals."

12. Gómez-Quiñones, *Chicano Politics*, p. 62.

13. Márquez, *LULAC*, p. 20.

14. It should be noted that the line between mainstream Mexican American liberals and later Chicano radicals could be porous. Before founding the Crusade for Justice, for example, Rodolfo "Corky" Gonzáles was an active participant in mainstream Democratic Party politics in Colorado, serving as a Democratic district captain. Interestingly, Gonzáles's background as a boxing champion led to a form of local sports celebrity that served as a stepping-stone to his political career both among Anglos in the Democratic Party and later among Mexican Americans and Chicano activists. See Romero, "Wearing the Red, White, and Blue Trunks of Aztlán," pp. 96, 101.

15. This is not to say that there was no leftist presence in the Mexican American community during this era. Activists such as Josefina Fierro de Bright and Luisa Moreno founded the Spanish-Speaking Congress in 1938. This organization represented the attempt of some members of this generation to form a working-class movement in coalition with other progressive liberals. But the largest and most visible organizations during this era were

liberal-centrist (LULAC, American G.I. Forum, etc.). For more information about this era, see García's *Mexican Americans*.

16. Barrera, "The Historical Evolution of Chicano Ethnic Goals," p. 10.

17. The American G.I. Forum was organized after a funeral home in Texas refused burial services for a Mexican American veteran, Felix Longoria. Anger over the incident led to the 1949 founding of the organization by Hector García (a physician, surgeon, and World War II veteran), attorney Gus Garcia, and other Mexican American veterans. See Gómez-Quiñones, *Chicago Politics*, p. 60.

18. Muñoz, *Youth, Identity, Power*, pp. 47–48.

19. Muñoz, *Youth, Identity, Power*, pp. 64–65.

20. In 1968, for example, more than a thousand students walked out of Abraham Lincoln High School in East Los Angeles to protest staggeringly high dropout rates, inadequate facilities, and a tracking system that steered them toward unskilled, low-paying jobs. These walkouts (or "blowouts," as they were dubbed by the organizers) lasted eight days and ultimately involved more than 3,500 Chicano high school students. The protests disrupted the nation's largest school district and captured front-page headlines and national attention. In terms of numbers, the student strike represented "the first major mass protest ever undertaken by Mexican-Americans" (Muñoz, *Youth, Identity, Power*, p. xi). Three months after the blowouts, thirteen of the strike organizers were indicted by the Los Angeles County grand jury for conspiracy to "willfully disturb the peace and quiet" of the city of Los Angeles and disrupt the education process. The defendants became publicly known as the Los Angeles 13, and their trial marked the early use of conspiracy charges leveled against activists. Later that same year, the Chicago Seven would become another group of activists charged with conspiracy, for their protest activities at the 1968 Democratic National Convention. Similar student walkouts occurred in other states. See Barrera, "The 1968 Edcouch-Elsa High School Walkout," pp. 83–115.

21. Pulido, *Black, Brown, Yellow, and Left*, p. 75.

22. Oboler, *Ethnic Labels, Latino Lives*, p. 64.

23. Chávez, *¡Mi Raza Primero! (My People First!)*, p. 118.

24. Oboler, *Ethnic Labels, Latino Lives*, pp. 61–62.

25. According to Ignacio García, José Angel Gutiérrez was a political science graduate student at St. Mary's University in San Antonio. Selected as the chief coordinator of the emerging political party, Gutiérrez was a veteran activist of the Chicano movement and had also grown up in Crystal City. The other leader of the Crystal City effort was Mario Compeán, a former migrant farmworker in his late twenties who was then a freshman political science major at St. Mary's. In winter 1969, a successful student strike at a Crystal City high school provided the political base to officially launch the party in January 1970. That year, the party put up three candidates (including Gutiérrez) for the school board and two candidates for city council. The Gutiérrez-led ticket swept the three seats with 55 percent of the vote. A week later, the two candidates for city council won with 60 percent of the vote. When two Mexican American incumbents—one on the school board and one on the city council—shifted allegiance from the Democratic Party to La Raza Unida, Chicanos officially had political control of the city. For the first time in Texas history, Mexican Americans controlled the schools in a heavily Mexican town. See Garcia, *United We Win*, pp. 15–16, 59.

26. Oboler, *Ethnic Labels, Latino Lives*, pp. 67–68.

27. Some examples of this cultural renaissance include musical bands such as Santana, Malo, War, and La Onda Chicana; authors such as Rudolfo Anaya, Tomás Rivera, and Oscar "Zeta" Acosta; playwrights such as Luis Valdez (founder of Teatro Campesino); poets such as Alurista, José Montoya, and Jimmy Santiago Baca; and art collectives such as the Royal Chicano Air Force.

28. Given the significance of the student movement to the Chicano movement's ideological development and overall success, my research focuses on student-led organizations and the significant political and theoretical documents produced by, for, and about Chicano students, including the previously discussed *El Plan Espiritual de Aztlán* (1969), *El Plan de Santa Barbara* (1969), and the political poem/manifesto "Yo Soy Joaquín/I Am Joaquín" (1967).

29. García, *Chicanismo*, p. 3.

30. Ibid.

31. Vigil, *The Crusade for Justice*.

32. *El Plan Espiritual Aztlán*, in *Aztlán*, pp. 1–5.

33. This geographic region is composed of the territory that Mexico ceded in 1848 in the Treaty of Guadalupe Hidalgo.

34. Klor de Alva, "Aztlán, Borinquen and Hispanic Nationalism in the United States," p. 149.

35. Ibid.

36. Rodríguez-Morazzani, "Political Cultures of the Puerto Rican Left in the United States," p. 33.

37. Falcon, "A History of Puerto Rican Politics in New York City," p. 19.

38. By 1894, there were 3,000 cigar factories in New York City. In 1916, *tabaqueros* made up 60 percent of the Puerto Rican population in the city. By 1918, there were more than 4,500 Puerto Ricans in cigar-maker unions in New York. See Falcon, "A History of Puerto Rican Politics in New York City," p. 23.

39. The intellectual and political impact of the *lector* tradition is powerfully portrayed by Bernardo Vega in *Memoirs of Bernardo Vega*. Describing his experience in 1916 working at the cigar factory "El Morito" on Eighty-sixth Street off Third Avenue in Manhattan, he writes:

> "El Morito" seemed like a university. At the time the official "reader" was Fernando García. He would read to us for one hour in the morning and one in the afternoon. He dedicated the morning session to current news and events of the day. . . . The afternoon sessions were devoted to more substantial readings of a political and literary nature. A Committee on Reading suggested the books to be read, and their recommendations were voted on by all the workers in the shop. The readings alternated between works of philosophical, political, or scientific interest, and novels, chosen from the writings of Zola, Dumas, Victor Hugo, Flaubert, Jules Verne, Pierre Loti, Vargas Vila, Pérez Galdós, Palacio Valdés, Dostoyevski, Gogol, Gorky or Tolstoy. All these authors were well known to the cigarworkers at the time.
>
> It used to be that a factory reader would choose the texts himself, and they were mostly light reading, like the novels of Pérez Escrich, Luis Val, and the like. But as they developed politically, the workers had more and more to say in the selection. Their preference for works of social theory won out. From then on the readings were most often from books by Gustave LeBon, Ludwig Buchner, Darwin, Marx, Engels, Bakunin. . . .

The practice [of factory readings] began in the factories of Viñas & Co., in Bejucal, Cuba, around 1864. . . . Emigrants to Key West and Tampa introduced the practice into the United States around 1869. . . . In Puerto Rico the practice spread with the development of cigar production, and it was Cubans and Puerto Ricans who brought it to New York. It is safe to say that there were no factories with Hispanic cigarworkers without a reader. Things were different in the English-speaking shops where, as far as I know, no such readings took place. (*Memoirs of Bernardo Vega*, pp. 21–22)

40. Flores, "Translator's Preface," in Vega, *Memoirs of Bernardo Vega*, p. x.

41. Falcon, "A History of Puerto Rican Politics in New York City," p. 23.

42. Following the Depression and World War II, the remainder of the Puerto Rican left fell victim to McCarthyism and the general shift to a more conservative national political climate. The terrorist attacks on President Harry Truman and on congressmen in the U.S. House of Representatives by Puerto Rican nationalists in 1950 and 1954 also made supporting Puerto Rican independence and other radical causes less acceptable politically. In 1950, Puerto Rican nationalists attacked the Blair House in Washington, D.C., in an effort to assassinate President Truman (who was living at Blair House while the White House was being remodeled). Truman was not hurt, but the incident drew global attention to Puerto Rican nationalism. Following the assassination attempt, in 1954, three Puerto Rican nationalists fired eight shots from the gallery of the House of Representatives. Five congressmen were injured, and the nationalists (led by Lolita Lebron) were captured and sent to prison. Following the attacks, Puerto Rican nationalists and socialists were placed under increased surveillance, and FBI agents visited the homes of suspected terrorists. During the period, many Puerto Rican civic elites sought to distance themselves from these violent events and from the independence movement and left-wing politics more generally. See Rodríguez-Morazzani, "Political Cultures of the Puerto Rican Left in the United States," p. 32; Baver, "Puerto Rican Politics in New York City," p. 45.

43. Torres, "Political Radicalism in the Diaspora," p. 5.

44. Ibid.

45. Sánchez, *Boricua Power*, p. 131.

46. Sánchez, *Boricua Power*, p. 205.

47. Sánchez, *Boricua Power*, p. 202.

48. Sánchez, *Boricua Power*, p. 207.

49. In addition to the work of Sánchez, my analysis of the significance of the Young Lords Party to the Puerto Rican movement is based in part on the claim that the activism and mass resistance that characterized the Young Lords "left a mark" on the collective memory of U.S.-raised Puerto Ricans. Scholars such as Agustín Laó-Montes and Juan Flores cite a number of recent examples in which Puerto Rican activists lay claim to the Young Lords' historical mantle. Writes Laó-Montes: "I remembered the young leaders of the CUNY student strikes of the early nineties claiming to be acting in the spirit of the Young Lords; the Latino anti–Gulf war group in Brooklyn called Young Latinos for Peace, honoring the acronym YLP (Young Lords Party); and recent newspaper articles on two East Harlem gangs (Netas & Latin Kings) who, admittedly inspired by the Lords, moved their ranks to work in a local electoral campaign" (Laó-Montes, "Resources of Hope," p. 35). Similarly, Juan Flores cites the Young Lords as an inspiration and model of "militancy and righteous defiance" for a new generation of politically engaged Latinos:

[T]hat heyday is long past, no longer even a living memory for young Latinos. But the Brown Berets and the Young Lords party, the Chicano Moratorium and the Lincoln Hospital takeover are still an inspiration, a model of militancy and righteous defiance for the present generation of Latinos of all nationalities as they sharpen their social and political awareness. For although the immediacy, intensity, and cultural effervescence has no doubt waned in the intervening decades, Latinos in the United States have just as assuredly continued to grow as a social movement to be reckoned with, nationally and internationally, in the years ahead. ("The Latino Imaginary: Meanings of Community and Identity," in *From Bomba to Hip-Hop*, p. 191)

50. Morales, "Palante, Siempre Palante! The Young Lords," p. 215.

51. Melendez, *We Took the Streets*, p. 87. Leaders in the Young Lords also initiated contact with other radical organizations, including the Weather Underground. Eventually, concern for their own safety and the possible need for self-defense led the Young Lords to organize what Melendez described as a "combat ready underground organization able to coordinate actions in New York and Puerto Rico . . . to draw attention to the colonial status of our home country and the injustices we suffered on the mainland" (pp. 130–31). As commander of the underground in charge of recruiting, training, and arming the organization, Melendez describes this nascent aspect of the organization involving weapons training as well as the establishing of safe houses (p. 134).

52. Laó-Montes, "Resources of Hope," p. 41.

53. Morales, "Palante, Siempre Palante! The Young Lords," p. 215; Melendez, *We Took the Streets*, pp. 126, 168.

54. Morales, "Palante, Siempre Palante! The Young Lords," pp. 220–22.

55. Guzmán, "La Vida Pura," p. 158.

56. Serrano, "'Rifle, Cañon, y Escopeta!'" p. 133.

57. Melendez, *We Took the Streets*, p. 192.

58. Flores, *Divided Borders*, p. 183.

59. Young Lords Party and Abramson, *Palante*, p. 73.

60. Young Lords Party and Abramson, *Palante*, p. 12; Laó-Montes, "Resources of Hope," p. 43.

61. García, *Chicanismo*, p. 4.

62. Pietri, "Puerto Rican Obituary," pp. 433, 438.

63. Melendez, *We Took the Streets*, p. 85.

64. *El Plan de Santa Barbara*, in Muñoz, *Youth, Identity, Power*, p. 191.

65. Muñoz, *Youth, Identity, Power*, p. 61.

66. Barrera, "The Historical Evolution of Chicano Ethnic Goals," p. 23.

67. Morales, "Palante, Siempre Palante! The Young Lords," p. 215.

68. Barrera, "The Historical Evolution of Chicano Ethnic Goals," p. 23.

69. *El Plan Espiritual de Aztlán*, in *Aztlán*, pp. 2–3.

70. *El Plan de Santa Barbara*, in Muñoz, *Youth, Identity, Power*, p. 196.

71. Young Lords Party and Abramson, *Palante*, p. 57.

72. Laó-Montes, "Resources of Hope," p. 36; Melendez, *We Took the Streets*, pp. 84, 86.

73. Young Lords Party and Abramson, *Palante*, p. 9.

74. *El Plan de Santa Barbara*, in Muñoz, *Youth, Identity, Power*, pp. 191–92.

75. Garcia, *Chicanismo*, p. 133.

76. Pablo Puente was initially disqualified by the city attorney because he did not own property, as the city charter required. The Mexican American Legal Defense and Education Fund managed to restore him to the ballot in time for the election. See García, *United We Win*, p. 57.

77. García, *United We Win*, p. 74.

78. García, *United We Win*, p. 58.

79. Laó-Montes, "Resources of Hope," p. 40.

80. Torres, "Political Radicalism in the Diaspora," p. 13.

81. In recent years, the paranoid literalism of right-wing critics has led them to interpret the concept of Aztlán as proof that many Latinos in the United States are members of a radical secessionist movement called "the *reconquista*." See Buchanan, *The Death of the West* and *State of Emergency*.

82. Melendez, *We Took the Streets*, p. 120.

83. Young Lords Party and Abramson, *Palante*, p. 83.

84. Laó-Montes, "Resources of Hope," p. 41.

85. Melendez, *We Took the Streets*, p. 120.

86. Melendez, *We Took the Streets*, p. 190.

87. Laó-Montes, "Resources of Hope," p. 41.

88. Morales, "PALANTE, SIEMPRE PALANTE! The Young Lords," p. 221.

89. Young Lords Party and Abramson, *Palante*, p. 158.

90. This desire to construct a progressive narrative of resistance and unity is visible in the Young Lords' history of Puerto Rico. According to Laó-Montes, the "genealogy of anti-colonial resistance" constructed by the Young Lords involves an ideologically selective reading of Puerto Rican political history (including what Laó-Montes describes as an "acrobatic historical jump" between "El Grito de Lares" in 1868 and the Nationalist Party of the 1930s. Laó-Montes also describes the Young Lords as practicing a "conspiracy theory of imperial power" to explain the lack of success of the Nationalist Party in Puerto Rico ("Resources of Hope," p. 41).

91. Laó-Montes, "Resources of Hope," pp. 41.

92. Melendez, *We Took the Streets*, p. 193.

93. Morales, "PALANTE, SIEMPRE PALANTE! The Young Lords," p. 222.

94. Melendez, *We Took the Streets*, p. 193.

95. Morales, "PALANTE, SIEMPRE PALANTE! The Young Lords," p. 221.

96. Laó-Montes describes how the group "degenerated" from a "popular radical left" to a "strict ideological left." See "Resources of Hope," p. 44.

97. According to Laó-Montes, the Young Lords' tendency to conflate "party with people" was linked to the organization's desire for an "unmediated relationship between state and capital" that left little space for difference and contradiction. See Laó-Montes, "Resources of Hope," p. 41.

98. Morales, "PALANTE, SIEMPRE PALANTE! The Young Lords," p. 221.

99. Melendez, *We Took the Streets*, p. 197.

100. Muñoz, *Youth, Identity, Power*, p. 101.

101. *El Plan Espiritual de Aztlán*, in *Aztlán*, p. 2.

102. Gonzáles, "Chicano Nationalism," pp. 425–26.

103. *El Plan Espiritual de Aztlán*, in *Aztlán*, p. 3.

104. Gonzáles, "Chicano Nationalism," p. 426.

105. Zinn, "'Political Familism,'" p. 16.

106. Ibid.

107. *El Plan Espiritual de Aztlán*, in *Aztlán*, p. 1.

108. Luis Leal, "In Search of Aztlán," in Anaya and Lomeli, *Aztlán: Essays on the Chicano Homeland*, p. 8.

109. *El Plan Espiritual de Aztlán*, in *Aztlán*, p. 2.

110. Muñoz, *Youth, Identity, Power*, p. 25.

111. *El Plan Espiritual de Aztlán*, in *Aztlán*, p. 2.

112. García, *Chicanismo*, p. 54.

113. Muñoz, *Youth, Identity, Power*, p. 120.

114. Muñoz, *Youth, Identity, Power*, p. 101.

115. Gonzáles, "Chicano Nationalism," p. 427.

116. Lack of unity is certainly not the only reason given for the decline of these movements. In researching *Youth, Identity, Power: The Chicano Movement*, Carlos Muñoz obtained FBI documents describing how movement organizations were targets of political surveillance and infiltration by police and FBI agents. For Muñoz, the role of J. Edgar Hoover's COINTELPRO program played a significant role in the decline of the Chicano student movement (see p. 172). These movements were also sometimes victims of their own success. Affirmative action, Chicano and Puerto Rican studies programs, and new antipoverty programs in low-income communities were all movement demands that had mobilized Chicano and Puerto Rican communities. The end of the Vietnam War was another positive development that simultaneously removed a significant factor that mobilized and radicalized U.S. youth movements.

Nevertheless, despite the many challenges faced by Chicano and Puerto Rican activists, movement scholars are in consistent agreement that the lack of group unity is one of the most significant reasons for the political decline of the mid-1970s.

117. Muñoz, *Youth, Identity, Power*, p. 123.

118. Muñoz, *Youth, Identity, Power*, p. 103.

119. García, *United We Win*, p. 222.

120. García, *United We Win*, p. xv.

121. Chávez, *¡Mi Raza Primero! (My People First!)*, p. 7.

122. Young Lords Party and Abramson, *Palante*, p. 52.

123. Hawkesworth, "Women's Struggle for Political Equality in the United States," p. 77.

124. Jorge, "The Black Puerto Rican Woman in Contemporary American Society," p. 135.

125. Recent scholarship on women's activism within particular organizations during the Chicano movement includes Chavez's "'We Lived and Breathed and Worked the Movement'" and Espinoza's "'Revolutionary Sisters,'" pp. 17–58.

126. Baca Zinn, "Political Familism," p. 24.

127. Espinoza, "'Revolutionary Sisters,'" pp. 17–18.

128. Gonzáles, "Chicano Nationalism," in Rosaldo, Calvert, and Seligmann, *Chicano*, pp. 424–25.

129. See Vásquez, "The Women of La Raza," p. 29.

130. Mirande and Enríquez, *La Chicana*, p. 237.

131. NietoGomez, "La Femenista," p. 88.

132. Anonymous, "Chicanas Take Wrong Direction," p. 13.

133. NietoGomez, "La Femenista," p. 90.

134. NietoGomez, "La Femenista," p. 91.

135. NietoGomez, "La Femenista," p. 90.

136. NietoGomez, "La Femenista," p. 87.

137. For an excellent overview of this topic, see Gutiérrez, "Policing 'Pregnant Pilgrims.'"

138. The suit, *Madrigal v. Quilligan*, was filed on June 18, 1975. See Gutiérrez, "Policing 'Pregnant Pilgrims,'" p. 392.

139. Sosa-Riddell, "Chicanas and El Movimiento," p. 94.

140. Cotera, "Our Feminist Heritage, 1973," p. 42.

141. Espinoza, "'Revolutionary Sisters,'" p. 39.

142. Point 5 of the Young Lords Party thirteen-point program and platform initially read: "We want equality for women. *Machismo* must be revolutionary . . . not oppressive" (Melendez, *We Took the Streets*, p. 236).

143. Young Lords Party and Abramson, *Palante*, p. 52.

144. For example, Chicana feminists and loyalists both referred to the women's movement as the "Anglo women's movement," while women in the Young Lords spoke of the "women's liberation movement." See Young Lords Party and Abramson, *Palante*, p. 50.

145. Young Lords Party and Abramson, *Palante*, p. 50.

146. Young Lords Party and Abramson, *Palante*, p. 51.

147. Melendez, *We Took the Streets*, pp. 174–75.

148. Young Lords Party and Abramson, *Palante*, pp. 46–47.

149. Pulido, *Black, Brown, Yellow, and Left*, p. 182.

Chapter 2

1. Young, *Justice and the Politics of Difference*, pp. 226–27.

2. Young, *Justice and the Politics of Difference*, p. 10.

3. Young, *Justice and the Politics of Difference*, p. 229.

4. Young, *Justice and the Politics of Difference*, pp. 229, 234–35.

5. Young, *Justice and the Politics of Difference*, p. 117. Additional significant writings on deliberative democracy include Barber, *Strong Democracy*; Benhabib, *Democracy and Difference*; Bessette, *The Mild Voice of Reason*; Bohman and Rehg, *Deliberative Democracy*; Dryzek, *Discursive Democracy*; Fishkin, *Democracy and Deliberation*; Fishkin and Ackerman, *Deliberation Day*; Cohen, *Associations and Democracy* (with Joel Rogers); and Elster, *Deliberative Democracy*.

6. See Young, *Inclusion and Democracy*.

7. Young, *Justice and the Politics of Difference*, p. 184.

8. Young, *Justice and the Politics of Difference*, pp. 231–32.

9. Young, *Justice and the Politics of Difference*, p. 233.

10. Young, *Justice and the Politics of Difference*, pp. 231–32.

11. Young, *Justice and the Politics of Difference*, p. 25.

12. Young, *Justice and the Politics of Difference*, pp. 185, 188–89.

13. Young, *Justice and the Politics of Difference*, p. 95.

14. Young, *Justice and the Politics of Difference*, pp. 185, 188–89.

15. Young, *Justice and the Politics of Difference*, pp. 186–87.

16. Young, *Justice and the Politics of Difference*, p. 43.

17. Young, *Justice and the Politics of Difference*, p. 13.

18. Young, *Justice and the Politics of Difference*, p. 234.

19. Young, *Justice and the Politics of Difference*, pp. 238–39.

20. Dean, *Solidarity of Strangers*, p. 179.

21. Young Lords Party and Abramson, *Palante*, p. 158.

22. Butler, *Bodies That Matter*, p. 188.

23. Some of the classic texts: Lorde, *Sister Outsider*; Anzaldúa, *Borderlands/La Frontera*; Moraga, *Loving in the War Years* and *The Last Generation*; Smith, *Home Girls*; Moraga and Anzaldúa, *This Bridge Called My Back*; Anzaldúa et al., *Making Face/Making Soul/Hacienda Caras*; Collins, *Black Feminist Thought*; Alarcón, *Chicana Critical Issues*; Sandoval, "U.S. Third World Feminism"; and Lugones and Spelman, "Have We Got a Theory for You!"

24. Bickford, "Anti-Anti-Identity Politics," p. 118.

25. See Sampaio, "Theorizing Women of Color in a New Global Matrix"; Dhamoon, *Identity/Difference Politics*; Coles, *Gated Politics*; Alarcón, "The Theoretical Subject(s) of *This Bridge Called My Back* and Anglo-American Feminism"; Barvosa, *Wealth of Selves*; Hancock, *The Politics of Disgust*; Phelan, *Getting Specific*; Ackelsberg, "Sisters or Comrades?" and *Resisting Citizenship*; Bickford, *The Dissonance of Democracy*; Crenshaw, Gotanda, Peller, and Thomas, *Critical Race Theory*; and Sparks, "Dissident Citizenship."

26. Dean, *Solidarity of Strangers*, p. 30.

27. Alarcón, "The Theoretical Subject(s) of *This Bridge Called My Back* and Anglo-American Feminism," pp. 364, 366.

28. Ferguson, *The Man Question*, p. 161.

29. Ferguson, *The Man Question*, p. 163.

30. Lorde, *Sister Outsider*, p. 58.

31. Lorde, *Between Ourselves*.

32. Anzaldúa, *Borderlands/La Frontera*, p. 44.

33. Sandoval, "U.S. Third World Feminism," p. 5.

34. Moraga, "Foreword: Refugees of a World on Fire."

35. Young, *Justice and the Politics of Difference*, p. 229.

36. Young, *Justice and the Politics of Difference*, p. 234.

37. Reagon, "Coalition Politics," p. 344.

38. Reagon, "Coalition Politics," p. 346.

39. Reagon, "Coalition Politics," pp. 344–45.

40. Reagon, "Coalition Politics," p. 348.

41. Reagon, "Coalition Politics," p. 349.

42. Anzaldúa, "Bridge, Drawbridge, Sandbar or Island: Lesbians-of-Color *Hacienda Alianzas*," p. 218. See also Anzaldúa's poem "Never, Momma."

43. Honig, *Democracy and the Foreigner*, p. xiii.

44. As Honig notes, this desire relates to larger issues in democratic theory having to do with foreignness, freedom, agency, community, and solidarity. See *Democracy and the Foreigner*, p. xiv.

45. Young, *Justice and the Politics of Difference*, p. 15.

46. Wolin, "Fugitive Democracy," p. 11.

47. Ibid.

48. Wolin, "Fugitive Democracy," p. 23.

49. Wolin, "Fugitive Democracy," pp. 17, 23.

50. Wolin, *Politics and Vision*, pp. 602, 601.

51. Wolin, *Politics and Vision*, p. 601.

52. Wolin, *Politics and Vision*, p. 603.

53. Wolin, "Fugitive Democracy," p. 24.

54. Keenan, *Democracy in Question*, pp. 3–4.

55. Keenan, *Democracy in Question*, pp. 11, 53.

56. Wolin, "Fugitive Democracy," p. 23.

57. Keenan, *Democracy in Question*, p. 7.

58. Keenan, *Democracy in Question*, pp. 12, 14.

59. Keenan, *Democracy in Question*, pp. 11, 53.

60. Wolin, "Fugitive Democracy," p. 18.

61. Of course, Wolin himself is sometimes a critic of identity politics, arguing that "the politics of difference and the ideology of multiculturalism have contributed to rendering suspect the language and possibilities of collectivity, common action, and shared purposes." Interestingly, he notes that this same attention to difference can also lead to "the illusion of internal unity within each difference." See Wolin, "Democracy, Difference, and Re-cognition," pp. 481, 477. I find Wolin's reading here both astute and limited, for while I share his critique of the unitary assumptions that sometimes animate the turn to difference, I also share William Connolly's concern that Wolin is sometimes less attentive to how "the weight of the common itself often poses barriers to the political extension of democracy" and is invoked "to marginalize or liquidate challenges to that order." See Connolly, "Politics and Vision," p. 16.

62. Keenan, *Democracy in Question*, p. 13.

63. Keenan, *Democracy in Question*, pp. 11–13.

64. Ibid.

65. Xenos, "Momentary Democracy," p. 36.

66. Dallmayr, "Beyond Fugitive Democracy," p. 74.

67. Wolin, "Fugitive Democracy," p. 23.

Chapter 3

1. Cullen, *Freedom in Rousseau's Political Philosophy*, p. 24.

2. Rousseau, "Dedication to the Second Discourse," in *The First and Second Discourses*, p. 79.

3. Marso, *(Un)Manly Citizens*, p. 136.

4. Orwin, "Rousseau and the Discovery of Political Compassion," p. 297.

5. In the *Discourse on the Origin and Foundations of Inequality*, Rousseau writes: "Pity . . . carries us without reflection to the aid of those whom we see suffer. . . . [I]t is in this natural sentiment rather than in subtle arguments, that we must seek the cause of the repugnance every man would feel in doing evil" (*The First and Second Discourses*, p. 133).

6. Melzer, "Rousseau and the Modern Cult of Sincerity," p. 289.

7. Rousseau, *The First and Second Discourses*, p. 132.

8. Ibid.

9. Orwin, "Rousseau and the Discovery of Political Compassion," p. 299.

10. As Orwin notes, "It is not merely that Enlightenment thought overestimates the possibilities of reason, but that it underestimates those of sentiment" ("Rousseau and the Discovery of Political Compassion," p. 299).

11. Rousseau, *The Government of Poland*, p. 10.

12. Rousseau, *The Government of Poland*, p. 11.

13. *El Plan de Santa Barbara*, p. 198.

14. Cullen, *Freedom in Rousseau's Political Philosophy*, p. 118.

15. Ibid.

16. Riley, *The General Will before Rousseau*, p. 241.

17. Ibid.

18. Rousseau, *Social Contract*, p. 59.

19. Rousseau, *Social Contract*, p. 61.

20. Ibid.

21. Riley, *The General Will before Rousseau*, p. 212.

22. Riley, *The General Will before Rousseau*, p. 124.

23. Ibid.

24. This joining of democracy and harmony—democracy and *stability*—is an example of how Rousseau transformed the debate surrounding democracy and the nature of political agreement. Prior to Rousseau, democracy was more commonly portrayed in terms of chaos, violence, and mob rule. In *Rousseau: Dreamer of Democracy*, James Miller discusses Rousseau's impact in recasting the terms of debate:

> Formerly the picture of disunity and decadence . . . democracy now connoted harmony and regeneration. . . . [Democracy] became a name for popular sovereignty, extending to all the promise of a personally fulfilling freedom, exercised in cooperation with others. (p. 202)

25. Rousseau, *Social Contract*, p. 108.

26. Graham, "Rousseau's Concept of Consensus," p. 94.

27. Rousseau, *Social Contract*, p. 128.

28. Rousseau, *Social Contract*, p. 109.

29. Rousseau, *Social Contract*, p. 108.

30. For Rousseau, public gatherings have the tendency to inflame man's *amour propre* (pride)—the sociability of the assembly inflames man's desire to see and be seen ("to look at the others and to want to be looked at himself"). Moreover, if not properly constituted, the assembly has the tendency to expose and exacerbate differences of ability and social location. The result is unhealthy competition, inequality, and an increased dependency on others for approval and approbation.

31. Rousseau, *The First and Second Discourses*, p. 149.

32. Rousseau, *The First and Second Discourses*, p. 37.

33. Rousseau, *The First and Second Discourses*, p. 46.

34. Rousseau, *The First and Second Discourses*, p. 48.

35. Rousseau, *Social Contract*, p. 61.

36. Describing this idealization of unanimity, Allen writes:

> Lying beneath the ideology of "oneness" is a philosophical tradition that idealizes unanimity. The social contract tradition, out of which our political institutions arise, dreams of

an ur-moment of total consent as the legitimating foundation of liberal institutions. In some state of nature, all men will unite and consent unanimously to establish a shared government. A close look at this tradition reveals, however, that this idealization of unanimity brings with it a severely impoverished understanding of language as the medium of politics. (*Talking to Strangers*, p. 54)

37. Cullen, *Freedom in Rousseau's Political Philosophy*, p. 29.

38. Shklar, *Men and Citizens*, p. 20.

39. Ibid.

40. Vasquez, "The Women of La Raza," p. 29.

41. Wingrove, *Rousseau's Republican Romance*, p. 5. According to Wingrove, if women's proper performance of femininity is constitutive of Rousseau's republican politics, then sexuality and sexual identities are central to the deep structure of Rousseau's political thought.

42. Wingrove, *Rousseau's Republican Romance*, p. 167.

43. Crocker, *Rousseau's "Social Contract,"* p. 139.

44. Rousseau, *Social Contract*, p. 77.

45. Strong, *Jean-Jacques Rousseau*, p. 55.

46. Strong, *Jean-Jacques Rousseau*, p. 61.

47. Ibid.

48. Cullen, *Freedom in Rousseau's Political Philosophy*, p. 24.

49. Rousseau, *Politics and the Arts*, pp. 99, 105.

50. Miller, *Rousseau*, p. 35.

51. Rousseau, *Politics and the Arts*, p. 105.

52. Starobinski, *Jean-Jacques Rousseau*, p. 86.

53. Miller, *Rousseau*, p. 36.

54. Miller, *Rousseau*, p. 109.

55. Miller, *Rousseau*, p. 36.

56. Alurista, "Poem in Lieu of a Preface," p. 3.

57. Pérez-Torres, *Movements in Chicano Poetry*, p. 216.

58. In addition to poetry, visual art—particularly in the form of public murals—was another public, political, and emotive yet nondeliberative practice that emerged from the movement. Inspired by Diego Rivera and David Alfaro Siqueiros, the muralist movement provided Chicanos with a revised history in which they could see themselves as both heroic and larger than life.

59. García, *Chicanismo*, p. 105.

60. Laó, "Resources of Hope," p. 36.

61. Pérez-Torres, *Movements in Chicano Poetry*, p. 47.

62. Pérez-Torres, *Movements in Chicano Poetry*, p. 100.

63. Gonzales, *Yo Soy Joaquín/I Am Joaquín*, p. 3.

64. Pérez-Torres, *Movements in Chicano Poetry*, p. 47.

65. Muñoz, *Youth, Identity, Power*, p. 52.

66. Candelaria, *Chicano Poetry*, p. 77.

67. Ybarra-Frausto, "Alurista's Poetics," p. 118.

68. This commitment to community readings endures today: poetry readings continue to be a staple of Chicano student conferences, political rallies, and marches.

69. Pérez-Torres, *Movements in Chicano Poetry*, p. 175.

70. In movement politics, the speaking of Spanish can be understood as a Rousseauian attempt to achieve transparency and a "union of hearts." Armando Rendon's portrayal of language in *Chicano Manifesto* is typical in this regard; in this passage, the speaking of Spanish is portrayed in romantic and familial terms:

> I did well in the elementary grades and learned English quickly. Spanish was off limits in school anyway, and teachers and relatives taught me early that my mother tongue would be of no help in making good grades and becoming a success. Yet Spanish was the language I used in playing and arguing with friends. Spanish was the language I spoke with my *abuelita*, my dear grandmother, as I ate *atole* on those cold mornings when I used to wake at dawn to her clattering dishes in the tiny kitchen. (pp. 320–21)

In this movement treatise, Rendon invokes Spanish as a way of distinguishing public (assimilated) life from the more familial and authentic experiences of his childhood. For him, Spanish evolves from being the familial language of his childhood to a form of public speech that offers the promise of transparency. In his discussions with other Chicano and Mexican men, Rendon reconciles public speech with the Rousseauian desire for "communication without dissimulation."

The linking of Spanish with the "heart" was so successful in movement discourse that its presence is apparent even in the more conservative Latino political narratives that emerged in the postmovement era. In his 1982 memoir *Hunger of Memory*, essayist Richard Rodriguez argues against bilingual education while waxing rhapsodic about the emotive power of Spanish in his childhood. Like earlier movement authors, Rodriguez equates Spanish with transparency. In a passage that evokes sexual release almost as much as familial affection, he writes:

> I remember many nights when my father would come back from work, and I'd hear him call out to my mother in Spanish, sounding relieved. In Spanish, he'd sound light and free notes he never could manage in English. Some nights I'd jump up just at hearing his voice. With *mis hermanos* I would come running into the room where he was with my mother. Our laughing (so deep was the pleasure!) became screaming. Like others who know the pain of public alienation, we transformed the knowledge of our public separateness and made it consoling—the reminder of intimacy. Excited, we joined our voices in a celebration of sounds. *We are speaking now the way we never speak out in public. We are alone—together....*
>
> Some nights, no one seemed willing to loosen the hold sounds had on us. At dinner, we invented new words. (Ours sounded Spanish, but made sense only to us.) We pieced together new words by taking, say, an English verb and giving it Spanish endings.... Tongues explored the edges of words, especially the fat vowels. And we happily sounded that military drum roll, the twirling roar of the Spanish *r*. Family language: my family's sounds. The voices of my parents and sister and brother.... Voices singing and sighing, rising, straining, then surging, teeming with pleasure that burst syllables into fragments of laughter. At times it seemed there was steady quiet only when, from another room, the rustling whispers of my parents faded and I moved closer to sleep. (p. 18)

Like Rendon, Rodriguez shares the Rousseauian belief that the heart is in need of civic education. Unlike Rendon, however, Rodriguez sees Spanish as a powerfully *private* language that keeps Chicanos from fully participating in the social and political life of America. For Rodriguez, Chicano hearts must renounce the private (Spanish) for the public (English). But despite their very different views on language policy, Rodriguez shares the movement's assumption that Spanish is deeply implicated in civic life—a signifier of both intimacy and transparency.

71. Calderón, "At the Crossroads of History, on the Borders of Change," p. 218.

72. Kelly, "Rousseau and the Case against (and for) the Arts," p. 31.

73. Starobinski, *Jean-Jacques Rousseau*, p. 90.

74. Rousseau, *Social Contract*, p. 68.

75. Keenan, *Democracy in Question*, p. 11.

76. Keenan, *Democracy in Question*, p. 12.

77. Riley, *The General Will before Rousseau*, p. 126.

78. Ibid.

79. Rousseau, *Social Contract*, p. 67.

80. Strong, *Jean-Jacques Rousseau*, p. 62.

81. Rousseau, *Politics and the Arts*, p. 126.

82. Cullen, *Freedom in Rousseau's Political Philosophy*, p. 10.

83. Starobinski, "Rousseau and Modern Tyranny," p. 20.

84. Shklar, *Men and Citizens*, p. 160.

85. Miller, *Rousseau*, p. 35.

86. Cullen, *Freedom in Rousseau's Political Philosophy*, p. 135.

87. Rousseau, *Politics and the Arts*, pp. 135–36.

88. Strong, *Jean-Jacques Rousseau*, p. 62.

89. Strong, *Jean-Jacques Rousseau*, pp. 62–63.

90. Strong, *Jean-Jacques Rousseau*, p. 61.

91. Strong, *Jean-Jacques Rousseau*, p. 10.

92. Laó, "Resources of Hope," p. 35.

93. Miller, *Rousseau*, p. 35.

94. In *Letter to d'Alembert*'s famous footnote, for example, the festival reaches its emotional zenith when the wives and children enter and join in the spectacle.

95. Stavans, *The Hispanic Condition*, pp. 100–101.

96. Kelly, "Rousseau and the Case against (and for) the Arts," p. 32.

97. Quoted in Muñoz, *Youth, Identity, Power*, p. 78.

98. See Rousseau, *La nouvelle Héloise* (part 5, letter 7), quoted in Starobinski, *Jean-Jacques Rousseau*, p. 87.

99. Starobinski, *Jean-Jacques Rousseau*, p. 88.

100. Ibid.

101. Cullen, *Freedom in Rousseau's Political Philosophy*, p. 118.

102. Shklar, "Jean-Jacques Rousseau and Equality," p. 20.

103. Young, *Justice and the Politics of Difference*, p. 233.

104. See Holloway Sparks, review of Young's *Inclusion and Democracy*, *Signs* 30, no. 2 (Winter 2005): 1674–75.

105. Young, *Inclusion and Democracy*, p. 132.

106. Rousseau, *The First and Second Discourses*, pp. 115–16.

107. Keenan, *Democracy in Question*, p. 13.

Chapter 4

1. See Chávez, *¡Mi Raza Primero! (My People First!)*; Mariscal, *Brown-Eyed Children of the Sun*; Villarreal and Hernandez, *Latinos and Political Coalitions*; García, *Latinos and the Political System*; and Gómez-Quiñones, *Chicano Politics*.

2. Ortiz, "Chicana/o Organizational Politics and Strategies in the Era of Retrenchment," p. 123.

3. Ortiz, "Chicana/o Organizational Politics and Strategies in the Era of Retrenchment," p. 117.

4. See Dávila, *Latinos, Inc.*; Marquez, *Constructing Identities in Mexican American Political Organizations*.

5. Villarreal and Hernandez, *Latinos and the Political System*, p. xviii. For a similar critique, see Dávila, *Latinos, Inc.*

6. To some extent, the immigrant-rights protests of 2006 expanded the discussion beyond the electoral realm to include the politics of protest and mobilization. However, as I discuss in the next chapter, even this democratic moment of mass action was often reframed in terms of representation—as a precursor to what would eventually be a large and influential voting bloc.

7. Keenan, *Democracy in Question*, pp. 8, 12.

8. Flores, *From Bomba to Hip-Hop*, p. 150.

9. See Oboler, *Ethnic Labels, Latino Lives*, p. 5. For a more extended analysis of how the Hispanic-origin question came to be added to the census, see Victoria Hattam's *In the Shadow of Race*, pp. 111–28.

10. See Skerry, *Counting on the Census?* pp. 37–38; Hattam, *In the Shadow of Race*, chapter 5. As both Hattam and Skerry note, a Mexican American member of the U.S. Interagency Committee on Mexican American Affairs demanded that a specific Hispanic-origin question be included on the census. The White House (which had recently inaugurated Hispanic Heritage Week) was eager to court this pool of voters, so the question was quickly added.

11. Skerry, *Counting on the Census?* p. 38.

12. Ibid.

13. Sánchez Korrol, "Latinismo among Early Puerto Rican Migrants in New York City," p. 151.

14. Sánchez Korrol, "Latinismo among Early Puerto Rican Migrants in New York City," p. 152.

15. Flores, *From Bomba to Hip-Hop*, p. 148.

16. Flores, *From Bomba to Hip-Hop*, p. 149.

17. Fox, *Hispanic Nation*.

18. Ramos, *The Latino Wave*, p. xvii.

19. Brian Grow et al., "Hispanic Nation," *BusinessWeek* online, March 15, 2004.

20. Ramos, *The Latino Wave*, p. xxiii.

21. Remarks of Senator Robert Menendez at the National Council of La Raza Annual Conference, July 23, 2007, Miami.

22. Senator Robert Menendez, July 23, 2007, Miami.

23. Hernandez, "Hispanic Voters Gain New Clout with Democrats."

24. Santillan, "The Latino Community in State and Congressional Redistricting," p. 329.

25. Santillan, "Styles and Strategies," p. 477.

26. Foreword from National Council of La Raza's *State of Hispanic America 2004*, p. iii.

27. "Hispanic" is the generic term the Bureau of the Census uses to identify persons with Spanish surnames. It is also the term often used to identify the Spanish-language minority in the United States.

28. Giménez, "Latino/Hispanic—Who Needs a Name?" p. 559.

29. Ibid.

30. Giménez, "Latino/Hispanic—Who Needs a Name?" p. 560.

31. Nelson, Candace, and Marta Tienda, "The Structuring of Hispanic Ethnicity: Historical and Contemporary Perspectives," *Ethnic and Racial Studies* 8 (1985): 49–74 (cited in Oboler, *Ethnic Labels, Latino Lives*, p. 3)

32. Oboler, *Ethnic Labels, Latino Lives*, p. 2.

33. Nelson and Tienda, "The Structuring of Hispanic Ethnicity" (cited in Oboler, *Ethnic Labels, Latino Lives*, p. 3)

34. Acosta-Belén and Sjostrom, *The Hispanic Experience in the United States*, p. 84.

35. Oboler, *Ethnic Labels, Latino Lives*, p. 15.

36. Oboler, *Ethnic Labels, Latino Lives*, p. 83.

37. Klor de Alva, "Aztlán, Borinquen and Hispanic Nationalism," p. 107.

38. Calderón, "'Hispanic' and 'Latino,'" p. 42.

39. Gómez-Quiñones, *Chicano Politics*, p. 185.

40. For many critics, the word "Hispanic" overemphasizes the European (Spanish) over the indigenous aspects of Spanish-speaking society.

41. Calderón, "'Hispanic' and 'Latino,'" pp. 42–43.

42. Flores, *From Bomba to Hip-Hop*, p. 142.

43. Flores, *From Bomba to Hip-Hop*, p. 154.

44. Flores, *From Bomba to Hip-Hop*, p. 162.

45. Flores, *From Bomba to Hip-Hop*, p. 164.

46. Flores, *From Bomba to Hip-Hop*, p. 165.

47. Ibid.

48. Flores, *From Bomba to Hip-Hop*, p. 164.

49. Ibid.

50. Bowler and Segura, *Diversity in Democracy*, pp. 9–10.

51. Garcia, *Latinos and the Political System*, pp. 499–500.

52. de la Garza, DeSipio, Garcia, Garcia, and Falcon, *Latino Voices*, p. 4. The survey began in August 1989 and ended in April 1990.

53. de la Garza et al., *Latino Voices*, p. 16.

54. DeSipio, *Counting on the Latino Vote*, p. 176.

55. This was Mexican Americans saying they had common political concerns with Puerto Ricans. See de la Garza et al., *Latino Voices*, p. 144.

56. DeSipio, *Counting on the Latino Vote*, pp. 176–77.

57. de la Garza et al., *Latino Voices*, p. 13.

58. DeSipio, *Counting on the Latino Vote*, p. 177.

59. Examining the political behavior of Puerto Ricans and other Latinos in New York City, for example, author James Jennings states: "Comparison of political and social attitudes of different Latino groups seems to suggest major differences between Cubans,

Dominicans, and Puerto Ricans." Citing research by Dale Nelson, Jennings writes: "[T]he term 'Hispanic' political attitudes was of little conceptual help in describing the attitudes analyzed, at least in reference to Puerto Ricans, Cubans and Dominicans in New York City." See Jennings, "Future Directions for Puerto Rican Politics in the U.S. and Puerto Rico," p. 495.

60. DeSipio, *Counting on the Latino Vote*, p. 177.

61. Ibid.

62. Ibid.

63. Oboler, *Ethnic Labels, Latino Lives*, p. xiv.

64. Ibid.

65. de la Garza et al., *Latino Voices*, p. 14.

66. de la Garza et al., *Latino Voices*, p. 16.

67. de la Garza et al., *Latino Voices*, p. 15.

68. Later in this chapter, I look to Maurilio Vigil's *Hispanics in Congress* as an example of this tendency to presume pan-ethnic consciousness in Latino political discourse. Other texts that share this presumption include Stavans, *The Hispanic Condition*; Trueba, *Latinos Unidos*; Heyck, *Barrios and Borderlands*; and Flores and Benmayor, *Latino Cultural Citizenship*.

69. During the movement heyday, for example, Chicano and Puerto Rican activists were inspired by the Black Power movement, often emulating its radical and performative politics. The Black Panther Party inspired the dramatic militancy of both the Brown Berets and the Young Lords. Yet such emulation and inspiration have been tinged with resentment regarding the ongoing invisibility of the history of racism against Latinos.

70. Quoted in Pierce, Neal R. and Jerry Hagstrom, "The Hispanic Community—A Growing Force to Be Reckoned With," in Garcia, *Latinos and the Political System*, p. 12.

71. Hawkesworth, "Congressional Enactments of Race-Gender," p. 546.

72. Yzaguirre, "Keys to Hispanic Empowerment," p. 181.

73. Interestingly, prior to the Chicano and Puerto Rican movements, Latinos sought to portray themselves as *unlike* African Americans and more akin to white ethnic groups such as Italian or Irish (see chapter 2). By the mid-1960s, however, Latinos began to consistently define themselves as a nonwhite minority in need of federal assistance and protections similar to those granted African Americans. No longer a group to distance oneself from, African Americans became the racial group to emulate.

74. Garcia, "The Chicano Movement," p. 92.

75. Garcia, "The Chicano Movement," p. 101.

76. Ibid.

77. After passage of the Voting Rights Act of 1965, for example, Latino activists and elected officials lobbied for extensions in the VRA to designate Latinos as linguistic minorities. According to John Garcia, "It was only after passage of the VRA extensions of 1970 and 1975 with their designation of linguistic minorities that Chicanos could make effective use of this legislation. Organizations such as the Mexican American Legal Defense and Education Fund (MALDEF) and the Southwest Voter Registration and Education Project (SWVREP) initiated litigation to alter election systems, improve access to voter registration, and challenge redistricting plans." See Garcia, "The Chicano Movement," pp. 94–95.

78. Executive Summary of the Hispanic Public Policy Agenda published by the National Hispanic Leadership Agenda (1999), p. 1.

79. Such characterizations of cohesiveness implicitly echo the political practice of black voters. Moreover, such comparisons are self-consciously explicit as well. In describing the rapid growth of Spanish-origin subgroups, Latino civic elites consistently contrast the growth of the Latino electorate with that of African Americans, emphasizing how Latinos have overtaken African Americans as the nation's largest minority. Such articulations of demographic displacement and political replacement reflect the varied and conflicting reactions that emerge when Latino civic elites confront the black political experience.

80. Vigil, *Hispanics in Congress*, p. vii.

81. The Congressional Hispanic Caucus Web site, www.chci.org ("About the CHC").

82. www.chci.org.

83. Vigil, *Hispanics in Congress*, p. 85.

84. Vigil, *Hispanics in Congress*, p. 87.

85. Twenty-five years after the founding of the Congressional Hispanic Caucus, the National Hispanic Leadership Agenda continues to organize Latinos based on the belief that a pan-ethnic political agenda can serve all Latinos equally well. Describing their mission, the association states:

> The National Hispanic Leadership Agenda (NHLA) was founded in 1991 as a non-partisan coalition of major Hispanic national organizations, as well as distinguished Hispanic leaders from across the nation. The NHLA represents all major ethnic groups in the Hispanic community: Mexican Americans, Puerto Ricans, Cuban Americans, and Americans whose countries of origin are in the Caribbean and Central and/or South America. Governing the NHLA is a 37-member board comprised of the chief executive officers of 31 national Hispanic organizations, along with elected officials, corporate executives, and other prominent Hispanic professionals. NHLA's mission calls for a spirit of unity among Latinos nationwide to provide the Hispanic community with greater visibility and a clearer, stronger voice in our country's affairs. NHLA seeks a consensus among Hispanic leaders to help frame policy and promote public awareness of the major issues facing Latinos nationally. (NHLA Mission Statement. Congressional Scorecard, 106th Congress, Second Session. 2000)

86. Vigil, *Hispanics in Congress*, p. 92.

87. Vigil, *Hispanics in Congress*, p. 88.

88. Vigil, *Hispanics in Congress*, p. 97.

89. Vigil, *Hispanics in Congress*, p. 95.

90. Vigil, *Hispanics in Congress*, p. 97.

91. See Gonzáles, "Chicano Nationalism," in Rosaldo, Calvert, and Seligmann, *Chicano*, pp. 425–26.

92. See Garcia, *Latino Politics in America*, p. 2; García Bedolla, *Latino Politics*, p. 4.

93. Suro et al., *2002 National Survey of Latinos*, p. 23.

94. Suro et al., *2002 National Survey of Latinos*, p. 33.

95. Suro et al., *2002 National Survey of Latinos*, p. 23.

96. See http://depts.washington.edu/uwiser/LNS.shtml.

97. See the Woodrow Wilson International Center for Scholars, December 7, 2006, www.wilsoncenter.org/index.cfm?topic_id=1427&;fuseaction=topics.event_summary&event_id=201793; Latino National Survey (LNS), http://depts.washington.edu/uwiser/LNS.shtml, LNS Toplines 2007.

98. See http://depts.washington.edu/uwiser/LNS.shtml, LNS Toplines 2007, p. 35.

99. See the Woodrow Wilson International Center for Scholars, December 7, 2006, www.wilsoncenter.org/index.cfm?topic_id=1427&;fuseaction=topics.event_summary&event_id=201793.

100. For a discussion of the debate over the percentage of the Latino vote Bush won in 2004, see Leal, Barreto, Lee, and de la Garza, "The Latino Vote in the 2004 Election," pp. 42–47; Dávila, *Latino Spin*, pp. 46–70.

101. Segura, "Symposium Introduction," p. 277.

102. Daniels and Martinez de Castro, *The Latino Electorate*, pp. 5.

103. For an excellent overview and scholarly analysis of the role Latino voters played in the 2008 Democratic primary, see Barreto, Fraga, Manzano, Martinez-Ebers, and Segura, "Should They Dance with the One Who Brung 'Em?" pp. 753–60. For additional analysis of how Latinos are viewed as "cultural" rather than ideological voters, see Dávila, *Latino Spin*, pp. 59–66.

104. For more on this depiction of Hillary Clinton as "*la fría*," see Sanchez, *Los Republicanos*.

105. Heilemann, "The Evita Factor."

106. See Judis, "Hillary Clinton's Firewall"; and Reno, "Black-Brown Divide."

107. See Martinez, "Clinton's Hispanic Edge."

108. See Preston, Julia. "In Big Shift, Latino Vote Was Heavily for Obama," *New York Times*, November 6, 2008.

109. See Cobble and Velasquez, "Obama's Latino Vote Mandate."

110. See Gary Langer, "The Hispanic Vote," ABC News, June 28, 2008.

111. Dávila, *Latino Spin*, p. 50.

112. Daniels and Martinez de Castro, *The Latino Electorate*, p. 12.

113. Alvarez and García Bedolla, "The Foundations of Latino Voter Partisanship," p. 37.

114. Alvarez and García Bedolla, "The Foundations of Latino Voter Partisanship," p. 40.

115. Dávila, *Latino Spin*, pp. 29, 53.

116. Vigil, *Hispanics in Congress*, p. 95.

117. Brown, *States of Injury*, p. 75.

Chapter 5

1. Flores, "Undocumented Immigrants and Latino Cultural Citizenship," pp. 255–77.

2. Arendt, *The Human Condition*, p. 206.

3. Barber, *Strong Democracy*, p. 123

4. As Ted Wang and Robert Winn of the Four Freedoms Fund note, H.R. 4437 raised the stakes "not only for immigrants and advocates, but also for faith-based organizations, social service agencies, employers, and other groups that work closely with immigrants and recognize their contributions to U.S. communities" (*Groundswell Meets Groundwork*, p. 2.).

5. As Ruth Milkman notes in "Critical Mass," a number of factors led to the "massive outpouring of activism manifested in spring 2006." Labor unions clearly played a key role, as did the Catholic Church, immigrant hometown associations, and student organizations. Spanish-language media also played a crucial role in the marches; two Latino radio hosts, in particular, were credited with helping to mobilize hundreds of thousands to the various marches and protests: Los Angeles disc jockeys El Piolín (Tweetybird) and El Cucuy (The

Boogeyman). Both Mexican native Piolín (whose actual name is Eddie Sotelo) and Honduran-born El Cucuy (Renán Almendárez Coello) are popular and widely known figures in Spanish-language radio; they broadcast nationally and were instrumental in raising awareness of the various demonstrations, offering participants advice regarding how they should present themselves to the larger public. Moreover, both men publicly revealed that they had been illegal immigrants in the United States themselves. See Reuters, "Powerful Latino DJs to Mount Immigrant Voter Drive," July 7, 2006.

6. Wang and Winn, *Groundswell Meets Groundwork*, p. 6.

7. In analyzing the immigrant-rights protests, it is clear that the demonstrations involved a large number of non-Latino populations from Asia, Africa, the Caribbean, and beyond. While I do not want to replicate the mass media's erasure of these populations from the protests, my research focus is on Latino immigrants (with a particular focus on the undocumented). In doing this, my research draws on the insights of Mae Ngai and Nicholas de Genova, who note that in the United States, the social condition of illegality has often rendered "Mexican" the distinctive national/racialized name for such undocumented subjectivity. Like Ngai and de Genova, this chapter seeks to engage this particular racialization of the undocumented. See Ngai's *Impossible Subjects*; de Genova's "Migrant 'Illegality' and Deportability in Everyday Life."

8. Of course, not all scholars viewed the marches as a continuation of the Chicano movement. In their *Urban Affairs Review* article on the 2006 marches, for example, Matt A. Barreto, Sylvia Manzano, Ricardo Ramírez, and Kathy Rim argue that the immigrant pro-test marches were distinct from Chicano movement activism. According to the authors, "Whereas the Chicano movement inherently challenged the status quo with respect to working conditions, quality of education, and access to political representation, the immi-gration protest rallies were first and foremost focused on maintaining the status quo with a secondary push for an improvement of the status quo through a call for a path to legaliza-tion." See Barreto, Manzano, Ramírez, and Rim, "Mobilization, Participation, and *Soli-daridad*," pp. 746–47.

9. See Gonzales, "The 2006 Mega-Marchas in Greater Los Angeles," pp. 30–59.

10. See Buchanan, *State of Emergency* and *The Death of the West*.

11. Warner, *Publics and Counterpublics*, pp. 66–67, 88.

12. Wolin, *Politics and Vision*, p. 603.

13. Wolin, *Politics and Vision*, p. 602.

14. Wolin, *Politics and Vision*, p. 602, 603.

15. See Honig, *Democracy and the Foreigner*, p. 99.

16. For a discussion of these issues, see Mary Dietz's essay "Feminist Receptions of Han-nah Arendt." Among Arendt's critics on this point, see especially Wolin, "Hannah Arendt"; Benhabib, *The Reluctant Modernism of Hannah Arendt*; Pitkin, *The Attack of the Blob*; Canovan, *Hannah Arendt*.

17. Reinhardt, *The Art of Being Free*, p. 146.

18. Arendt, *On Revolution*, p. 94.

19. As Linda Zerilli has noted, Arendt's tendency "to define all issues related to the body as dangerous forms of necessity that are best kept private if not hidden" has made her "a controversial figure on the progressive Left and in contemporary feminism." See Zerilli, *Feminism and the Abyss of Freedom*, p. 3.

20. See Warner, *Publics and Counterpublics*, p. 61; Benhabib, "Kantian Questions, Arendtian Answers," p. 173. See also Butler and Spivak, *Who Sings the Nation-State?* p. 27; Bernstein, "Did Hannah Arendt Change Her Mind?" p. 127.

21. Warner, *Public and Counterpublics*, p. 61.

22. See Benhabib, *The Rights of Others*; Butler and Spivak, *Who Sings the Nation-State?*

23. Parekh, "Hannah Arendt's Critique of Marx," pp. 85–87.

24. Alcoff, *Visible Identities*, pp. 5, 183.

25. Arendt, *The Origins of Totalitarianism*, p. 267.

26. Arendt, *The Human Condition*, p. 246.

27. Arendt, "What Is Freedom?" p. 151.

28. Arendt, *The Human Condition*, p. 8.

29. Arendt, *The Human Condition*, p. 176.

30. Arendt, *The Human Condition*, p. 197.

31. Zerilli, *Feminism and the Abyss of Freedom*, p. 20.

32. Arendt, *The Human Condition*, pp. 178–79.

33. Bickford, Susan, "In the Presence of Others," in Honig, *Feminist Interpretations of Hannah Arendt*, p. 315.

34. Markell, "The Rule of the People," p. 10.

35. Wang and Winn, *Groundswell Meets Groundwork*, pp. 2, 5–6.

36. For a more developed discussion of the mobilizing structures that helped facilitate the protests, see Barreto, Manzano, Ramírez, and Rim, "Mobilization, Participation, and *Solidaridad*," p. 746.

37. Arendt, "What Is Freedom?" p. 169.

38. Wang and Winn, *Groundswell Meets Groundwork*, p. 6.

39. http://nylatinojournal.com/home/politics/americas/a_multitude_in_chicago_for_immigrant_rights.html

40. Arendt, *The Human Condition*, p. 197.

41. Arendt, *The Origins of Totalitarianism*, p. 287.

42. Burke, *Reflections on the Revolution in France*.

43. Arendt, *The Origins of Totalitarianism*, p. 300.

44. Benhabib, "Kantian Questions, Arendtian Answers," p. 192.

45. Arendt, *The Origins of Totalitarianism*, p. 286.

46. Arendt, *The Origins of Totalitarianism*, pp. 295–96.

47. Arendt, *The Origins of Totalitarianism*, pp. 297, 300–01.

48. Arendt, *The Origins of Totalitarianism*, p. 296.

49. As Richard Bernstein notes in his discussion of Arendt and her reading of the concentration and extermination camps, to make human beings superfluous "is to eradicate the very conditions that make humanity possible—to destroy human plurality, spontaneity, natality, and individuality" ("Did Hannah Arendt Change Her Mind?" p. 135).

50. Lima, *The Latino Body*, pp. 168–69.

51. For more on how immigrants serve to renationalize the state, see chapter 4 in Honig's *Democracy and the Foreigner* ("The Myth of Immigrant America").

52. Bosniak, *The Citizen and the Alien*, p. 117.

53. Bosniak, *The Citizen and the Alien*, pp. 3, 118.

54. In "Who Is the Subject of the Rights of Man?" Rancière takes issue with what he describes as Arendt's "rigid opposition between the realm of the political and the realm of private life" in *The Origins of Totalitarianism*. For Rancière, Arendt's position depoliticizes matters of power and repression, setting them in "an anthropological sphere of sacrality beyond the reach of political dissensus." Intriguingly, in an analysis of Giorgio Agamben's *Homo Sacer*, Rancière notes that while Agamben's view of the camp as the "nomos for modernity" may seem quite removed from Arendt's view of political action, in fact "the radical suspension of politics in the exception of bare life is the ultimate consequence of Arendt's archipolitical position, of her attempt to preserve the political from the contamination of private, social, apolitical life" ("Who Is the Subject of the Rights of Man?" pp. 299, 301).

55. In his reading of *The Origins of Totalitarianism*, Agamben's depiction of the biopolitical nature of sovereign power goes far beyond Arendt in producing a fatalistic and rectilinear account of history. For an excellent account of Agamben's theory of history, his representation of time, and its relationship to sovereignty in *Homo Sacer*, see Kalyvas, "The Sovereign Weaver," pp. 107–34.

56. Rancière, "Who Is the Subject of the Rights of Man?" p. 304.

57. Ibid.

58. Quoted in Swarns, "Immigrants Rally in Scores of Cities for Legal Status."

59. Ibid.

60. Quoted in Bill Hackwell, "Largest Demonstration in California History," *San Francisco Bay Area Independent Media Center*, March 26, 2006, http://www.indybay.org/newsitems/2006/03/26/18111081.php.

61. Arendt, *On Revolution*, p. 119.

62. Quoted in Arendt, *On Revolution*, p. 119.

63. Arendt, *On Revolution*, p. 69.

64. Quoted in Arendt, *On Revolution*, p. 69.

65. Allen, *Talking to Strangers*, p. 101.

66. Apostolidis, "Feminist Theory, Immigrant Workers' Stories, and Counterhegemony in the United States Today," p. 545.

67. Pitkin, "Justice," p. 332.

68. Arendt, *The Human Condition*, p. 186.

69. Sparks, "Dissident Citizenship," p. 76.

70. Sparks, "Dissident Citizenship," p. 93.

71. Sparks, "Dissident Citizenship," p. 92.

72. Arendt, *On Revolution*, p. 119.

73. Swarns, "Immigrants Rally in Scores of Cities for Legal Status."

74. Russ Rymer, Editor's Note, "Mañana Votamos," *Mother Jones*, July/August 2006.

75. I should note that such efforts at purging the demonstrations of any negative display of emotion were also a way to avoid any negative *consequences* from the protests. Aware of the risks immigrants were taking in claiming the public realm, many liberal advocates encouraged protesters to display explicit forms of patriotism alongside cultural displays that emphasized family, tradition, and festiveness. By de-emphasizing the marches' radical and agonistic quality, activists sought to protect protesters from the violent power of the state.

76. Honig, *Democracy and the Foreigner*, p. 8. Honig's suggestion that "taking may be the very thing that immigrants have to give us" challenges the more "consensual" notion of citizenship common among democratic theorists. Michael Walzer, for example, approaches membership as a social good that members distribute and give out to strangers:

> Membership as a social good is constituted by our understanding; its value is fixed by our work and conversation; and then we are in charge (who else could be in charge?) of its distribution. But we don't distribute it among ourselves; it is already ours. We give it out to strangers. Hence the choice is also governed by our relationships with strangers. (*Spheres of Justice*, p. 32)

Walzer's treatment of membership as a good that is possessed reflects a logic invested in the idea of intentional and deliberate distribution. Yet as Charles T. Lee has argued, this seemingly democratic notion of consensual citizenship "fortifies rather than loosens the binary distinction of citizens and outsiders." See Lee, "Tactical Citizenship: Domestic Workers, the Remainders of Home, and Undocumented Citizen Participation in the Third Space of Mimicry," *Theory & Event* 9, no. 3 (2006).

By privileging the idea of mutuality, Walzer is less able to account for the more contentious practices involved in gaining political membership. As Honig notes, practices of taking are always viewed as illegitimate from the perspective of the current governing order. Moreover, membership is itself a precarious concept, particularly when considering the dynamics of race and citizenship. Latinos have often found themselves in a stigmatized and subordinate position, regardless of citizenship status. From the deportations of U.S.-born Mexicans during the mass repatriation of Mexican immigrants in the 1930s to the anti-Latino rhetoric of backers of Proposition 187 in California, the civic history of Latinos has shown that "being a citizen guarantees neither full membership in society nor equal rights" (see Flores, "Undocumented Immigrants and Latino Cultural Citizenship," 225). In other words, Walzer's claim that membership is "already ours" is complicated by conditions of inequality and racial difference. Despite the fact that Walzer is sympathetic to the rights of noncitizens and promotes their naturalization, his language of mutual consent is unable to account for contested notions of membership and racialized political action.

77. Allen discusses Ellison by quoting from *Invisible Man*. In the novel, the protagonist starts his life story by recollecting his grandfather's deathbed words:

> "Son, after I'm gone I want you to keep up the good fight. I never told you, but our life is a war and I have been a traitor all my born days, a spy in the enemy's country ever since I give up my gun back in the Reconstruction. Live with your head in the lion's mouth. I want you to overcome 'em with yeses, undermine 'em with grins, agree 'em to death and destruction, let 'em swoller you till they vomit or bust wide open.... Learn it to the younguns." (Ellison, *Invisible Man*, p. 16)

78. Allen, *Talking to Strangers*, p. 115.
79. Bickford, "In the Presence of Others," p. 316.
80. Bickford, "In the Presence of Others," p. 318.
81. Bickford, "In the Presence of Others," p. 317.
82. Bickford, "In the Presence of Others," p. 320.
83. See Habermas, *The Structural Transformation of the Public Sphere.*

84. Warner, *Publics and Counterpublics*, pp. 62, 65.

85. Warner, *Publics and Counterpublics*, p. 56.

86. Chambers, "Democracy and (the) Public(s)," p. 131.

87. Warner, *Publics and Counterpublics*, pp. 75, 119.

88. Warner, *Publics and Counterpublics*, pp. 118, 113. Also see Fraser, "Rethinking the Public Sphere."

89. Warner, *Publics and Counterpublics*, p. 118.

90. Bruyneel, *The Third Space of Sovereignty*, p. 217.

91. See Oboler, *Ethnic Labels, Latino Lives*; Flores and Benmayor, *Latino Cultural Citizenship*; C. Muñoz, *Youth, Identity, Power*.

92. Warner, *Publics and Counterpublics*, 58.

93. Flores, "Undocumented Immigrants and Latino Cultural Citizenship," pp. 276, 273.

94. Flores, "Undocumented Immigrants and Latino Cultural Citizenship," p. 263.

95. Flores, "Undocumented Immigrants and Latino Cultural Citizenship," p. 258.

96. See Constable, "Latinos Unite to Turn Fear into Activism."

97. Warner, *Publics and Counterpublics*, p. 63.

98. Warner, *Publics and Counterpublics*, pp. 57–58.

99. For an example of depictions of the undocumented as political pawns of larger left-wing forces (including "veteran, hard-core Marxists," the Ford Foundation, the Carnegie Endowment, George Soros, and Bill Gates), see Jasper, "Pawns in a Losing Game."

100. Warner, *Publics and Counterpublics*, p. 62.

101. Ibid.

102. "Spanish 'Banner' Draws Protest," USA Today.com, April 29, 2006.

103. Holusha, "Bush Says Anthem Should Be in English."

104. Butler and Spivak, *Who Sings the Nation-State?* p. 60.

105. Markell, "The Rule of the People," p. 10.

106. Ibid.

107. See Parekh, "Hannah Arendt's Critique of Marx," p. 77.

108. Levin, "On *Animal Laborans* and *Homo Politicus* in Hannah Arendt," p. 525.

109. Levin, "On *Animal Laborans* and *Homo Politicus* in Hannah Arendt," p. 523.

110. Arendt, *The Human Condition*, p. 87.

111. Arendt, *The Human Condition*, p. 101.

112. Wright, *Disposable Women and Other Myths of Global Capitalism*, p. 2.

113. Wright, *Disposable Women and Other Myths of Global Capitalism*, pp. 73, 88.

114. Ibid.

115. Wright, *Disposable Women and Other Myths of Global Capitalism*, p. 151. For a discussion of the concept of "death by culture," see Uma Narayan's "Cross-Cultural Connections, Border-Crossings, and 'Death by Culture,'" in *Dislocating Cultures*.

116. Apostolidis, "Hegemony and Hamburger," p. 650.

117. Ibid.

118. de Genova, "The Legal Production of Mexican/Migrant 'Illegality,'" p. 179.

119. Behdad, *A Forgetful Nation*, p. 159.

120. See Santa Ana, *Brown Tide Rising*.

121. Bernstein, "Did Arendt Change Her Mind?" p. 132.

122. Warner, *Publics and Counterpublics*, p. 63.

123. Shklar, *American Citizenship*, p. 68.

124. Shklar, *American Citizenship*, p. 79.

125. Barber, Review of *American Citizenship* in *Political Theory*, pp. 146–53.

126. "Remarks by the President on Comprehensive Immigration Reform," August 3, 2006. http://georgewbush-whitehouse.archives.gov/news/releases/2006/08/20060803-8.html

127. Suderman, "Rove's Quotes."

128. See Kirkpatrick, "Demonstrations on Immigration Are Hardening Divide."

129. Butler and Spivak, *Who Sings the Nation-State?* p. 113.

130. Butler and Spivak, *Who Sings the Nation-State?* p. 67.

131. Wolin, "Fugitive Democracy," pp. 23–24.

132. Arendt, *The Human Condition*, p. 206.

133. Rancière, "Who Is the Subject of the Rights of Man?" p. 302.

134. Ibid.

135. Markell, "The Rule of the People," p. 12.

Conclusion

1. See Spivak, *Outside in the Teaching Machine*.

2. Arendt, *The Human Condition*, p. 15.

3. Butler, "Contingent Foundations," pp. 15–16.

4. Butler, *Gender Trouble*, p. 3.

5. Butler, *Gender Trouble*, p. 4.

6. Butler, *Gender Trouble*, p. 5.

7. Butler, "Contingent Foundations," p. 8.

8. Butler, "Contingent Foundations," p. 15.

9. Butler, *Gender Trouble*, p. 148.

10. Ferguson, *The Man Question*, p. 158.

11. Ferguson, *The Man Question*, p. 159.

12. Ferguson, *The Man Question*, p. 178.

13. Phelan, *Getting Specific*, p. 139.

14. Phelan, *Getting Specific*, pp. 140, 149.

15. Ibid.

16. Phelan, *Getting Specific*, p. 154.

17. Dean, *Solidarity of Strangers*, p. 179.

18. Keenan, *Democracy in Question*, p. 7.

19. Dallmayr, "Beyond Fugitive Democracy," p. 74.

20. Keenan, *Democracy in Question*, pp. 11–13.

21. Ferguson, *The Man Question*, p. 183.

22. Mathiowetz, "'Interest' Is a Verb," p. 622.

23. Mathiowetz, "'Interest' Is a Verb," p. 624.

24. Mathiowetz, "'Interest' Is a Verb," p. 632.

25. Mathiowetz, "'Interest' Is a Verb," p. 626.

26. Truman, David B. *The Governmental Process: Political Interests and Public Opinion.* New York: Knopf, 1951.

27. Mathiowetz, "'Interest' Is a Verb," p. 626.

28. Mathiowetz, "'Interest' Is a Verb," p. 628.

29. Mathiowetz, "'Interest' Is a Verb," pp. 631–33.

30. Young, *Justice and the Politics of Difference*, pp. 188–89, 95.

31. Young, *Justice and the Politics of Difference*, pp. 186–87, 43.

32. Deleuze and Guattari, *A Thousand Plateaus*, p. 15.

33. Dallmayr, "Beyond Fugitive Democracy," p. 74.

34. This work is productively influenced by *Juana* María Rodríguez and her discussion of rhizomatic approaches to reading in *Queer Latinidad* (see p. 22). Yet in turning to Deleuze, my project seeks to elaborate on what it might mean not only to read rhizomatically but to consider how the very practice of *Latinidad* can be understood in both arboreal and rhizomatic terms.

35. Deleuze and Guattari, *A Thousand Plateaus*, pp. 6–7, 9, 12.

36. Deleuze and Guattari, *A Thousand Plateaus*, p. 212.

37. Deleuze and Guattari, *A Thousand Plateaus*, p. 5.

38. Deleuze and Guattari, *A Thousand Plateaus*, p. 21.

39. Deleuze and Guattari, *A Thousand Plateaus*, p. 15.

40. Deleuze and Guattari, *A Thousand Plateaus*, p. 25.

41. Deleuze and Guattari, *A Thousand Plateaus*, p. 12.

42. Deleuze and Guattari, *A Thousand Plateaus*, p. 7.

43. Deleuze and Guattari, *A Thousand Plateaus*, p. 12, 15.

44. Connolly, "The Evangelical-Capitalist Resonance Machine," pp. 870, 873. Also see Connolly, *Capitalism and Christianity, American Style*, particularly chapter 2.

45. Connolly, "The Evangelical-Capitalist Resonance Machine," p. 879.

46. Connolly, "The Evangelical-Capitalist Resonance Machine," p. 869.

47. Connolly, "The Evangelical-Capitalist Resonance Machine," p. 872.

48. Connolly, "The Evangelical-Capitalist Resonance Machine," p. 875.

Bibliography

Ackelsberg, Martha A. *Resisting Citizenship: Feminist Essays on Politics, Community, and Democracy*. New York: Routledge, 2009.

———. "Sisters or Comrades? The Politics of Friends and Families." In Irene Diamond, ed., *Families, Politics, and Public Policy*. London: Longman, 1983.

Ackerman, Bruce, and James S. Fishkin. *Deliberation Day*. New Haven, Conn.: Yale University Press, 2005.

Acosta-Belén, Edna, and Barbara Sjostrom, eds. *The Hispanic Experience in the United States: Contemporary Issues and Perspectives*. New York: Praeger, 1988.

Affigne, Tony, et al. "Symposium: Latino Politics in the United States." *PS: Political Science & Politics* 33 (September 2000): 520–567.

Aizenman, N. C. "Immigration Debate Wakes a 'Sleeping Latino Giant.'" *Washington Post*, April 6, 2006.

Alarcón, Norma. *Chicana Critical Issues*. Berkeley, Calif.: Third Woman Press, 1993.

———. "The Theoretical Subject(s) of *This Bridge Called My Back* and Anglo-American Feminism." In Gloria Anzaldúa, ed., *Making Face, Making Soul/Haciendo Caras: Creative and Critical Perspectives by Feminists of Color*. San Francisco: Aunt Lute Foundation Books, 1990.

Alcoff, Linda Martín. *Visible Identities: Race, Gender, and the Self*. New York: Oxford University Press, 2006.

Allen, Danielle. *Talking to Strangers: Anxieties of Citizenship Since Brown v. Board of Education*. Chicago: University of Chicago Press, 2004.

Alurista. "Poem in Lieu of a Preface." In Alurista, F. A. Cervantes, and Juan Gomez-Quiñones, eds., *Festival de Flor y Canto*, p. 3. Los Angeles: University of Southern California Press, 1976.

Alvarez, R. Michael, and Lisa García Bedolla. "The Foundations of Latino Voter Partisanship: Evidence from the 2000 Elections." *Journal of Politics* 65, no. 1 (2003): 31–49.

Anaya, Rudolfo, and Francisco Lomeli, eds. *Aztlán: Essays on the Chicano Homeland*. Albuquerque: University of New Mexico Press, 1989.

Anonymous. "Chicanas Take Wrong Direction." *El Popo Femenil* [Chicano student newspaper]. California State University at Northridge, May 1974, p. 13.

Anzaldúa, Gloria. *Borderlands/La Frontera: The New Mestiza.* San Francisco: Aunt Lute Foundation Books, 1987.

———. "Bridge, Drawbridge, Sandbar or Island: Lesbians-of-Color *Hacienda Alianzas.*" In Lisa Albrecht and Rose M. Brewer, eds., *Bridges of Power: Women's Multicultural Alliances*, pp. 216–31. Philadelphia: New Society Publishers, 1990.

———, ed. *Making Face, Making Soul/Haciendo Caras: Creative and Critical Perspectives by Feminists of Color.* San Francisco: Aunt Lute Foundation Books, 1990.

———. "Never, Momma." In Norma Alarcón, Ana Castillo, and Cherríe Moraga, eds., *The Sexuality of Latinos*, special issue of *Third Woman* 4 (1989).

Aparicio, Frances R., and Susan Chávez-Silverman. *Tropicalizations: Transcultural Representations of Latinidad.* Hanover, N.H.: University Press of New England, 1997.

Apostolidis, Paul. "Feminist Theory, Immigrant Workers' Stories, and Counterhegemony in the United States Today." *Signs: Journal of Women in Culture and Society* 33, no. 3 (2008): 545–68.

———. "Hegemony and Hamburger: Migration Narratives and Democratic Unionism among Mexican Meatpackers in the U.S. West." *Political Research Quarterly* 58, no. 4 (2005): 647–58.

Arendt, Hannah. *The Human Condition.* Chicago: University of Chicago Press, 1981 [1958].

———. *On Revolution.* New York: Viking Compass, 1965.

———. *The Origins of Totalitarianism.* San Diego: Harcourt, 1985 [1951].

———. "What Is Freedom?" In *Between Past and Future: Eight Exercises in Political Thought.* New York: Penguin Books, 2006 [1968].

Arteaga, Alfred, ed. *An Other Tongue: Nation and Ethnicity in the Linguistic Borderlands.* Durham, N.C.: Duke University Press, 1994.

Baca Zinn, Maxine. "'Political Familism': Toward Sex Role Equality in Chicano Families." *Aztlan: International Journal of Chicano Studies Research* 6, no. 1 (Spring 1975): 13–26.

Barber, Benjamin R. *Strong Democracy: Participatory Politics for a New Age.* Berkeley: University of California Press, 1984.

Barrera, B. James. "The 1968 Edcouch-Elsa High School Walkout: Chicano Student Activism in a South Texas Community." *Aztlán: A Journal of Chicano Studies* 29, no. 2 (Fall 2004): 93–122.

Barrera, Mario. "The Historical Evolution of Chicano Ethnic Goals: A Bibliographic Essay." *Sage Race Relations Abstracts* 10 (1988): 1–48.

Barreto, Matt A. "Si Se Puede! Latino Candidates and the Mobilization of Latino Voters." *American Political Science Review* 101 (August 2007): 425–41.

Barreto, Matt A., Luis Fraga, Sylvia Manzano, Valerie Martinez-Ebers, and Gary Segura. "Should They Dance with the One Who Brung 'Em? Latinos and the 2008 Presidential Election." *PS: Political Science & Politics* 41 (October 2008): 753–60.

Barreto, Matt A., Sylvia Manzano, Ricardo Ramírez, and Kathy Rim. "Mobilization, Participation, and *Solidaridad*: Latino Participation in the 2006 Immigration Protest Rallies." *Urban Affairs Review* 44, no. 5 (May 2009): 736–64.

Barvosa, Edwina. *Wealth of Selves: Multiple Identities, Mestiza Consciousness, and the Subject of Politics.* College Station: Texas A&M University Press, 2008.

Baver, Sherrie. "Puerto Rican Politics in New York City: The Post–World War II Period." In James Jennings and Monte Rivera, eds., *Puerto Rican Politics in Urban America.* Westport, Conn.: Greenwood Press, 1984.

Behdad, Ali. *A Forgetful Nation: On Immigration and Cultural Identity in the United States.* Durham, N.C.: Duke University Press, 2005.

———. "INS and Outs: Producing Delinquency at the Border." *Aztlán: A Journal of Chicano Studies.* 23, no. 1 (Spring 1998): 103–13.

Benhabib, Seyla, ed. *Democracy and Difference: Contesting Boundaries of the Political.* Princeton, N.J.: Princeton University Press, 1996.

———. "Kantian Questions, Arendtian Answers: Statelessness, Cosmopolitanism, and the Right to Have Rights." In Seyla Benhabib and Nancy Fraser, eds., *Pragmatism, Critique, Judgment: Essays for Richard J. Bernstein,* p. 173. Cambridge, Mass.: MIT Press, 2004.

———. *The Reluctant Modernism of Hannah Arendt.* New ed. Lanham, Md.: Rowman & Littlefield, 2000.

———. *The Rights of Others: Aliens, Residents and Citizens.* Cambridge: Cambridge University Press, 2004.

Bernstein, Richard J. "Did Hannah Arendt Change Her Mind? From Radical Evil to the Banality of Evil." In Larry May and Jerome Kohn, eds., *Hannah Arendt: Twenty Years Later.* Cambridge, Mass.: MIT Press, 1997.

Bessette, Joseph M. *The Mild Voice of Reason: Deliberative Democracy and American National Government.* Chicago: University of Chicago Press, 1994.

Bickford, Susan. "Anti-Anti-Identity Politics: Feminism, Democracy and the Complexities of Citizenship." *Hypatia* 12, no. 4 (1997): 111–31.

———. *The Dissonance of Democracy: Listening, Conflict, and Citizenship.* Ithaca, N.Y.: Cornell University Press, 1996.

Bohman, James, and William Rehg. *Deliberative Democracy: Essays on Reason and Politics.* Cambridge, Mass.: MIT Press, 1997.

Bosniak, Linda. *The Citizen and the Alien: Dilemmas of Contemporary Membership.* Princeton, N.J.: Princeton University Press, 2006.

Botwinick, Aryeh, and William E. Connolly, eds. *Democracy and Vision: Sheldon Wolin and the Vicissitudes of the Political.* Princeton, N.J.: Princeton University Press, 2001.

Bowler, Shaun, and Gary M. Segura, eds., *Diversity in Democracy: Minority Representation in the United States.* Charlottesville: University of Virginia Press, 2005.

Brown, Wendy. *Edgework: Critical Essays on Knowledge and Politics* Princeton, N.J.: Princeton University Press, 2005.

———. *States of Injury: Power and Freedom in Late Modernity.* Princeton, N.J.: Princeton University Press, 1995.

Bruyneel, Kevin. *The Third Space of Sovereignty: The Postcolonial Politics of U.S.-Indigenous Relations.* Minneapolis: University of Minnesota Press, 2007.

Buchanan, Patrick J. *The Death of the West: How Dying Populations and Immigrant Invasions Imperil Our Country and Civilization.* New York: St. Martin's/Griffin, 2002.

———. *State of Emergency: The Third World Invasion and Conquest of America.* New York: Thomas Dunne Books, 2006.

Burke, Edmund. *Reflections on the Revolution in France.* Translated by J. C. D. Clark. Stanford, Calif.: Stanford University Press, 2001 [1790].

Butler, Judith. *Bodies That Matter: On the Discursive Limits of Sex.* New York: Routledge, 1993.

————. "Contingent Foundations: Feminism and the Question of 'Postmodernism.'" In Judith Butler and Joan Scott, eds., *Feminists Theorize the Political*. New York: Routledge, 1992.

————. *Gender Trouble: Feminism and the Subversion of Identity*. New York: Routledge, 1990.

Butler, Judith, and Gayatri Chakravorty Spivak, *Who Sings the Nation-State? Language, Politics, Belonging*. New York: Seagull Books, 2007.

Calderón, Hector. "At the Crossroads of History, on the Borders of Change: Chicano Literary Studies Past, Present, and Future." In Lennard J. Davis and M. Bella Mirabella, eds., *Left Politics and the Literary Profession*. New York: Columbia University Press, 1990.

Calderón, José. "'Hispanic' and 'Latino': The Viability of Categories for Panethnic Unity." *Latin American Perspectives* 19, no. 4 (Fall 1992): 37–44.

————. *Hybrid Cultures: Strategies for Entering and Leaving Modernity*. Minneapolis: University of Minnesota Press, 1995.

Candelaria, Cordelia. *Chicano Poetry: A Critical Introduction*. Westport, Conn.: Greenwood Press, 1986.

Canovan, Margaret. *Hannah Arendt: A Reinterpretation of Her Political Thought*. New ed. Cambridge: Cambridge University Press, 2002.

Chambers, Samuel A. "Democracy and (the) Public(s): Spatializing Politics in the Internet Age." *Political Theory* 33, no. 1 (2005): 125–36.

Chavez, Ernesto, *"¡Mi Raza Primero!" (My People First): Nationalism, Identity, and Insurgency in the Chicano Movement in Los Angeles, 1966–1978*. Berkeley: University of California Press, 2002.

Chavez, Marisela R. "'We Lived and Breathed and Worked the Movement': The Contradictions and Rewards of Chicana/Mexicana Activism in el Centro de Accion Social Autonomo-Hermandad General de Tabajadores (CASA-HGT), Los Angeles, 1975–1978." In Vicki L. Ruiz, ed., *Las Obreras: Chicana Politics of Work and Family*, pp. 83–105. Los Angeles: UCLA Chicano Studies Research Center, 2000.

Cobble, Steve, and Joe Velasquez. "Obama's Latino Vote Mandate." *Nation*, November 18, 2008.

Cohen, Joshua. "Deliberative Democracy and Democratic Legitimacy." In Alan Hamlin and Philip Pettit, eds., *The Good Polity: Normative Analysis of the State*, pp. 17–34. Oxford: Blackwell, 1991.

Cohen, Joshua, and Joel Rogers, eds. *Associations and Democracy*. London: Verso, 1995.

Coles, Romand. *Beyond Gated Politics: Reflections for the Possibility of Democracy*. Minneapolis: University of Minnesota Press, 2005.

Collins, Patricia Hill. *Black Feminist Thought: Knowledge, Consciousness, and the Politics of Empowerment*. New York: Routledge, 1991.

Connolly, William E. *Capitalism and Christianity, American Style*. Durham, N.C.: Duke University Press, 2008.

————. "The Evangelical-Capitalist Resonance Machine." *Political Theory* 33, no. 6 (December 2005): 869–86.

————. "Politics and Vision." In Aryeh Botwinick and William E. Connolly, eds. *Democracy and Vision: Sheldon Wolin and the Vicissitudes of the Political*. Princeton, N.J.: Princeton University Press, 2001.

Constable, Pamela. "Latinos Unite to Turn Fear into Activism." *Washington Post*, July 28, 2007.

Cotera, Martha. "Our Feminist Heritage, 1973." In Martha Cotera, ed., *The Chicana Feminist*. Austin, Tex.: Information Systems Development, 1977.

Crenshaw, Kimberlé, Neil Gotanda, Gary Peller, and Kendall Thomas, eds. *Critical Race Theory: The Key Writings That Formed the Movement*. New York: New Press, 1996.

Crocker, Lester. *Rousseau's "Social Contract": An Interpretive Essay*. Cleveland, Ohio: Case Western University Press, 1968.

Cullen, Daniel. *Freedom in Rousseau's Political Philosophy*. DeKalb: Northern Illinois University Press, 1993.

Dallmayr, Fred. "Beyond Fugitive Democracy: Some Modern and Postmodern Reflections." In Aryeh Botwinick and William E. Connolly, eds., *Democracy and Vision: Sheldon Wolin and the Vicissitudes of the Political*. Princeton, N.J.: Princeton University Press, 2001.

Daniels, Lindsay, and Clarissa Martinez de Castro. *The Latino Electorate*. Washington, D.C. National Council of La Raza, Latino Empowerment and Advocacy Project, 2007.

Dávila, Arlene. *Barrio Dreams: Puerto Ricans, Latinos and the Neoliberal City*. Berkeley: University of California Press, 2004.

———. *Latino Spin: Public Image and the Whitewashing of Race*. New York: New York University Press, 2008.

———. *Latinos, Inc.: The Making and Marketing of a People*. Berkeley: University of California Press, 2001.

De Genova, Nicholas. "Migrant 'Illegality' and Deportability in Everyday Life." *Annual Review of Anthropology* 31 (2002): 419–47.

———. "The Legal Production of Mexican/Migrant 'Illegality.'" *Latino Studies* 2, no. 2 (2004): 160–85.

De Genova, Nicholas, and Ana Y. Ramos-Zayas. *Latino Crossings: Mexicans, Puerto Ricans, and the Politics of Race and Citizenship*. New York: Routledge, 2003.

de la Garza, Rodolfo O. "Chicano Elites and National Policymaking, 1977–1980: Passive or Active Representatives." In F. Chris Garcia, ed., *Latinos and the Political System*. Notre Dame, Ind.: University of Notre Dame Press, 1988.

———. "The Political Socialization of Chicano Elites: A Generational Approach." *Social Science Quarterly* 65 (June 1984): 290–307.

de la Garza, Rodolfo O., and Louis DeSipio. *Awash in the Mainstream: Latino Politics in the 1996 Election*. Boulder, Colo.: Westview Press, 1999.

———. *Barrio Ballots: Latino Politics in the 1990 Elections*. Boulder, Colo.: Westview Press, 1994.

———. *Ethnic Ironies: Latino Politics in the 1992 Election*. Boulder, Colo.: Westview Press, 1996.

———. *From Rhetoric to Reality: Latino Politics and the 1988 Elections*. Boulder, Colo.: Westview Press, 1992.

———. *Muted Voices: Latinos and the 2000 Election*. Lanham, Md.: Rowman & Littlefield, 2004.

de la Garza, Rodolfo O., Louis DeSipio, F. Chris Garcia, John Garcia, and Angelo Falcon. *Latino Voices: Mexican, Puerto-Rican, and Cuban Perspectives on American Politics*. Boulder, Colo.: Westview Press, 1992.

Dean, Jodi. *Solidarity of Strangers: Feminism after Identity Politics*. Berkeley: University of California Press, 1996.

Deleuze, Gilles, and Félix Guattari. *A Thousand Plateaus: Capitalism and Schizophrenia.* Translated by Brian Massumi. Minneapolis: University of Minnesota Press, 1987.

DeSipio, Louis. *Counting on the Latino Vote: Latinos as a New Electorate.* Charlottesville: University of Virginia Press, 1996.

DeSipio, Louis, and Rodolfo O. de la Garza. "Forever Seen as New: Latino Participation in American Elections." In Marcelo M. Súarez-Orozco and Mariela M. Páez, eds., *Latinos: Remaking America.* Berkeley: University of California Press, 2002.

Dhamoon, Rita. *Identity/Difference Politics: How Difference Is Produced, and Why It Matters.* Vancouver: University of British Columbia Press, 2009.

Dietz, Mary. "Feminist Receptions of Hannah Arendt." In Bonnie Honig, ed., *Feminist Interpretations of Hannah Arendt.* University Park: Pennsylvania State University Press, 1995.

Dorsey, Margaret E. *Pachangas: Borderlands Music, U.S. Politics, and Transnational Marketing.* Austin: University of Texas Press, 2006.

Dryzek, John S. *Discursive Democracy: Politics, Policy, and Political Science.* Cambridge: Cambridge University Press, 1994.

Ellison, Ralph. *Invisible Man.* New York: Random House, 1952.

Elster, Jon, ed. *Deliberative Democracy.* Cambridge: Cambridge University Press, 1998.

Espino, Rodolfo, David L. Leal, and Kenneth J. Meier, eds. *Latino Politics: Identity, Mobilization, and Representation.* Charlottesville: University of Virginia Press, 2007.

Espinoza, Dionne. "'Revolutionary Sisters': Women's Solidarity and Collective Identification among Chicana Brown Berets in East Los Angeles, 1967–1970." *Aztlán: A Journal of Chicano Studies* 26, no. 1 (Spring 2001): 17–58.

Falcon, Angelo. "A History of Puerto Rican Politics in New York City: 1860s to 1945." In James Jennings and Monte Rivera, eds., *Puerto Rican Politics in Urban America.* New York: Greenwood Press, 1984.

Ferguson, Kathy. *The Man Question: Visions of Subjectivity in Feminist Theory.* Berkeley: University of California Press, 1993.

Fishkin, James S. *Democracy and Deliberation: New Directions for Democratic Reform.* New Haven, Conn.: Yale University Press, 1991.

Flores, Juan. *Divided Borders: Essays on Puerto Rican Identity.* Houston: Arte Público Press, 1993.

———. *From Bomba to Hip-Hop: Puerto Rican Culture and Latino Identity.* New York: Columbia University Press, 2000.

Flores, William V. "Undocumented Immigrants and Latino Cultural Citizenship." In William V. Flores and Rina Benmayor, eds., *Latino Cultural Citizenship: Claiming Identity, Space, and Rights,* pp. 255–77. Boston: Beacon Press, 1997.

Flores, William V, and Rina Benmayor, eds. *Latino Cultural Citizenship: Claiming Identity, Space, and Rights.* Boston: Beacon Press, 1997.

Fox, Geoffrey. *Hispanic Nation: Culture, Politics, and the Constructing of Identity.* Secaucus, N.J.: Birch Lane Press, 1996.

Fraga, Luis R., John A. Garcia, Rodney Hero, Michael Jones-Correa, and Valerie Martinez-Ebers. "Su Casa Es Nuestra Casa: Latino Politics Research and the Development of American Political Science." *American Political Science Review* 100, no. 4 (2006): 515–22.

Fraga, Luis R., John A. Garcia, Rodney Hero, Michael Jones-Correa, Valerie Martinez-Ebers, and Gary M. Segura. Latino National Survey. http://depts.washington.edu/uwiser/LNS.shtml.

Fraser, Nancy. "Rethinking the Public Sphere: A Contribution to the Critique of Actually Existing Democracy." In Craig Calhoun, ed., *Habermas and the Public Sphere*. Cambridge, Mass.: MIT Press, 1992.

Fusco, Coco. *English Is Broken Here: Notes on Cultural Fusion in the Americas*. New York: New Press, 1995.

Garcia, Alma, ed. *Chicana Feminist Thought: The Basic Writings*. New York: Routledge, 1997.

García, F. Chris, ed. *Latinos and the Political System*. Notre Dame, Ind.: University of Notre Dame Press, 1988.

———, ed. *Latinos and the Political System*. Notre Dame, Ind.: University of Notre Dame Press, 1988.

———. *Pursuing Power: Latinos and the Political System*. Notre Dame, Ind.: University of Notre Dame Press, 1997.

García, Ignacio. *Chicanismo: The Forging of a Militant Ethos among Mexican-Americans*. Tucson: University of Arizona Press, 1997.

———. *United We Win: The Rise and Fall of La Raza Unida Party*. Tucson: University of Arizona Press, 1989.

Garcia, John A. "The Chicano Movement: Its Legacy for Politics and Policy." In David R. Maciel and Isidro D. Ortiz, eds., *Chicanas/Chicanos at the Crossroads*. Tucson: University of Arizona Press, 1996.

———. *Latino Politics in America: Community, Culture, and Interests*. Lanham, Md.: Rowman & Littlefield, 2003.

García, Mario. *Mexican Americans: Leadership, Ideology, and Identity: 1930–1960*. New Haven, Conn.: Yale University Press, 1989.

———, ed. *Latinos and the Political System*. Notre Dame, Ind.: University of Notre Dame Press, 1988.

García Bedolla, Lisa. *Fluid Borders: Latino Power, Identity, and Politics in Los Angeles*. Berkeley: University of California Press, 2005.

———. *Latino Politics*. Cambridge, Mass.: Polity Press, 2009.

García Canclini, Néstor. *Consumers and Citizens: Globalization and Multicultural Conflicts*. Minneapolis: University of Minnesota Press, 2001.

Giménez, Martha. "Latino/Hispanic—Who Needs a Name? The Case against a Standard Terminology." *International Journal of Health Services* 19 (1989): 557–71.

Godsell, Geoffrey. "Hispanics in the US: Ethnic 'Sleeping Giant' Awakens." *Christian Science Monitor*, April 28, 1980.

Gómez-Peña, Guillermo. *The New World Border: Prophecies, Poems and Loqueras for the End of the Century*. San Francisco: City Lights, 1996.

———. *Warriors for Gringostroika*. St. Paul, Minn.: Graywolf Press, 1993.

Gómez-Quiñones, Juan. *Chicano Politics: Reality and Promise, 1940–1990*. Albuquerque: University of New Mexico Press, 1990.

Gonzales, Alfonso. "The 2006 Mega-Marchas in Greater Los Angeles: Counter-hegemonic Moment and the Future of El Migrante Struggle." *Latino Studies* 7, no. 1 (2009): 30–59.

Gonzáles, Rodolfo "Corky." "Chicano Nationalism: The Key to Unity for La Raza." In Renato Rosaldo, Robert A. Calvert, and Gustav L. Seligmann, eds., *Chicano: The Evolution of a People*. Minneapolis, Minn.: Winston Press, 1973.

———.*Yo Soy Joaquín/I Am Joaquín: An Epic Poem*. New York: Bantam Books, 1972.

Gosse, Van, and Richard Moser, eds. *The World the Sixties Made: Politics and Culture in Recent America*. Philadelphia: Temple University Press, 2003.

Graham, George. "Rousseau's Concept of Consensus." *Political Science Quarterly* 85 (1970): 80–98.

Gutiérrez, Elena R. "Policing 'Pregnant Pilgrims': Situating the Sterilization Abuse of Mexican-Origin Women in Los Angeles County." In Georgina Feldberg, Molly Ladd-Taylor, Alison Li, and Kathryn McPherson, eds., *Women, Health, and Nation: Canada and the United States since 1945*. Montreal: McGill-Queen's University Press, 2003.

Gutiérrez, José Angel. *The Making of a Chicano Militant*. Madison: University of Wisconsin Press, 1998.

Guzmán, Pablo. "La Vida Pura: A Lord of the Barrio." In Andrés Torres and José E. Velázquez, eds., *The Puerto Rican Movement: Voices from the Diaspora*. Philadelphia: Temple University Press, 1998.

Habell-Pallán, Michelle, and Mary Romero. *Latino/a Popular Culture*. New York: New York University Press, 2002.

Habermas, Jürgen. *The Structural Transformation of the Public Sphere: An Inquiry into a Category of Bourgeois Society*. Translated by Thomas Burger with the assistance of Frederick Lawrence. Cambridge, Mass.: MIT Press, 1991 [1962].

Hancock, Ange-Marie. *The Politics of Disgust: The Public Identity of the Welfare Queen*. New York: New York University Press, 2004.

Hardy-Fanta, Carol. *Latina Politics, Latino Politics: Gender, Culture, and Political Participation in Boston*. Philadelphia: Temple University Press, 1993.

Hardy-Fanta, Carol, and Jeffrey N. Gerson. *Latino Politics in Massachusetts: Struggles, Strategies and Prospects*. New York: Routledge, 2001.

Hattam, Victoria. *In the Shadow of Race: Jews, Latinos, and Immigrant Politics in the United States*. Chicago: University of Chicago Press, 2007.

Hawkesworth, Mary. "Congressional Enactments of Race-Gender: Toward a Theory of Raced-Gendered Institutions." *American Political Science Review* 97, no. 4 (2003): 529–50.

———. "Women's Struggle for Political Equality in the United States." In Jane Bayes, Patricia Begné, Laura Gonzalez, Lois Harder, Mary Hawkesworth, and Laura Macdonald, eds., *Women, Democracy, and Globalization in North America: A Comparative Study*. New York: Palgrave Macmillan, 2006.

Heilemann, John. "The Evita Factor." *New York*, February 1, 2008.

Hernandez, Raymond. "Hispanic Voters Gain New Clout with Democrats." *New York Times*, June 10, 2007.

Hero, Rodney E. *Latinos and the U.S. Political System: Two-Tiered Pluralism*. Philadelphia: Temple University Press, 1992.

Heyck, Denis Lynn Daly. *Barrios and Borderlands: Cultures of Latinos and Latinas in the United States*. New York: Routledge, 1994.

Holusha, John. "Bush Says Anthem Should Be in English." *New York Times*, April 28, 2006.

Honig, Bonnie. *Democracy and the Foreigner*. Princeton, N.J.: Princeton University Press, 2003.

———, ed., *Feminist Interpretations of Hannah Arendt*. University Park: Pennsylvania State University Press, 1995.

Huntington, Samuel P. *Who Are We? The Challenges to America's National Identity*. New York: Simon and Schuster, 2004.

Jaspar, William F. "Pawns in a Losing Game." *New American*, May 29, 2006.

Jennings, James. "Future Directions for Puerto Rican Politics in the U.S. and Puerto Rico." In F. Chris Garcia, ed., *Latinos and the Political System*. Notre Dame, Ind.: University of Notre Dame Press, 1988.

Johnson, Kevin. "Vasquez Tells Latinos Their Time Has Come." *Los Angeles Times* (Orange County edition), March 7, 1991.

Jones-Correa, Michael. *Between Two Nations: The Political Predicament of Latinos in New York City*. Ithaca, N.Y.: Cornell University Press, 1998.

Jorge, Angela. "The Black Puerto Rican Woman in Contemporary American Society." In Edna Acosta-Belen, ed., *The Puerto Rican Woman: Perspectives on Culture, History, and Society*. New York: Praeger, 1979.

Joseph, May, and Jennifer Natalya Fink. *Performing Hybridity*. Minneapolis: University of Minnesota Press, 1999.

Judis, John B. "Hillary Clinton's Firewall: Will Barack Obama's Anemic Standing among Latinos Be His Undoing?" *New Republic*, December 18, 2007.

Kalyvas, Andreas. "The Sovereign Weaver: Beyond the Camp." In Andrew Norris, ed., *Politics, Metaphysics, and Death: Essays on Giorgio Agamben's Homo Sacer*, pp. 107–34. Durham, N.C.: Duke University Press, 2005.

Keenan, Alan. *Democracy in Question: Democratic Openness in a Time of Political Closure*. Stanford, Calif.: Stanford University Press, 2003.

Kelly, Christopher. "Rousseau and the Case against (and for) the Arts." In Clifford Orwin and Nathan Tarcov, eds., *The Legacy of Rousseau*. Chicago: University of Chicago Press, 1997.

Kirkpatrick, David. "Demonstrations on Immigration Are Hardening Divide." *New York Times*, April 17, 2006.

Klor de Alva, J. Jorge. "Aztlán, Borinquen and Hispanic Nationalism in the United States." In Rudolfo Anaya and Francisco Lomelí, eds., *Aztlán: Essays on the Chicano Homeland*. Albuquerque: El Norte Publications/Academia, 1989.

Langer, Gary. "The Hispanic Vote." ABC News, June 28, 2008.

Laó-Montes, Agustín. "Resources of Hope: Imagining the Young Lords and the Politics of Memory." *Centro* 8, no. 1 (1995): 35–49.

Laó-Montes, Agustín, and Arlene Dávila. *Mambo Montage: The Latinization of New York*. New York: Columbia University Press, 2001.

Leal, David, Matt Barreto, Jongho Lee, and Rodolfo de la Garza. "The Latino Vote in the 2004 Election." *PS: Political Science & Politics* 38 (January 2005): 41–49.

Lee, Charles T. "Tactical Citizenship: Domestic Workers, the Remainders of Home, and Undocumented Citizen Participation in the Third Space of Mimicry." *Theory & Event* 9, no. 3 (2006).

Levin, Martin. "On *Animal Laborans* and *Homo Politicus* in Hannah Arendt: A Note." *Political Theory* 7, no. 4 (1979): 521–31.

Lima, Lazáro. *The Latino Body: Crisis Identities in Literary and Cultural Memory.* New York: New York University Press, 2007.

Liu, Eric. *The Accidental Asian: Notes of a Native Speaker.* New York: Random House, 1998.

Lorde, Audre. *Between Ourselves.* San Francisco: Eidolon Editions, 1976.

———. *Sister Outsider: Essays and Speeches.* Berkeley, Calif.: Crossing Press, 1984.

Lugones, Maria, and Elizabeth Spelman. "Have We Got a Theory for You! Feminist Theory, Cultural Imperialism, and the Demand for 'The Woman's Voice.'" *Women's Studies International Forum* 6, no. 6 (1983): 573–81.

Maciel, David, and Isidro D. Ortiz. *Chicanas/Chicanos at the Crossroads: Social, Economic, and Political Change.* Tucson: University of Arizona Press, 1996.

Mariscal, George. *Brown-Eyed Children of the Sun: Lessons from the Chicano Movement, 1965–1975.* Albuquerque: University of New Mexico Press, 2005.

Markell, Patchen. "The Rule of the People: Arendt, Arche, and Democracy." *American Political Science Review* 100, no. 1 (February 2006): 1–14.

Marquez, Benjamin. *Constructing Identities in Mexican American Political Organizations: Choosing Issues, Taking Sides.* Austin: University of Texas Press, 2003.

———. *LULAC: The Evolution of a Mexican American Political Organization.* Austin: University of Texas Press, 1993.

Marso, Lori Jo. *(Un)Manly Citizens: Jean-Jacques Rousseau's and Germaine de Staël's Subversive Women.* Baltimore: Johns Hopkins University Press, 1999.

Martinez, Gebe. "Clinton's Hispanic Edge." *Politico,* January 24, 2008.

Mathiowetz, Dean. "'Interest' Is a Verb: Arthur Bentley and the Language of Interest." *Political Research Quarterly* 61, no. 4 (2008): 622–35.

McWilliams, Carey. *North from Mexico: The Spanish-Speaking People of the United States.* Philadelphia: Lippincott, 1948.

Melendez, Miguel "Mickey." *We Took the Streets: Fighting for Latino Rights with the Young Lords.* New York: St. Martin's Press, 2003.

Melzer, Arthur M. "Rousseau and the Modern Cult of Sincerity." In Clifford Orwin and Nathan Tarcov, eds., *The Legacy of Rousseau.* Chicago: University of Chicago Press, 1997.

Michaelsen, Scott, and David E. Johnson. *Border Theory: The Limits of Cultural Politics.* Minneapolis: University of Minnesota Press, 1997.

Milkman, Ruth. "Critical Mass: Latino Labor and Politics in California." *North American Congress on Latin America* 40, no. 3 (May/June 2007): 30–36.

Miller, James. *Rousseau: Dreamer of Democracy.* New Haven, Conn.: Yale University Press, 1984.

Mirande, Alfredo, and Evangelina Enríquez. *La Chicana: The Mexican American Woman.* Chicago: University of Chicago Press, 1979.

Montoya, Lisa J. "The Sleeping Giant in Latino Electoral Politics." In Richard Flores, ed., *Reflexiones 1999: New Directions in Mexican American Studies.* Austin, Tex.: CMAS Books, 1999.

Moraga, Cherríe. "Foreword: Refugees of a World on Fire." In Cherríe Moraga and Gloria Anzaldúa, eds., *This Bridge Called My Back: Writings by Radical Women of Color.* 2nd ed. New York: Kitchen Table: Women of Color Press, 1984.

————. *The Last Generation: Prose and Poetry*. Toronto: Canadian Scholars Press, 1993.

————. *Loving in the War Years*. Cambridge, Mass.: South End Press, 1983.

Moraga, Cherríe, and Gloria Anzaldúa, eds. *This Bridge Called My Back: Writings by Radical Women of Color*. 2nd ed. New York: Kitchen Table: Women of Color Press, 1984.

Morales, Iris. "PALANTE, SIEMPRE PALANTE! The Young Lords." In Andrés Torres and José E. Velázquez, eds., *The Puerto Rican Movement: Voices from the Diaspora*. Philadelphia: Temple University Press, 1998.

Muñoz, Carlos. *Youth, Identity, Power: The Chicano Movement*. London: Verso, 1989.

Muñoz, Jose Esteban. *Disidentifications: Queers of Color and the Performance of Politics*. Minneapolis: University of Minnesota Press, 1999.

Narayan, Uma. *Dislocating Cultures: Identities, Traditions, and Third World Feminism*. New York: Routledge, 1997.

National Council of La Raza. *State of Hispanic America 2004: Latino Perspectives on the American Agenda*. Washington, D.C.: National Council of La Raza. February 2004.

Ngai, Mae M. *Impossible Subjects: Illegal Aliens and the Making of Modern America*. Princeton, N.J.: Princeton University Press, 2004.

NietoGomez, Anna. "La Femenista." In Alma Garcia, ed., *Chicana Feminist Thought: The Basic Writings*. New York: Routledge, 1997.

Noriega, Chon. *Chicanos and Film: Representation and Resistance*. Minneapolis: University of Minnesota Press, 1992.

Oboler, Suzanne. *Ethnic Labels, Latino Lives: Identity and the Politics of (Re)presentation in the United States*. Minneapolis: University of Minnesota Press, 1995.

Oropeza, Lorena. *¡Raza Sí! ¡Guerra No! Chicano Protest and Patriotism during the Viet Nam War Era*. Berkeley: University of California Press, 2005.

Ortiz, Isidro D. "Chicana/o Organizational Politics and Strategies in the Era of Retrenchment." In Isidro D. Ortiz and David Maciel, eds., *Chicanas/Chicanos at the Crossroads: Social, Economic, and Political Change*. Tucson: University of Arizona Press, 1996.

Orwin, Clifford. "Rousseau and the Discovery of Political Compassion." In Clifford Orwin and Nathan Tarcov, eds., *The Legacy of Rousseau*. Chicago: University of Chicago Press, 1997.

Parekh, Bhikhu. "Hannah Arendt's Critique of Marx." In Melvyn A. Hill, ed., *Hannah Arendt: The Recovery of the Public World*. New York: St. Martin's Press, 1979.

Pérez-Torres, Rafael. *Movements in Chicano Poetry: Against Myths, against Margins*. Cambridge: Cambridge University Press, 1995.

Phelan, Shane. *Getting Specific: Postmodern Lesbian Politics*. Minneapolis: University of Minnesota Press, 1994.

Pietri, Pedro. "Puerto Rican Obituary." In Adalberto López, ed., *The Puerto Ricans: Their History, Culture, and Society*. Cambridge, Mass.: Schenkman, 1980.

Pitkin, Hanna Fenichel. *The Attack of the Blob: Hannah Arendt's Concept of the Social*. Chicago: University of Chicago Press, 1998.

————. "Justice: On Relating Private and Public." *Political Theory* 9, no. 3 (1981): 327–52.

Poblete, Juan. *Critical Latin American and Latino Studies*. Minneapolis: University of Minnesota Press, 2003.

Pulido, Laura. *Black, Brown, Yellow, and Left: Radical Activism in Los Angeles*. Berkeley: University of California Press, 2006.

Ramos, Jorge. *The Latino Wave: How Hispanics Will Elect the Next American President*. New York: HarperCollins, 2004.

Rancière, Jacques. "Who Is the Subject of the Rights of Man?" *South Atlantic Quarterly* 103, nos. 2/3 (Spring/Summer 2004): 297–310.

Reagon, Bernice Johnson. "Coalition Politics: Turning the Century." In Barbara Smith, ed., *Home Girls: A Black Feminist Anthology*. New Brunswick, N.J.: Rutgers University Press, 1983.

Reinhardt, Mark. *The Art of Being Free: Taking Liberties with Tocqueville, Marx, and Arendt*. Ithaca, N.Y.: Cornell University Press, 1997.

Rendon, Armando B. *Chicano Manifesto: The History and Aspirations of the Second Largest Minority in America*. New York: Macmillan, 1971.

Reno, Jamie. "Black-Brown Divide." *Newsweek*, January 26, 2008.

Riley, Patrick. *The General Will before Rousseau: The Transformation of the Divine into the Civic*. Princeton, N.J.: Princeton University Press, 1986.

Rodríguez, Juana María. *Queer Latinidad: Identity Practices, Discursive Spaces*. New York: New York University Press, 2003.

Rodriguez, Richard. *Hunger of Memory: The Education of Richard Rodriguez*. Boston: David R. Godine, 1982.

Rodríguez-Morazzani, Roberto. "Political Cultures of the Puerto Rican Left in the United States." In Andrés Torres and José E. Velázquez, eds., *The Puerto Rican Movement: Voices from the Diaspora*. Philadelphia: Temple University Press, 1998.

Romero, Mary, Pierrette Hondagneu-Sotelo, and Vilma Ortiz. *Challenging Fronteras: Structuring Latina and Latino Lives in the U.S.* New York: Routledge, 1997.

Romero, Tom I., II. "Wearing the Red, White, and Blue Trunks of Aztlán: Rodolfo 'Corky' Gonzales and the Convergence of American and Chicano Nationalism." *Aztlán: A Journal of Chicano Studies* 29, no. 1 (Spring 2004): 83–117.

Rosaldo, Renato, Robert A. Calvert, and Gustav L. Seligmann, eds. *Chicano: The Evolution of a People*. Minneapolis, Minn.: Winston Press, 1973.

Rosales, Arturo. *Chicano! The History of the Mexican American Civil Rights Movement*. Houston, Tex.: Arte Público Press, 1996.

Rosales, Rodolfo. *The Illusion of Inclusion: The Untold Political Story of San Antonio*. Austin: University of Texas Press, 2000.

Rousseau, Jean-Jacques. ———. *The First and Second Discourses*. Translated by Roger D. and Judith R. Masters; edited by Roger D. Masters. New York: St. Martin's Press, 1964.

———. *The Government of Poland*. Translated by Wilmoore Kendall. Indianapolis, Ind.: Hackett, 1985.

———. *Politics and the Arts: Letter to M. d'Alembert on the Theatre*. Translated by Allan Bloom. Ithaca, N.Y.: Cornell University Press, 1960.

———. *Social Contract*. Translated by Judith R. Masters; edited by Roger D. Masters. New York: St. Martin's Press, 1978.

Sampaio, Anna. "Theorizing Women of Color in a New Global Matrix." *International Feminist Journal of Politics* 6, no. 2 (2004): 181–206.

Sánchez, José Ramón. *Boricua Power: A Political History of Puerto Ricans in the United States*. New York: New York University Press, 2007.

Sanchez, Leslie. *Los Republicanos: Why Hispanics and Republicans Need Each Other*. New York: Palgrave Macmillan, 2007.

Sánchez Korrol, Virginia. "Latinismo among Early Puerto Rican Migrants in New York City: A Sociohistoric Interpretation." In Edna Acosta-Belén and Barbara R. Sjostrom, eds., *The Hispanic Experience in the United States: Contemporary Issues and Perspectives*. New York: Praeger, 1988.

Sandoval, Chela. "U.S. Third World Feminism: The Theory and Method of Oppositional Consciousness in the Postmodern World." *Genders* 10 (Spring 1991): 1–24.

Santa Ana, Otto. *Brown Tide Rising: Metaphors of Latinos in Contemporary American Public Discourse*. Austin: University of Texas Press, 2002.

Santillan, Richard. "The Latino Community in State and Congressional Redistricting: 1961–1985." In F. Chris Garcia, ed., *Latinos and the Political System*. Notre Dame, Ind.: University of Notre Dame Press, 1988.

———. "Styles and Strategies." In F. Chris Garcia, ed., *Latinos and the Political System*. Notre Dame, Ind.: University of Notre Dame Press, 1988.

Sarlo, Beatriz. *Scenes from Postmodern Life*. Translated by Jon Beasley-Murray. Minneapolis: University of Minnesota Press, 2001.

Schmidt, Ronald, Sr. *Language Policy and Identity Politics in the United States*. Philadelphia: Temple University Press, 2000.

Schwartz, Joseph M. *The Permanence of the Political: A Democratic Critique of the Radical Impulse to Transcend Politics*. Princeton: Princeton University Press, 1995.

Segura, Gary M. "Symposium Introduction: Immigration and National Identity." *Perspectives on Politics* 4, no. 2 (June 2006): 277–78.

Segura, Gary M., Stephen P. Nicholson, and Adrian Pantoja. "Political Knowledge and Issue Voting among the Latino Electorate." *Political Research Quarterly* 59, no. 2 (2006): 259–71.

Serrano, Basilio. "'Rifle, Cañon, y Escopeta!': A Chronicle of the Puerto Rican Student Union." In Andrés Torres and José E. Velázquez, eds., *The Puerto Rican Movement: Voices from the Diaspora*. Philadelphia: Temple University Press, 1998.

Shklar, Judith. *American Citizenship: The Quest for Inclusion*. Cambridge, Mass.: Harvard University Press, 1991.

———. "Jean-Jacques Rousseau and Equality." In *Rousseau for Our Time*, special issue of *Daedalus: Journal of the American Academy of Arts and Sciences* 107, no. 3 (Summer 1978): 13–26.

———. *Men and Citizens: A Study of Rousseau's Social Theory*. Cambridge: Cambridge University Press, 1969.

Skerry, Peter. *Counting on the Census? Race, Group Identity, and the Evasion of Politics*. Washington, D.C.: Brookings Institution Press, 2000.

Smith, Barbara, ed. *Home Girls: A Black Feminist Anthology*. New Brunswick, N.J.: Rutgers University Press, 1983.

Sosa-Riddell, Adaljiza. "Chicanas and El Movimiento." In Alma García, ed., *Chicana Feminist Thought: The Basic Writings*, p. 29. New York: Routledge, 1997.

Sparks, Holloway. "Dissident Citizenship: Democratic Theory, Political Courage, and Activist Women." *Hypatia* 12, no. 4 (1997): 74–110.

Spivak, Gayatri Chakravorty. *Outside in the Teaching Machine*. New York: Routledge, 1993.

Starobinski, Jean. *Jean-Jacques Rousseau: Transparency and Obstruction*. Translated by Arthur Goldhammer. Chicago: University of Chicago Press, 1988.

————. "Rousseau and Modern Tyranny." *New York Review of Books*, November 29, 1973.

Stavans, Ilan. *The Hispanic Condition: Reflections on Culture and Identity in America*. New York: HarperCollins, 1995.

Strong, Tracy. *Jean-Jacques Rousseau: The Politics of the Ordinary*. Lanham, Md.: Rowman & Littlefield, 1994.

Suderman, Peter. "Rove's Quotes," from "The Corner." *National Review Online*, February 12, 2007. http://corner.nationalreview.com/post/?q=NTZhZDdiYmJlNDViYTAwOWE xNmUyMmQ5ODlmMWYwYTU.

Suro, Robert, et al. *2002 National Survey of Latinos*. Washington, D.C.: Pew Hispanic Center/ Kaiser Family Foundation, 2002. http://pewhispanic.org/reports/report.php?ReportID=15.

Swarns, Rachel L. "Immigrants Rally in Scores of Cities for Legal Status." *New York Times*, April 11, 2006.

Torres, Andrés. "Political Radicalism in the Diaspora." In Andrés Torres and José E. Velázquez, eds., *The Puerto Rican Movement: Voices from the Diaspora*. Philadelphia: Temple University Press, 1998.

Torres, Andrés, and José E. Velázquez, eds. *The Puerto Rican Movement: Voices from the Diaspora*. Philadelphia: Temple University Press, 1998.

Torres, Rodolfo, and George Katsiaficas. *Latino Social Movements: Historical and Theoretical Perspectives*. New York: Routledge, 1999.

Trueba, Enrique (Henry). *Latinos Unidos: From Cultural Diversity to the Politics of Solidarity*. Lanham, Md.: Rowman & Littlefield, 1999.

Uttal, Lynet. "Nods That Silence." In Gloria Anzaldúa, ed., *Making Face, Making Soul/ Haciendo Caras: Creative and Critical Perspectives by Feminists of Color*. San Francisco: Aunt Lute Foundation Books, 1990.

Vásquez, Enriqueta Longeaux y. "The Women of La Raza." In Alma García, ed., *Chicana Feminist Thought: The Basic Writings*, p. 29. New York: Routledge, 1997.

Vega, Bernardo. *Memoirs of Bernardo Vega: A Contribution to the History of the Puerto Rican Community in New York*. Edited by César Andreu Iglesias. New York: Monthly Review Press, 1984.

Vélez-Ibáñez, Carlos G., and Anna Sampaio. *Transnational Latina/o Communities: Politics, Processes, and Cultures*. Lanham, Md.: Rowman & Littlefield, 2002.

Vigil, Ernesto. *The Crusade for Justice: Chicano Militancy and the Government's War on Dissent*. Madison: University of Wisconsin Press, 1999.

Vigil, Maurilio E. *Hispanics in Congress: A Historical and Political Survey*. Lanham, Md.: University Press of America, 1996.

Vila, Pablo. *Ethnography at the Border*. Minneapolis: University of Minnesota Press, 2003.

Villarreal, Roberto, and Norma Hernandez, eds. *Latinos and Political Coalitions: Political Empowerment for the 1990s*. New York: Greenwood Press, 1991.

Waldron, Martin. "Farm Workers End Texas March for Wage Bill," *New York Times*, September 6, 1966.

Walzer, Michael. *Spheres of Justice: A Defense of Pluralism and Equality*. New York: Basic Books, 1983.

Wang, Ted, and Robert C. Winn. *Groundswell Meets Groundwork: Preliminary Recommendations for Building on Immigrant Mobilizations*. A special report from the Four Freedoms Fund and grantmakers concerned with immigrants and refugees. New York: The Four Freedoms Fund, June 2006.

Warner, Michael. *Publics and Counterpublics.* New York: Zone Books, 2005.

Wingrove, Elizabeth Rose. *Rousseau's Republican Romance.* Princeton, N.J.: Princeton University Press, 2000.

Wolin, Sheldon S. "Democracy, Difference, and Re-Cognition." *Political Theory* 21, no. 3 (August 1993): 464–83.

———. "Fugitive Democracy." *Constellations* 1, no. 1 (1994): 11–25.

———. "Hannah Arendt: Democracy and the Political." *Salmagundi* 60 (Summer 1983): 3–19.

———. *Politics and Vision: Continuity and Innovation in Western Political Thought.* Expanded edition. Princeton, N.J.: Princeton University Press, 2006.

Wright, Melissa W. *Disposable Women and Other Myths of Global Capitalism.* New York: Routledge, 2006.

Xenos, Nicholas. "Momentary Democracy." In Aryeh Botwinick and William E. Connolly, eds., *Democracy and Vision: Sheldon Wolin and the Vicissitudes of the Political.* Princeton, N.J.: Princeton University Press, 2001.

Ybarra-Frausto, Tomás. "Alurista's Poetics: The Oral, the Bilingual, the Pre-Columbian." In Ybarra-Frausto and Joseph Sommers, eds., *Modern Chicano Writers: A Collection of Critical Essays.* Englewood Cliffs, N.J.: Prentice-Hall, 1979.

Young, Iris Marion. *Inclusion and Democracy.* New York: Oxford University Press, 2000.

———. *Justice and the Politics of Difference.* Princeton, N.J.: Princeton University Press, 1990.

Young Lords Party and Michael Abramson. *Palante: Young Lords Party.* New York: McGraw-Hill, 1971.

Yúdice, George, Jean Franco, and Juan Flores. *On Edge: The Crisis of Contemporary Latin American Culture.* Minneapolis: University of Minnesota Press, 1992.

Yzaguirre, Raul. "Keys to Hispanic Empowerment." In Roberto Villarreal, ed., *Latinos and Political Coalitions: Political Empowerment for the 1990s.* New York: Greenwood Press, 1991.

Zerilli, Linda. *Feminism and the Abyss of Freedom.* Chicago: University of Chicago Press, 2005.

Index

CPSIA information can be obtained
at www.ICGtesting.com
Printed in the USA
BVHW030543141219
566631BV00002B/12/P